An Introduction to Historical Epistemology

An Introduction to Historical Epistemology

The Authority of Knowledge

Mary Tiles and Jim Tiles

BLACKWELL
Oxford UK & Cambridge USA

Copyright © Mary Tiles and Jim Tiles, 1993

The right of *Mary Tiles* and *Jim Tiles* to be identified as authors of this work has been asserted in accordance with the Copyright, Designs and Patents Act 1988.

First published 1993

Blackwell Publishers
238 Main Street, Suite 501
Cambridge, Massachusetts 02142
USA

108 Cowley Road
Oxford OX4 1JF
UK

All rights reserved. Except for the quotation of short passages for the purposes of criticism and review, no part of this publication may be reproduced, stored in a retrieval system, or transmitted, in any form or by any means, electronic, mechanical, photocopying, recording or otherwise, without the prior permission of the publisher.

Except in the United States of America, this book is sold subject to the condition that it shall not, by way of trade or otherwise, be lent, resold, hired out, or otherwise circulated without the publisher's prior consent in any form of binding or cover other than that in which it is published and without a similar condition including this condition being imposed on the subsequent purchaser.

Library of Congress Cataloging-in-Publication Data
Library of Congress data has been applied for.
ISBN 0-631-17514-8; 0-631-17515-6 (pbk.)

British Library Cataloguing in Publication Data
A CIP catalogue record for this book is available from the British Library.

Typeset in 10 on 12 pt Plantin by
Pure Tech Corporation, Pondicherry, India
Printed in Great Britain by Biddles Ltd., Guildford, Surrey.
This book is printed on acid-free paper

Contents

Acknowledgments   vii

Introduction   1

1 Plato and Bacon: *Two Challenges to Prevailing Authority*   7

1 Knowledge and Authority   7
    PLATO'S SCIENCE OF OBJECTIVE STANDARDS
2 Expertise   11
3 Opinion and Understanding   15
4 Forms   19
    FRANCIS BACON'S GREAT INSTAURATION
5 Redefining the Goal of Knowledge   24
6 Retooling the Study of Nature   29
7 Idols and Ideas   36

2 Idols of the Tribe: *Perception and Prejudice*   43

1 "Scientifically Objective Knowledge"   43
2 Subversive Philosophy   48
3 From Ancient Skepticism to Modern Philosophy   53
4 Democritus and the School of Epicurus   58
5 The Latter-day "School of Democritus"   63
6 Idols, Ideas, and Cartesian Epistemology   68
7 Cartesian Epistemology and Stoicism   74
8 Theory, Practice, and Experiment   78

3 Idols of the Theater: *Metaphysics and the Aim of Inquiry*   84

1 Metaphysics   84
2 Aristotle's Speculative Knowledge   87
3 Practical Knowledge and Explanation   93
4 "Mechanism" and the Rejection of Teleology   98
5 The Foundations of Cartesian Method   103
6 The Metaphysics of Representation   108
7 The Unavoidability of Metaphysics   114
8 The Demands of Practical Thought   120

4 Idols of the Market Place: *Language and Representation*   127

1 The Tyranny of Words   127
2 Of Trees and Harmonies   130
3 Signs and the Chemical Philosophy   135
4 From Signs to Representations via the Way of Ideas   142
5 Natural Representations   148
6 Losing the Way (of Ideas)   152
7 Ideal Languages and the Linguistic Turn   158
8 An Inadequate Ideal?   163

5 Idols of the Cave: *Human Science and Human History*   169

1 Human Nature and Human Knowledge   169
2 Epistemology as an Empirical Science of Human Nature   172
3 Epistemology as an Experimental Science of Human Nature   179
4 Humans as Historical Beings   186
5 Humans as Self-Creators   192
6 Epistemology as Idol Knowledge   202
7 Skeptical Strategies   205

Authorities   208

Name Index and Biographical Glossary   213

Subject Index   217

Acknowledgments

We are grateful to Simon Prosser for suggesting that we undertake this project and to Blackwell Publishers for their support. Peter Manicas read drafts of over half of this book and reminded us of our obligations to our readers. We know we have not laid to rest all his concerns, but if we have managed to discharge our obligations at all satisfactorily, then our readers should be as grateful to him as we are.

Introduction

Epistemology loosely defined is the philosophical discussion of knowledge. "Knowledge" here labels something of value in our lives, something we make efforts to acquire, something which we admire in others, something to which we defer. But "knowledge" is a very general, not to say vague, label. It is not always clear that we have acquired what we sought or have sought for the right thing or have gone about our inquiries in the right way. It is not always clear that what we admire in others really deserves respect. It is not always clear when, instead of deferring, we should ask questions or pay no attention. This is why knowledge itself becomes the topic of the sort of very general discussion which we call "philosophical."

"Philosophical" discussions occur in two contexts; relaxed conversations lubricated perhaps by alcohol ("bull sessions") and institutionalized discussion between professional academics or serious amateurs. It is not surprising that both contexts presuppose leisure, for even when what is known or not known is the key to some problem, we seldom can afford time or energy to reflect on whether we are operating with an adequate general conception of knowledge. Relaxed conversation by and large does not pursue any really difficult question far enough to come to a satisfactory resolution; the results seldom become public and do not accumulate. Academic discussion is on the whole disciplined; much of it is published or actually carried out in a published form, and it is cumulative.

This is not to say that academic discussions of knowledge leave the impression of getting somewhere. To outsiders who try to follow such discussions, they frequently appear both to go around in interminable circles and to be bogged down in intractable disagreements. This impression belies the extent to which academic discussion generates its own stable objects, if not of admiration, at least of deference. No group of people can go around in circles together and lock themselves into disagreements without agreeing (at least tacitly) on a framework, which determines what counts as an issue, what counts as a decisive consideration and what counts as a relevant consideration. This framework is not visible in the discussion, but many outsiders, who try not merely to follow a conversation but to contribute to it, are frequently made to feel their ignorance of the framework.

It is the framework of philosophic discussions of knowledge which embodies what passes for knowledge about knowledge – it is, after all, what is assumed not to need questioning – and this is true not just among the participants. Educated people in other disciplines learn enough about these discussions (sometimes only in their undergraduate days) to carry some sense of what passes for knowledge about knowledge. This experience contributes perhaps a little to their own habits of inquiry and somewhat more to their habits of deferring to some, but not to others, of those in society, who claim authoritative knowledge of some matter.

Philosophical discussion is not one conversation but an overlapping network of conversations; and there is no single fixed framework which governs all these discussions. One can feel the framework shift as one moves from discussions held within one tradition to those conducted within another. Within different traditions, issues and assumptions about knowledge have different degrees of importance. In the tradition broadly identified as "analytic," assumptions about what constitutes knowledge and what can and cannot be known influence discussions about almost every other issue. Discussions about knowledge, even when not seeming to get anywhere, reinforce a framework and serve to keep those assumptions in place.

Challenges to that framework of assumptions can take the form of challenging the importance of engaging in epistemology. Those disposed to make such challenges may try to appeal to the sense, which many people have, that discussions about knowledge appear to progress only in the direction of becoming increasingly remote from anything in non-academic life, or indeed from any other form of academic life. The motive for challenging the very enterprise of epistemology may be the desire (more or less self-consciously articulated) to alter or replace what is perceived to be the dominant framework of discussion. It may also be a more diffuse hostility to any idea that one framework should dominate, the discussions carried out within it thus being able to pretend to special authority.

Recently, resistance to the idea that there should be any dominant framework, dictating for example artistic style, has come to be called "postmodernism." It is not inappropriate to apply this term in philosophy, since it is common to conceive philosophy as taking its "modern" form early in the seventeenth century and the history of the issues, problems, and standards of relevance which now preoccupy "Western" philosophers appears to have taken a decisive turn in the hands of Descartes. That turn not only made certain assumptions about knowledge integral to discussions of other philosophical issues. It also moved to sever the pursuit of knowledge – as well as discussions of knowledge, of what it is, how to acquire it and of how to justify claims to possess it – from the influence of practical concerns, of beliefs supported by tradition and of any bias encouraged by the social, political and economic interests of participants in discussions of knowledge. It encouraged, in other words, participants in philosophical discussions to adopt an Olympian standpoint, which not only hid from them the possibility that the framework of their discussion was culturally limited, it made this suggestion appear positively impertinent. And it underwrote the assumption, particularly among those who sought knowledge of the natural world (natural philosophers, or "scientists" as they came to be called in the nineteenth century) that their efforts could be conducted in an atmosphere insulated from questions of practical consequences and narrow cultural perspectives.

So a move to dismantle wholesale the epistemology industry is a move against a form (however modest) of cultural hegemony. But it is both hazardous and unnecessary to leave in its place nothing but loose, undisciplined discussion ("edifying conversation" according to a gloss favored by Richard Rorty, a prime mover against epistemology). It is unnecessary because it is possible to open up the framework in which knowledge is discussed; epistemology (as opposed to one familiar way of conducting it) is not the creation of Descartes and does not require his framework to be sustained. It is hazardous because claims to authoritative knowledge are increasingly integral to the power structure and to the fabric of social life. It is hazardous because even if there were no epistemologists reinforcing through their practice the assumption that knowledge can be pursued and secured without reference to practical concerns or cultural biases, this assumption would not go away. Those (women and minorities), who feel their voices, their perspectives and their potential contributions have been unjustifiably ignored (and in some cases rejected as unworthy) by a special perspective masquerading as universal, will not find that the institutions which have ignored (and demeaned) them will suddenly open their ears.

Consider the oft-heard phrase, "There is no scientific proof that. . ." The rôle of this phrase in settling practical policy questions in favor of entrenched interests is familiar. "Scientific" may not be as vague a word as "knowledge," but when closely examined it turns out to be importantly ambiguous. We have what we call "scientific proof" when enough empirical evidence is assembled. We also call it "scientific proof" when the cause is understood. These are two quite different ways of knowing some purported fact, ways which were recognized as distinct in antiquity and by many of those who contributed to the formation of modern philosophy (see Chapters 2.4 and 3.7). Clarity about this potential ambiguity is a simple but important defense against a misuse of rhetoric. It is common, however, for epistemology to obscure this difference, in many cases treating proof as the same as empirical evidence. And here the pretense that a view of what constitutes knowledge (sufficient proof) is independent of practical concerns makes it difficult for epistemology to acknowledge the rôle that its views may have in supporting one side in a practical dispute. A number of cases of cancer in a certain class of humans (children who live in the vicinity of a nuclear power station, police who use hand-held radar units) may not be "statistically significant," and may not constitute scientific proof in the sense of understanding the causal connections. But the cases may provide strong empirical evidence for a causal connection and cannot fail to be significant for those involved.

"Scientific studies" of the innate abilities of certain classes in our society are not unnaturally suspected of bias. The claim made by those who conduct such studies is that scientific methods, properly used, can free an investigation from the taint of bias and generate "objective facts." That much of what has been done in the name of this enterprise has been manifestly bogus (see Gould, 1984) does not prove that it cannot be conducted properly, but how fanciful this hope is depends on just how easy it is to free oneself of bias by adopting a method. One of the strongest assumptions in the epistemological traditions which have descended from Descartes, is that adopting such a standpoint is a relatively easy matter. One of the benefits, we believe, of opening up the framework in which epistemology is conducted, is that this assumption will come to appear far from secure.

These indications of the hazards of not engaging at all in epistemology as a discipline, suggest that a wiser course would be to conduct it in a framework more comprehensive than is presently common. The problem is not only to indicate what that framework should be, but to demonstrate how to operate within it. Here the history of philosophy offers resources. This is not to say that contemporary epistemo-

Introduction

logy is wholly unmindful of its history; a view of its history is frequently taught to students as a vehicle for inducting them into the framework of its discussions. There are as a consequence many aspects of the history of our tradition which are commonly overlooked: historical figures such as Bacon and Vico as well as the Hellenistic philosophers, who are not commonly included in the canon of the history of epistemology; familiar figures such a Plato, Hume and Kant, whose concerns with the relation between knowledge and practice are frequently overlooked. This book is an attempt to reintroduce some of the silent voices and some of the overlooked preoccupations into the discussion of knowledge.

This is to say that this is not a history of epistemology, but an essay in (a "new introduction" to) historical epistemology, the discussion of matters of contemporary concern using the resources of history. It has been structured without concern for chronological order. It attempts to identify major historical elements in the framework of contemporary epistemology; it also attempts to place the whole framework within or alongside questions (also raised historically) about the practical relevance of knowledge and the extent to which we can aspire to knowledge from the standpoint of, and with the authority of, a universal perspective, one which transcends the contingencies of individual human situations or the human condition altogether.

To relocate the framework we have stepped back a generation from Descartes and made Francis Bacon a pivotal figure in our discussion. He is introduced in the first chapter in the company of one of the ancient philosophers, Plato, another man whose philosophy was shaped by practical problems and who provides an instructive contrast, which makes the nature of Bacon's revolutionary project clearer. Bacon is not only explicit about the kind of practical orientation which he desired for his new natural philosophy; he was mindful of the obstacles, the prejudices, the biases, the limitations of perspective and experience which stand in the way of improving our knowledge. He attempted a four-fold classification of these obstacles, which he designated "Idols" for rhetorical effect.

The classification itself does not bear up well under close scrutiny. There is the difficulty explored in chapter 5 of whether without a viable notion of human nature we can distinguish Idols of the Tribe from Idols of the Cave. The Idols of the Theater would appear to be a species of Idols of the Cave (Aristotle's philosophy is cited by Bacon as an instance of both kinds of Idol). The Idols of the Market Place are perhaps a species of the Idols of the Tribe, if language is essential to human beings, but if the Idols arise from differences local to different linguistic communities, they are also a species of Idols of the Cave.

Bacon's four-fold classification, nevertheless, proves to be a useful way to organize the bulk of our discussion, for associated with each class of Idols is an important source of obstacles to the improvement of knowledge, perception (Tribe), philosophic tradition (Theater), language (Market Place), and history (Cave). These are, we argue, obstacles which we cannot ever wholly transcend, in short because they are also the material out of which we are condemned (if that is the right word) to fashion ourselves, to remake our material and cognitive lives.

1
Plato and Bacon: *Two Challenges to Prevailing Authority*

1 Knowledge and Authority

Authorities are people who have a claim to be followed in some matter. In its most unrefined form this claim may be based on nothing more than the power to coerce people; that is, the power to make life unpleasant if those claiming authority are not obeyed. Authority, however, is not always imposed; in some cases it is accepted willingly, because those claiming authority possess charm (charisma) or because it is believed they possess superior knowledge about the affairs in which they are expected to be followed. Authority, however, is seldom based purely on one of these unrefined forms; more often it is embedded in human institutions which allow these forms to be mixed and amplified. People, who by themselves are weak, can coerce if they are able to call on the support of others. People, whose personalities do not impress others, acquire stature from symbols of office. People, who individually know very little, may have sources of knowledge provided by institutional connections, which can be called upon when needed.

Coercion breeds resentment. Even with the amplification afforded by institutions, the power to coerce is not a source of stable authority, unless those who exercise it are believed to be acting as they should. Charm is a fickle ally, which depends on the mood of those who are to be charmed, and the trappings of office can become hollow and contemptible to those who feel that authority is being exercised arbitrarily. People may not spontaneously follow those whom they believe to know what is the best course of action, but very few of those who claim authority can wholly dispense with the basis afforded by the belief that they are people who know enough to avoid bringing ruin to those who accept their claim. And their authority in turn will be vulnerable to those who appear to know how to increase the prosperity of those who accept their rival claim to authority.

Anyone who wishes to understand the issues which surround the concept of knowledge must bear in mind the contribution which knowledge makes to the constitution of authority. It is because an important part of what guides our conduct is what we (think we) know, and because we each recognize that what we as individuals know is very limited, that we are prepared to follow (acknowledge the authority of) someone who claims to know what we do not. It is because an important function of human institutions is to channel knowledge, so that we prosper and avoid ruin, that challenges to the authority of individuals and to the very institutions themselves turn from time to time on the allegation that those exercising authority are ignorant of what they should know.

On at least two memorable occasions in the history of Western Europe attempts were made to indict those in authority on a charge of ignorance and to criticize the institutions, which sustained their authority, for failing to encourage the discovery of what was needed to be known if humans were to flourish. The first of these occurred early in the fourth century BC in Athens and the second, two thousand years later, in the late sixteenth century AD in England. The two would-be reformers, Plato and Francis Bacon, were absorbed in political issues, which they approached with the outlook of aristocrats. Both drew inspiration from the intelligence which artisans invest in their work. Both wrote descriptions of ideal societies (what are now known as "utopias") as alternatives to the structures of institutional authority, which they wished to supplant.

In many respects, however, their lives and doctrines faced in different directions. Bacon's political fortunes took him to high public office in a kingdom that managed to contain its internal tensions and successfully defended itself against external aggression. Political infighting eventually led to Bacon's downfall and disgrace, but he was not by birth a political outsider. The aristocratic Plato was born into the political wilderness of democratic Athens and grew up during a period when the policies of successive democratic leaders of his city generated humiliating military defeats, vicious civil strife and general hardship.

Like many members of his social class Plato traced the source of his city's ills to its being governed by men who were not fit to govern. But unlike most members of his social class Plato did not equate belonging to the recognized aristocracy with being fit to govern. What makes men fit to govern, what would qualify them as true aristocrats, is knowledge. It would be both true and misleading to say that this would be for Plato "knowledge of how to govern," misleading because this suggests *savoir faire*, political shrewdness, perhaps only low cunning. But Plato believed that the most important thing which any group of people would know, if they knew how to govern, was their proper goals – what they should aim for and try to maintain in their policies. Of course they would need "know how" (*Republic* 484d), but even here the most important item was knowledge of how to control themselves so that private interests did not interfere with the public interest.

Thus Plato indicted a wide range of authorities in his society, from political, religious and military leaders to educators and dramatists, with ignorance of the ends toward which they should guide society. Bacon, on the other hand, indicted a narrower range of authorities, specifically those who claimed knowledge of the natural world, with failing to discover the means to the material improvement of mankind. In doing this Bacon had to get his intended audience to accept that improvement in the material conditions of mankind was indeed one important end toward which society should be organized. He clearly hoped this end would be recognized as an objective goal, but he placed no stress on the process by which ends (goals, aims, policies, etc.) are made determinate and recognized as having objective validity.

For Plato the primary lesson to be learned from the procedures of craftsmen was the importance of possessing a precise and accurate concept of one's goal. Those who succeeded did so because they possessed a clear idea of the aim of their activities and judged all of their efforts by reference to this standard. He did not otherwise go out of his way as Bacon did to valorize the knowledge possessed by craftsmen. Bacon lived at a time when the knowledge possessed by craftsmen was beginning to be written down and published so that it could accumulate and be more widely disseminated. The accumulated learning of the ages appeared empty and pretentious to Bacon when set against the potential material benefits to be reaped from acquiring knowledge of things which, like the magnetic compass, gunpowder and the printing press, had application to commerce, warfare and communication.

To Plato what we think of as the quality of life was insignificant compared to the quality of the people who would live and, even more importantly, govern that life. Indeed, in Plato's view material wealth was a serious threat to the health of society and the character of its citizens (*Republic* 372e–373a; cp. 399e). His *Republic* (the oldest surviving utopian work) is concerned almost entirely with describing the moral and intellectual character of a class of rulers and with the provisions by which it would reproduce itself over generations. The argument was that this arrangement will secure the best life for the community as a whole by ensuring that those whose decisions matter are sufficiently insulated from the corrupting influence of wealth and comfort. Bacon's utopian work, *New Atlantis*, presents a religious community, organized as a commonwealth, which is also aimed at securing the best life for the community as a whole. It is clear from what was expected of its community of scholars, who devote themselves to scientific inquiry, that wealth and comfort were regarded as, although not ends in themselves, entirely positive.

We have come close to realizing Bacon's plan for communities of scholars devoted to scientific research, and episodes of recent history, such as the Manhattan Project, have dramatically illustrated the power of fundamental science to create new effects and provide us with a hold, however tenuous, on enormously powerful natural forces. Bacon's voice, however, was not the only one in seventeenth century Europe to urge an intense and systematic study of nature. Others viewed the project as a moral or religious duty. God was believed by some to be revealed in his Work (Nature) as much as in his Word (scripture) and the study of Nature was one way to bring mankind closer to God. Others viewed human cognitive faculties as gifts which God had bestowed on us and which we had a duty to use to whatever limited extent we could. The idea that an understanding of the natural world is an end in itself has survived the secularization which has taken place since Bacon's time, and stands in an uneasy relationship with the motive championed by Bacon. Many of our research institutions are publicly supported. They are commonly viewed from the outside as generating new knowledge to improve the material conditions of our lives. This meshes neatly with the widespread modern idea that political authority is, and should be, based on a knowledge of the available means to obtain what the voters want. But those inside research institutions frequently see themselves as disinterestedly pursuing knowledge of the natural world and thus as able to disclaim any responsibility for the use or misuse of what they discover.

Plato's attempt to ground political authority in a grasp of the true goals of human life, in a "science of objective standards," is by contrast so remote from our thinking that it appears either quaintly obscure or outrageously absurd. It is no longer possible to apply the word "knowledge" to a claim of this sort; how society should be organized, what policies we should all adopt, how all people should act, are no longer conceived of as possible objects of knowledge. We expect to be able to know how things are, but not how they ought to be. It will be worthwhile to begin by looking carefully at the thought of both Plato and Bacon in order to locate some of our own most pervasive assumptions about knowledge. Plato advocated something which although once widely accepted in our culture is now alien to us, viz, that the ends of human endeavor are possible objects of knowledge. Bacon sought to put in place something which we now take for granted, viz. that the ability to improve our material conditions is a crucial test of having made a worthwhile advance in knowledge, is a sign of cognitive progress; and, it should be noted, this notion of "progress" retains a moral dimension. Possession of superior technology based on scientific knowledge is used as a basis to claim moral superiority, a claim which is based on a specific conception of the "destiny" of mankind.

PLATO'S SCIENCE OF OBJECTIVE STANDARDS

2 *Expertise*

As a consequence of associating with Socrates during his formative years, Plato acquired the idea that what made people succeed at any endeavor was either on the one hand some form of good fortune or divine favor or on the other hand something called *"epistêmê."* Over the former people have very little control; fortune or favor may desert one as mysteriously as it is bestowed. The latter, however, Plato took to be stable and completely reliable, thus his starting point was that in order to be fit to rule one needs to possess the appropriate *epistêmê*.

"Epistêmê" is a noun, derived from a Greek verb *"epistasthai,"* which means "to know how to [do something]" or "to be capable of [doing something]." The traditional translation of *"epistêmê"* into English as "knowledge" tends to obscure the links which the Greek has to "know-how." It also helps to obscure the link between this notion and another which figures prominently when Plato portrays Socrates in the process of cross-examining certain self-proclaimed experts concerning the basis of their authority. Socrates' examination proceeds in many cases by considering what is possessed by an undisputed expert in some field, whether it be medicine or navigation. What qualifies such an expert is the possession of a *"technê."* The translation of this word into English as "skill" or "craft" fails to convey what

Plato explicitly says he intends (*Gorgias* 465a), namely that the exercise of a *technê* involves a process of thought which can generate an account of what it offers, as well as explanations of its procedure based on the nature of those objectives. It is "know-how" backed up by thought which is able to articulate reasons.

Plato's pupil, Aristotle, later distinguished *technê* from *epistêmê* by defining each as a disposition for exercising discursive thought, the former directed to producing something such as a temple or a flute, and the latter directed to generating only rational discourse of a certain form, a form called "demonstration," which served to communicate *epistêmê*. Plato did not sharply distinguish between these two concepts and on occasion used them interchangeably. His initial interest in "knowledge" was an interest in how the sort of thought, which is able to articulate reasons, can succeed in establishing a reliable practice and succeed thereby in establishing the authority of someone to govern that practice. His theorizing about knowledge begins with an interest in expertise.

In the *Apology* (21c ff.), Plato has Socrates recount how, having recognized his own ignorance, he went around Athens looking for someone who had the wisdom which he lacked. Everyone in Athens turned out to be as ignorant as Socrates – more so since all people except Socrates seemed unaware of their own ignorance. The only class of people for whom Socrates has any kind words are those skilled in handcrafts (*cheirotechnai*, 22c), who knew something in their own fields, although they often imagined that this equipped them to pronounce on matters outside their fields, about which they were as ignorant as anybody else. No other class of supposed experts had the necessary rational foundation for their practice. This included three important groups – politically prominent citizens, dramatic poets and professional educators – which together embodied the political and moral establishment of Athens. It is against this establishment that one must try to assess the break which Plato was trying to make with what preceded him.

Professional educators in Athens were known as "sophists" (*sophistai*). Originally this term applied to anyone who could claim to be the master of some practice. In the generation before Plato's birth a class of émigrés collected in Athens, who as non-citizens could not participate directly in political life, but who gained influence through offering to teach citizens what we now call "communication skills" and through offering to write speeches for them. Plato was also acutely aware of the place which dramatic poets had in shaping public consciousness both through the public performances of their works and through the use of their works as texts when children were taught to read. The dialogues, identified by scholars as among the first which Plato wrote, show us prominent citizens and non-citizens – generals, sophists, members of a family which owns a large manufacturing concern, a self-professed expert in religious observance and a man whose profession it is to recite the works of Homer – all confronted with a Socrates bent on discovering whether these authority figures have the *epistêmê* necessary to back up the judgments which they confidently make.

Socrates' expressions of limited regard for some experts, including physicians and navigators as well as those who work with their hands, does not reflect, as it does in Bacon, an interest in advancing their endeavors. Indeed, compared to the fields of those whom Socrates is portrayed as pursuing with his embarrassing questions, Plato probably held the work of such experts in relatively low regard. Whether, thanks to the know-how of a navigator, a man safely makes a journey by sea is less important than whether his life is worth living once he arrives (*Gorgias* 511c ff.). Plato's interest in expertise is in establishing it in this vital area where, he believes, only dangerous amateurs and charlatans operate.

The criterion of possessing a *technê*, which is set out in the *Gorgias*, makes it possible to detect a pretender without being an expert oneself. People who possess a *technê* can explain their procedure by reference to the results they are aiming to achieve and what it is that makes those results beneficial. This is what distinguishes possessing a *technê* from merely having experience based on trial and error (*empeiria*). When in *Republic I* Polemarchus argues that to do what is just requires an intelligent application of the principle "Give each man his due," Socrates takes it that a man, who is able to do this, must possess a *technê* and he proceeds to examine Polemarchus on the principles of this "*technê* of justice." Possessors of any *technê* must be able to specify the field of things which they are competent to treat and what benefit they aim to bestow on those things. Polemarchus is not able to give satisfactory answers, but he does not protest the line of questioning. Plato expected his audience to accept that a principle can be applied intelligently only if there is a clear idea available of what one is trying to achieve in applying it.

Viewed from this perspective the general procedure which Socrates is made to adopt in the early Platonic dialogues is extremely well motivated. To determine whether expertise claimed by people is based on *technê*, one needs to hear them give an account of their enterprise. (In the *Protagoras* Socrates asks a sophist, "What is a sophist?" In the *Gorgias* he asks an orator, "What is oratory?") If the nature of the enterprise is obvious, one can move to the next step of asking for the practitioners' account of their principal objective (In *Republic I*, "What is doing the right thing with respect to your fellow men (justice, *dikaiosunê*)?" In the *Euthyphro*, "What is doing the right thing with respect to the gods (piety, *hosiotês*)?") If the objective is obvious, as it is obvious that a general's objective is to win battles, the next step is to ask for an account of the personal characteristics which must be used in the course of pursuing that objective (thus in the *Laches* Socrates asks two generals, "What is courage?").

There is nothing in this line of questioning which assumes that, until a definition has been established for a word, people have no idea what the word means. What is assumed is that unless people can articulate an account of the standards by which they judge their practice, they cannot claim rational understanding of what they are doing. Good fortune, divine favor, hearsay, or experience based on trial and error may have given them an intuitive feel for what will produce a beneficial outcome, but Plato holds that judgments made on that sort of basis are insecure (*Meno* 97e–98a) and exposed to a kind of corruption (*Gorgias* 464e, "pandering").

Physicians who rely on luck or supernatural guidance may be let down. If they rely on hearsay or trial and error experience, they will have to judge by appearances. This may leave them unable to recognize when their past experience is inapplicable and should not be relied upon, and it may well make them content to restore their patients only to what *appears to be* good health. Here is where a kind of corruption may overtake the physician's profession. If genuine health requires a course of treatment which patients find arduous, the physician who offers the easy route to the (temporary) appearance of health will attract gullible patients.

This is Plato's case against the political and educational establishment of Athens: they have led a gullible people toward the *mere appearance* of a flourishing and well-founded society. They have not educated the citizens to recognize what real justice, or what a genuinely admirable (*kalos*) life, would be, because they are not in a position to articulate the standards by which they or anyone else could judge whether a given policy would further these objectives. And those leaders who have the ability to discover the criteria of a genuinely just and admirable way of life, are themselves too content with appearances to undergo the discipline and meet the difficulties which acquiring real expertise would entail.

3 Opinion and Understanding

In order to explain how from an otherwise ill-equipped class of leaders there sometimes arise people who at least for a time display real excellence, Plato has Socrates introduce a contrast between "*epistêmê*" and "*orthê doxa*" (*Meno* 97a ff.). It is common to translate these into English as "knowledge" and "true belief," but we have already seen respects in which using the word "knowledge" for "*epistêmê*" obscures important connections in Plato's thought. We should consider what Plato says about the distinction before settling on a translation. For example, Plato has Socrates acknowledge that, for the purposes of succeeding at what one is doing, a correct *doxa* may serve just as well as *epistêmê* but the former is unstable, liable to escape, unless tethered down and turned into *epistêmê* by "working out the reasons" (*Meno* 98a). The *Meno* also appears to make the contrast in terms of first-hand acquaintance as opposed to hearsay. If I have never traveled the road to Larissa, the directions I give to another are based on *doxa*, whereas if I have traveled the road they are based on *epistêmê*. Now these two ways of explaining the relationship between *epistêmê* and *doxa* amount to a single coherent contrast only if the road to Larissa is treated as a metaphor for the train of reasoning which tethers *doxa* and turns it into *epistêmê*. To possess *epistêmê* one must go through the reasons oneself and not accept them on the authority of another person.

In the last book of the *Republic* (601c–602a) the contrast between *doxa* and *epistêmê* is made in what appears to be very different terms. Having noted that some *technai* produce, while others use, Socrates assigns true *doxa* to the former and *epistêmê* to the latter; thus bridle-makers have true *doxa* of bridles, while horsemen have *epistêmê*. The reason horsemen are said to be in this favored position is that it is the use to which they put the bridle which is the starting point of any reasoning which bridle-makers might undertake to determine how they will proceed. Bridle-makers must either take their specifications from people who know what is going to be done with this product, or must stop making things long enough to acquire the horserider's expertise. When bridle-makers explain their procedures, and why they adopt the materials and design which they do, they have to rely on principles which belong to this other area of expertise. If they do not possess the horserider's expertise, they must rely on the horserider's authority. In that case, when they explain their procedure, they are like the person who gives directions to Larissa on the basis of hearsay.

When a person knows the answer to some question, but lacks the ability to explain why that should be the right answer, we commonly say that such a person knows the answer but does not *understand* it. If we speak of people whose expertise we do not want to endorse, even when those people are sometimes obviously right, we may speak of deferring not to their expertise, but to their *opinions*, some of which, we have to admit, have been correct. These are the best English terms to identify Plato's contrast. The ability to explain why one's answers are right, why the aims and the procedures one has adopted are correct, is the ability we call *understanding* and Plato calls *epistêmê*. People who do not possess this ability, but who with hindsight we see were right, we speak of as having had a true or correct *opinion* (Plato, *doxa*).

This translation should serve to remind us of the quite specific interests which motivate what Plato says about knowledge-related topics. He did not start with an interest in all that could be said to be known, for example one's own name or the color of a mailbox, but with an interest in that high grade of knowledge (understanding), which constitutes a high level of expertise. And if we bear Plato's quite specific interest in mind, we can make better sense of the (at first sight bizarre) metaphysics which Plato links to this distinction.

The distinction between *epistêmê* and *doxa* is connected to Plato's metaphysics in *Republic* V. Starting at 474b Socrates attempts to say what it is that qualifies a philosopher to rule the ideal city which he has been describing. The answer in part is that a philosopher can claim understanding, where others possess only opinion. Plato's explanation of the difference dwells on the class of judgments to the effect that this or that thing is admirable (*kalos*). The person who lacks the qualifications of a philosopher is the person who makes such judgments without reference to what Plato calls "the admirable itself." By the end of Book V Plato has assigned to "the admirable itself" a supernatural grade of reality, declaring that it is without qualification admirable, while nothing in the natural world is without qualification admirable. (Indeed there turns out to be very little which something in the natural world can be said without qualification to be. Compare *Republic* 523c: a finger may be said to be a finger without qualification, but it cannot without qualification be said to be large or small, thick or thin, hard or soft.)

The way Plato chooses to express himself has unfortunate consequences, but his line of thought is not difficult to follow. To make matters easier it may help to change his example from "admirable" to "round." People who judge that an object is round, but are not able to say what justifies their judgment, have opinion, but cannot be said to have understanding. What they have to be able to do in order to justify their judgment is to appeal to some standard of what it is to be round. They might appeal to the definition given at *Parmenides* 137e: "Whatever has all the points of its edge equidistant from its center." This standard is not to be found by examining particular things in the natural world. It is partly to forestall this suggestion that Plato insists that however admirable some particular thing may be, it will appear the opposite (a matter for shame) in some other context or from some other perspective. In a similar vein he would insist that however round an object may be, it will always be possible to find one which is more (perfectly) round.

Now the formula for the criterion, by which one judges whether a thing is round and judges that for example an octagon is more round than a square is, has this peculiarity: we can state this formula, "Whatever has all the points of its edge equidistant from its center," and add "is round" without any qualification. That is, after all, what round is. But if we refer to some object in the natural world and say of it that it "is round" this has to be qualified in the sense that something could well be more (perfectly) round than it is. Plato appears to be more impressed with this comparison than he should be. He has a way of referring to the standard by which a thing is judged to be X (admirable, round, etc.); he calls it "the X itself." But there would appear to be two quite different senses of "is round," which allow Plato to say both that the X itself is round and that a ball is round. And it seems a pointless exaggeration to say, as Plato would insist (see *Republic* 479 ff.) that because any given thing may be less round than some other thing, that any round thing is therefore also "not round."

Whatever the drawbacks of this fancy metaphysical language, it does help Plato to articulate several important claims, for example that people who claim expertise will be able to justify their judgments (and thereby show that they have understanding of their area of expertise) only if they have a sufficient grasp of a standard by which to judge, and that this is not a standard which is embodied in any natural object, because no natural object ever perfectly exemplifies the standard by which natural objects are judged. When he refers to such a standard as "the X itself," and insists that it is unchanging and the same everywhere, he is saying that the standard by which an expert's judgments are made do not change from day to day or vary in different parts of the world. When he claims the X itself is more real than anything in the natural world, he is trying to make clear the role which this abstract standard plays in determining which things can claim to be really X and which are not really (but inferior, imitation, *ersatz*, or counterfeit) X. And when he stresses that acquiring *epistêmê* does not involve the use of the senses but the use of reason, he is simply pointing out the kind of mental activity which is involved in articulating and applying a definition such as that of "round."

In an effort to make clear the relationship between our ordinary mental activity and that required if a person is to gain the understanding needed to govern properly, Plato created one of the most memorable images in philosophy, the cave. In this parable the mental condition of most people is represented by a large crowd in the bowels of a cave chained to a wall and with their gaze fixed on a wall opposite. On this opposite wall there is a continual play of shadows, which are cast by a flickering fire falling on graven images paraded on a parapet above and behind the prisoners in chains. These shadows are the subject of continual conversation among the prisoners. A few of the prisoners break free of their chains and are able to examine the graven images and the fire which casts the shadows; fewer still escape the cave and once accustomed to the bright light of the sun are able to examine the living models from which the graven images in the cave have been fashioned.

Plato intended this to be an anything-but-flattering image of his own society, and it is doubtful he would view our own society in any kinder light. Were Plato to apply his parable to our society, he might make the following interpretation: The large crowd of prisoners at the bottom of the cave are ordinary citizens whose knowledge of the world derives from media such as newspapers and novels, cinema and television. For example, their knowledge of justice is derived from watching police, detective and courtroom dramas. Very few, even of those who on occasion come into direct contact with police and the courts, appreciate the actual workings of the legal system and the extent to which dramatic representations present partial and distorted pictures of how it works. And few among those, who understand the actual workings of the legal system, give any thought to how ideally it should be constituted. Few have extended their minds beyond the concrete reality of actual institutions (beyond the confines of the cave) to the abstract standards by which concrete practices should be judged. To most of us the study of how things really are, without a reduction to dramatic form or a gloss of artistic embellishment, has little appeal, but Plato's image suggests this is because we are prisoners of our appetites and habits. To us the abstractions beyond the cave appear obscure and indeterminate, but Plato's image suggests that this is because our mental vision is too weak to stand the light of the truth.

Physical escape from Plato's cave is impossible; only the mind can transcend the cave and explore the realm to which Plato assigns the all-important ideal standards by which people must judge if they are to claim understanding. Beyond this world, where things change and gain or lose characteristics depending on their context or on the perspective from which they are viewed, is a realm which only reason can reach and where characteristics are completely stable. This is the realm where what is said about the just, the admirable or the round does not depend on changes in perspective, context or material embodiment. This is the realm of the just itself, the admirable itself, the round itself. This is the standpoint we try to adopt whenever we try to judge ordinary things from the perspective of a definitive and unconditioned standard for assessing their characteristics. An object in this realm is also referred to in Plato's Greek as an *"idea,"* the closest English word to which is "form." In some contexts the Greek word suggests the appearance of a thing as opposed to its reality, but Plato used the word for what appears to our minds when they have correctly adopted the special perspective of judging things against an unconditioned standard. The special dignity of these objects, these standards, is often marked by capitalizing the English words "Form" and "Idea" when they are used to translate what Plato says about *"ideai."*

4 Forms

It is true to say that Plato's whole project stands or falls with the question of whether there are Forms. This question is often presented as a stark choice between accepting or rejecting the existence of things which are quite unlike others in our experience. Along with the presentation of this choice comes the suggestion that those with a mystical bent will be inclined to accept these peculiar objects on faith, while those reluctant to take leave of their senses will reject them. Plato's philosophy does require one to make choices, and the choices which favor his philosophy do involve a commitment akin to faith, but this way of phrasing the issues obscures the nature of the choices.

The first real issue one might take up with Plato is over the claim that expert authority should be capable of giving explicit reasons for its procedures and judgments, reasons which are based on clear accounts of the benefits sought. There are those who rightly point out that in circumstances where quick response is crucial to success, thinking out the reasons for what one does can lead to disaster. Plato can quite happily accommodate this point by recommending rational thought be invested in forming habits of instant response which rational thought will find itself happy to endorse after the fact. Others will insist that every practice requires a foundation of tacit habits of response and that no successful practice can reduce everything to a series of explicitly justified steps. Plato could reply that his intention is only to place the overall direction of an activity under rational guidance and to use reason to guide procedure by explicit standards only where it would otherwise fail to reach its objective.

But even after these doubts have been met, there will be people who prefer to trust to more "intuitive" ways of proceeding, who prefer not to think at all about what they are doing – or why – who have convinced themselves that they will be more successful without the assistance of reason. Someone sympathetic to Plato's general position might argue that possessing understanding makes one less liable to be fooled by appearances, but those hostile to Plato might protest that it is foolish arrogance to try to second guess appearances. Apart from suggesting (a suggestion which may simply be repudiated) that it is more characteristic of being human to try to distinguish between appearance and reality and to try to bring one's practices under rational guidance, there is little that can be said to these people.

If, however, one accepts Plato's claims about the sort of understanding and expertise which we should aspire to develop, then the next most pressing issue to be settled is the status of the standards on which that understanding and expertise must rest. Expertise based on understanding consists in the ability to explain one's judgments and procedures by reference to explicit standards. Plato speaks of these standards as though they were objects, which can be identified and described in such a way that the descriptions will provide the very principles to which experts must appeal when justifying their procedures or judgments. What led him to this assumption?

Plato knew enough of the mathematics of his day to know how the definition of "round" might figure in an argument of this sort: If I have a triangle whose base is the diameter of a circle and whose apex lies on the circumference, then if I connect the apex to the mid-point of the base, I will divide the triangle into two isosceles triangles (figure 1.1). Why? Because a circle, being perfectly round, has its extreme points (the three corners of the triangle) everywhere equidistant from its center (the mid-point of the diameter). And an isosceles triangle has two sides which are equal in length.

Two Challenges to Prevailing Authority

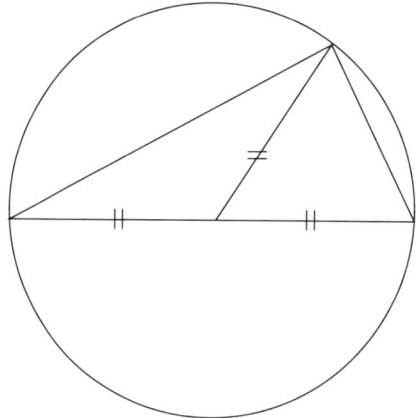

Figure 1.1

What Plato wanted was for all those who exercised authority to be able to justify what they said with this sort of rigor. Mathematicians had reached a consensus on what the round itself is, and on this and similar accounts had built an impressive body of practice. (Geometry in Plato's day was a collection of techniques for constructing figures with compasses and straight edge. Plato refers to geometry as a *technê* at *Republic* 551b.) What stands in the way of building a equally rigorous, equally impressive body of political practice based on understanding?

Two things might stand in the way. The first is that the Forms required to provide the standards, to which this practice would appeal, might simply not be there. Geometry might be evidence that a human mind can transcend the cave and acquire understanding of the sort Plato wanted, but when we reach beyond the cave for a grasp of the just itself or the admirable itself to add to our quite satisfactory grasp of the round itself, we might fail to find what we are looking for. It is important not to think of this simply in terms of the required Forms as "just not there (outside the cave)" as the clothes we are looking for are "just not there (in the closet)" because we gave them to a charity. To say that the Forms needed for political understanding are "not there" is to say (at least) that the procedure by which geometers arrived at a grasp of mathematical Forms will not generate a similar grasp of political Forms. But can one say that this is impossible in advance of trying to establish a body of political understanding?

Plato understood the procedure by which geometers arrived at a grasp of their key terms in this way: Accounts of the terms were laid down (Plato uses for this a Greek word from which our verb "hypothesize" is derived) and used in justifications until some difficulty was discovered with the formulation, at which point the accounts were taken up and modified so as to preserve what had been right about the old formulae and to incorporate the new requirements, and were laid down again until further problems emerged. This procedure took place in the context of a discussion which had the nature of a cooperative debate between mathematicians who were working on problems. Hence Plato referred to the general method by making use of a word for argumentative discourse (or rational conversation, *dialectikê*), which is rendered into English a "dialectic."

The first step in applying this procedure outside mathematics would be to offer an account of an important term of moral or political appraisal, such as "just," together with enough social theory to show how the account is meant to work. This is what Plato's *Republic* does. We may doubt that this procedure will ever lead to a definitive account of the standard by which actions or institutions may be called just or unjust; (this is what it is to doubt that there is anything we might speak of as "the just itself"). But Plato's account of "just" stands as a challenge and as soon as we try to say what is wrong with it, we engage in dialectic. There is no obvious reason why after a succession of criticisms and modifications we will not arrive at an account every bit as successful as the geometer's account of "round." But, of course, neither is there any guarantee of success.

If we are to conclude in advance of trying Plato's method that his project cannot succeed, the reason must lie in the second of the two obstacles, referred to above, which might stand in his way. This is the possibility that Plato has mistaken the nature of geometry, that its account of "round" does not describe anything Plato would want to call "the round itself," that there is no realm beyond the cave. The problem is not that geometers' accounts of terms such as "round" might always be subject to further refinement, in which case we could never be sure that no further refinement was needed. It may indeed be the case that in geometry, and consequently in Plato's projected *epistêmê* of politics, we will never be able to tell when no further development is possible. But this is a relatively minor worry compared to the suspicion that geometers have reached agreements, which are nothing more than conventions, about the terms on which they base justifications for their procedures. They have created a game played with compasses and straight edge, but they could conceivably have created a different game using perhaps bits of string and straight edges which pivot on one another. It is not that the account which geometers now give of "round" is wrong, but it might be irrelevant, if the game were different. And if Plato should succeed in reaching a satisfactory account of "just," the suspicion will remain that with a different form of life (corresponding to a different geometrical game) this account will simply have no place.

Plato's response to this worry is to assign to the method of dialectic a special responsibility, which if carried out would allay this suspicion once and for all and would also help to meet the other worries just canvassed. Dialectic is also intended by Plato to yield an account of a special Form, "the Good itself." This Form stands in a unique relationship to all the other Forms and a grasp of the Good itself is needed to underwrite any account given of any other Form. Plato's own account of the just itself is said to require an account of this Form (*Republic* 504b, cp. 435d) and the work of geometers is said to be incomplete until a dialectician finds in the Form of the Good a foundation for the principles which are used in geometry. Until it is found the principles which geometers use with complete confidence are still hypothetical (511).

The imagery which Plato uses to explain the rôle of the Good itself, is clearer than the literal way in which it is supposed to fulfill its function. The Good is compared to the sun, in that it illuminates the objects of the understanding, thereby enabling the understanding to comprehend them (508d). Given Plato's preference for explanations in terms of ends sought and purposes furthered, this appears to be a way of expressing the point that we understand through grasping the good of a thing, i.e., how it is supposed to be so that it fulfills its function. The Good is said to be the source of the "being and reality" of the objects of understanding (as the sun is the source of growth and nourishment, 509b). This it would be if an account of the Good itself enabled the dialectician to show why a certain way of doing geometry or a certain form of human association were unquestionably good. Then if a certain account of "round" or of "just" were obviously central to this way of doing geometry or this way of living, there would be no question about the reality of "the round itself" and "the just itself." This is because Plato insists that the Good itself is unique. There presumably could be no equally good alternative ways of doing geometry or of living with one another, for in that case there would be more than one account to be given of the Good.

So if Plato could produce the sort of account of the Good itself, which he thinks is possible, he could answer the worry that his Forms are not the uniquely authoritative objects which he claims them to be, because the Good would underwrite precisely one account of each important term of appraisal. And with an understanding of the Good itself it would be possible to determine when a completely satisfactory account of any term had been reached. And there would be no worry that there might be Forms to guide the practice of geometry but not to guide moral and political practice, for both would have a common foundation in a unique account of how everything should be.

Of course the prospect of giving an account of the Form of the Good only serves to create a space for Plato's program to be undertaken; it does not guarantee that it can be successfully completed. If we respond with criticism to any attempt by Plato to give an account of this Form, we will, as we noted above in discussing the Form of the just, be contributing to the dialectical advance of Plato's program. If we want no part of the program, we have to remain silent unless we can identify a flaw in its conception which would reveal it to be an impossible dream of reason.

FRANCIS BACON'S GREAT INSTAURATION

5 Redefining the Goal of Knowledge

Although there are many passages in Plato's dialogues where the argument turns on what is done by various experts from craftsmen to physicians, it is clear that Plato has no special interest in the further development of such bodies of expertise. His interest is in human conduct and social relations; the point of citing cases of acknowledged expertise is to argue for the indispensability of a certain kind of understanding, if our social institutions are to be well founded and our conduct properly judged. Plato's thought was that if potential rulers were made to study nature in the right way, this would develop in them a grasp of principles which govern the natural world. These principles are similar to those which are required to govern well and live righteously. It was common for later Greek philosophers, including those who rejected Plato's philosophy, to hold that the principles which govern the natural world contain the key to how humans should conduct their lives. In time Greek thought was incorporated into Christianity, where it is assumed that the natural world is the creation of a Being, who is also the source of the moral law to which all human conduct should conform.

Looking back over the two thousand years which separated him from Plato, Francis Bacon saw a philosophic tradition preoccupied either with theological speculation or moral philosophy. What made that preoccupation stand out for Bacon and made natural philosophy appear to him to have been by comparison sorely neglected (*Novum Organum* I LXXIX) was his interest in developing those spheres of expertise which might improve and transform the conditions of human life. Bacon was impressed by the transforming effects which three relatively simple inventions had had on the human world. These inventions were gunpowder, the magnetic compass and the printing press. Gunpowder was redefining the parameters of warfare; the compass, together with navigational techniques based on it, was opening up a new world to exploration, and the printing press was reshaping the intellectual space of Western Europe. It was, for example, becoming common for craftsmen and technicians to communicate important elements of their expertise to other experts and to the general public, not just to their apprentices. Books on mining (Georgius Agricola), metallurgy (Vannoccio Biringuccio), machines (Agostino Ramelli) and architecture (Andrea Palladio) were being published. It was becoming possible to conceive of know-how as something which could accumulate.

Bacon believed that the growth of this kind of knowledge could be facilitated, and the quality of life improved, only if the principles which govern nature were known in detail. He called for the adoption of a new goal for natural philosophy: "Now the true and lawful goal of the sciences is none other than this: that human life be endowed with new discoveries and powers" (*Novum Organum* I LXXXI: unless otherwise indicated, all references are to *Novum Organum*, by book and aphorism number.). Bacon appreciated, however, that his call would fall on deaf ears, unless it were generally accepted that concern for improving the material conditions of life was morally worthy, something which was compatible with human "dignity" and necessary to human fulfillment. He saw that he must overcome the opinion

> ...which though of long standing is vain and hurtful, namely, that the dignity of the human mind is impaired by long and close intercourse with experiments and particulars, subject to sense and bound in matter; especially as they are laborious to search, ignoble to meditate, harsh to deliver, illiberal to practice, indefinite in number, and minute in subtlety. So that it has come at length to this, that the true way is not merely deserted, but shut out and stopped up; experience being, I do not say abandoned or badly managed, but rejected with disdain. (I LXXXIII)

In arguing for more effort to be invested in the study of nature Bacon was very careful to limit the pretensions of natural philosophy in such a way as to exclude ethical and religious matters from its compass. At the beginning of *The Advancement of Learning* he argued that Adam and Eve were not expelled from Paradise for seeking knowledge of the natural world, but for presuming knowledge of good and evil. He was quite insistent that the human capacity for knowledge is limited and that our project cannot and should not be to "presume by the contemplation of nature to attain the mysteries of God" (*The Advancement of Learning* (1605) and the *New Atlantis* (1627) [ALNA], p. 9). Religious knowledge, whether mystical or moral, can only be attained by inspiration and revelation from God (ALNA, p. 241). But we can and should use our senses combined with our rational faculties to attain knowledge of the material world.

Although Bacon took pains to make his project appear incapable of leading to any challenges to existing moral, religious or political authority, it is important to recognize the extent to which Bacon was nevertheless advancing a specific moral vision – of mankind mastering nature – and a specific set of moral concerns, viz. for the material well-being of humanity as a whole. This is clear in his utopian story, *New Atlantis*. The society outlined there is a religious community, organized as a commonwealth; its institutions, including its community of scholars, devote themselves to scientific inquiry, which is expected to help in securing the best life for the community as a whole.

Bacon's defense of the pursuit of natural philosophy in part rests on a portrayal of the student of natural philosophy as disinterested and morally upright. The learned should not seek knowledge for personal gain, whether this is political power or commercial profit. They should, moreover, not treat other people as objects of scientific knowledge; the sort of knowledge one should have of other people is the knowledge one needs in order to be able to treat them with understanding, to be able to help or to be on guard against them. One should not seek the sort of knowledge which would make it possible to manipulate or dominate: "To be speculative into another man to the end to know how to work him or wind him, procedeth from a heart that is double and cloven and not entire and ingenuous" (ALNA, p. 25). This is in marked contrast to the attitude of, for example, Bacon's older contemporary, John Dee, who unsuccessfully sought power and influence in the Elizabethan court on the basis of his mathematical and astrological learning. Dee aspired to a mathematical-mystical knowledge of the sort that Bacon denied to be possible and believed to be the object of an illegitimate quest. Dee seems to have had little compunction about dominating others; those who do not develop their human potential by acquiring the knowledge which yields power are rightfully subject to domination by those who have achieved a higher estate: "Accordingly, whoever was able to fulfil, in a variety of ways, the office of both physician and musician could govern the bodies and minds of men almost according to his wish. But this surely is to be treated as a secret by discreet philosophers" (*Propaedeumata Aphoristica* XXIII).

In the seventeenth century context it was necessary to argue for the independence of natural philosophy from moral philosophy and theology in order to secure for it a place outside the jurisdiction of religious authorities. By insisting on a sharp division between natural science on the one hand and morals and theology on the other, Bacon hoped to persuade people of the moral neutrality of his project. But to succeed, his own arguments had to straddle that division, and the fact that Bacon's advocacy of his program for acquisition of knowledge of nature does rest on a moral vision, at the same time as proclaiming the autonomy of science from moral and political jurisdiction, means that there is an inherent source of tension within the project. On the one hand, if the autonomy of science is taken to be unconditional, i.e., not dependent on the moral vision which sets up the goal of knowledge as something which should be pursued (as a moral duty), then we have the conception of knowledge which should be pursued for its own sake, independently of all questions concerning the use to which it might be put. On the other hand, if it is recognized as a conditioned autonomy, the project is clearly vulnerable to criticism from those who do not share the vision on which it rests. Bacon himself does not defend the moral principles to which he appeals. They are simply taken for granted as principles, which will be recognized and approved by those for whom he is writing. He is justifying his project by reference to moral standards drawn from his social context.

It is well to bear this in mind in the light of what are now common attacks on Bacon by feminist writers, who reject the values inherent in adopting mastery over nature as the goal of human knowledge. Bacon is a natural target for criticism by feminists because he always treats nature as feminine and at one time called his project "The Masculine Birth of Time." By this he meant that technological advance, the active product ("birth" in the sense of thing born) of knowledge is made possible by a rational use of experience (time). Truth, regarded as something we are interested in only for the purposes of contemplation, is the passive, feminine birth of time (product of experience).

The question of whether these gendered metaphors are anything more than useful rhetorical devices, whether they result in Baconian science being inherently masculine, lies at the heart of feminist critiques of modern science and epistemology. This issue is too complex to be settled here, but it should be said that Bacon was proposing what seemed to him to be a very correct relationship. He also characterized the relation between the scientist and nature as one of holy wedlock, or lawful marriage, emphasizing that Nature must be respected before she can be dominated. He did not advocate the rape of Nature, although neither did he suggest partnership. He urged the unity of theory and practice, contemplation and action in order that "knowledge may not be as a courtesan, for pleasure and vanity only, or as a bondwoman, to acquire and gain to her master's use; but as a spouse, for generation, fruit, and comfort" (ALNA, pp. 42–3). The spouse metaphor is clearly expected to elicit moral approval from his readers, whom he (reasonably enough for the time) presumed would be male.

In assessing Bacon's attitude to nature, it should also be remembered that the Nature over which Bacon sought dominance has changed a great deal since he wrote. In the seventeenth century Nature was still full of threats; life in Europe at that time was very insecure. Natural disasters such as the great plague and fire, which ravaged London during Elizabeth's reign, were not uncommon; ships were lost at sea with great frequency; wolves still lurked in the forests. Nature then was hardly benign and still is not in regions of the planet subject to drought or earthquake, or where there is no money for the public health measures necessary to reduce the impact of infectious diseases. It is only as we have indeed dominated many of the aspects of the natural world which affect everyday life, constructing controlled environments for ourselves in which to live, that we can afford to take a more indulgent attitude to the natural world. Only from the apparent security of our controlled environments can it appear a world which does not pose immediate threats.

In trying to understand Bacon's project we should, therefore, distinguish between the rôle played by his rhetoric in his historical context and the appropriateness of that rhetoric in our own. What was appropriate rhetoric in the seventeenth century may no longer be so. A useful test of whether his metaphors of dominance (with violence) are obsolete, is to consider how easy it still is to speak of efforts to control ("combat") diseases such as cancer and AIDS as "the fight against cancer," etc. Is the language of violence and domination inappropriate in these cases?

6 Retooling the Study of Nature

Bacon is more deliberate and self-conscious about the style in which he presents his philosophy than is common for modern philosophers to be. Many intellectuals among his contemporaries and immediate predecessors took classical Greek and Roman authors as their models, spurning medieval philosophy as barbaric in its lack of style and elegance. Alive to the issue of the relation between style, content and function, Bacon chose to set out his views in the *Novum Organum* in the form of a sequence of aphorisms. The majority of his other writings do not have this form, and the thought behind his choice is set out in *The Advancement of Learning* (pp. 163–4). There Bacon observes that methodical presentation is appropriate for winning people over to your beliefs, but this is not a good way to prompt them to further action: ". . . aphorisms, representing a knowledge broken, do invite men to inquire further; whereas methods, carrying a show of a total, do secure men, as if they were at furthest" (ALNA, p. 164). Bacon has no system to present; he has a method which he wants people to pick up and use.

The title of this sequence of aphorisms, *Novum Organum*, is also chosen with care. Plato's influence was present from the time Christian apologists first felt the need for a philosophic framework in which to articulate Christian doctrine. It was quite a while before the writings of Plato's sometime student and junior colleague, Aristotle, were recognized as containing views strongly at odds with those of Plato. Four centuries before Francis Bacon lived many of Aristotle's writings which had been lost to Latin Christendom became available, and Aristotle came to be a dominant intellectual force in Western Europe, an influence which carried on into the Renaissance. In Bacon's time the rejection of medieval philosophy accompanied a revived interest in a fresh first-hand study of Aristotle's writings. Among Aristotle's most influential works were a number on logic and related subjects, known collectively as the *Organum*, from the Greek word for tool, "*organon.*" What Bacon's choice of title clearly indicated was that he was proposing a new intellectual tool, a method better suited to the new goal, which he was proposing for the study of nature.

Bacon accused Aristotle of having corrupted natural philosophy with his logic (*Novum Organum* I LXIII). He "fashioned the world out of categories" by laying down in an arbitrary way a network of distinctions – between density and rarity, act and power, proper and enforced motion – which set the framework within which the natural world had to be investigated and described. But it was not specific tenets of Aristotelian physics or metaphysics which rendered it a particularly inappropriate framework for the advancement of natural philosophy, but the way it encouraged people to approach the investigation of the natural world. Aristotle, Bacon believed, encouraged people to "anticipate nature" – that is, to make hasty generalizations from a few observations and give these generalizations the status of first principles – rather than to "interpret nature" with proper care. They were then urged to rely on deductive reasoning (syllogistic logic) to arrive at explanations of observed phenomena on the basis of first principles. This procedure is flawed, Bacon argues, because it is not possible to leap in one step from observations to first principles. The essences, or forms, of natural things are not open to view, are not outwardly displayed but, being hidden, must be gradually and methodically revealed.

What is required to "interpret nature" with proper care is worked out from Bacon's new identification of the goal of inquiry. Given that we are looking for practically useful knowledge of nature, what should we be looking for? Since to act is to bring about effects, clearly what we need is knowledge of how to bring about specific effects in the natural world, or how to prevent them occurring. This is knowledge of causes, where causes are viewed as the antecedent conditions which must be realized if a specific result is to be achieved. Such knowledge is important but on its own it will be of limited use. Knowing how to produce a specific effect (make strawberry jam), i.e., knowing what materials to use and what to do with them, is limited because it does not transfer to other situations (what if there are no strawberries but plenty of plums?) We will not have real power over Nature until we have the sort of generally applicable knowledge which can be adapted to varied situations.

It is clear from this that even though Bacon might claim that he is not proposing a metaphysical system, he cannot propose any method for acquiring knowledge of the natural world without presupposing a general conception of its causal structure, a conception which indicates to us what we should be looking for and which hence gives a direction to our inquiry. He simply states without argument:

> For though in nature nothing really exists besides individual bodies, performing pure individual acts according to fixed law, yet in philo-

sophy this very law, and the investigation, discovery and explanation of it, is the foundation as well of knowledge as of operation. And it is this law with its clauses that I mean when I speak of *forms*. (II II)

Here Bacon is rejecting the Aristotelian view of the world as made up of individual things (many of them living organisms), each of which is a composite of form and matter, and where it is the form of a natural thing (its principle of change) which we need to grasp if we are to understand how it will change if left to its own devices. Individual things, on this view, fall into natural kinds (species); all individuals of the same kind share the same form or nature.

Baconian forms are not forms of individual things but fundamental causal laws, which apply to all things. Suppose, for example, (Bacon's example) that we are inquiring after the nature of heat. What we would be looking for is an account which views heat as a special case of a more generally occurring phenomenon, such as motion, where we could say that whenever there is motion of such and such a kind, there we have heat, and whenever there is heat, there is motion of that kind. Then our grasp of the phenomena of heat will rest on our grasp of the phenomena of motion. The forms, or laws according to which all things operate, are thus to be the object of our inquiry.

The focus of the quest for knowledge of the natural world thus shifts in Bacon's hands as a result of the change he proposed in the conception of the goal of knowledge – in the reason for which knowledge is pursued. This change also entails that we should not rest content with natural history but must advance to experimental science. In natural history we aim for accurate and detailed observations of natural things and of natural processes where we have interfered as little as possible. Bacon argues that natural history, whilst still a necessary and important starting point, will not yield the kind of knowledge we want. By closely observing nature at work we may be able to reproduce certain natural effects, thus learning to imitate nature.

The ability to imitate nature is not, however, the ability to dominate or control. For this we must be able to make things which, left to its own devices, nature would not produce (such as electric light bulbs); we must be able to do things in ways which take less time than natural processes. To this end we need to devise experiments in which nature is forced out of her normal course. We need to do this in order to have any knowledge worthy of the name: "the nature of things betrays itself more readily under the vexations of art than in its natural freedom" (*Great Instauration*, [GI], p. 25). Such experiments will be necessary if we are to discover the fundamental laws governing events in the natural world.

> For a true and perfect rule of operation the direction will be *that it be certain, free and disposing, or leading to action*. . . . For a true and perfect axiom of knowledge, the direction will be *that another nature be discovered which is convertible with the given nature and yet is a limitation of a more general nature,* . . . these two directions, the one active and the other contemplative, are one and the same thing, and what in operation is most useful, that in knowledge is most true. (II IV)

As we must experiment in order to acquire genuine knowledge, so we must conform to the laws which we thereby discover, if we are to have any hope of effective action in the world – nature to be commanded must be obeyed. We are not relying on or looking for supernatural powers.

We must, moreover, conform to what laws we know if we are to experiment effectively. Experiments conducted haphazardly are "a mere groping, as of men in the dark. . . But the true method of experience, on the contrary, first lights the candle, and then by means of the candle shows the way; commencing as it does with experience duly ordered and digested, not bungling or erratic, and from it educing axioms, and from established axioms again new experiments" (I LXXXII).

Although Bacon rejected the atomism of such ancient philosophers as Democritus and Epicurus (on the grounds that it requires the existence of a vacuum) it is nonetheless clear that he subscribed to a view of the natural world according to which the events we observe are in fact complex, being made up of unobserved processes taking place at the level of the material particles out of which all observed objects are presumed to be composed. When physics searches after material and efficient causes, it is seeking to discover latent configurations and latent processes, the inner structures of specific things and the inner processes by which these are changed. Knowledge of forms, the task of metaphysics, however, is knowledge of the general laws governing the action of all the basic kinds of material and basic physical forces. It is knowledge of the kind that an engineer needs in order to be able to construct mechanical, electronic, or biological devices, not just the descriptive knowledge which would be revealed to a patient and meticulous observer.

The problem then is how do we go about acquiring this kind of knowledge? How can we penetrate beneath the level of what is directly observable?

Therefore a separation and solution of bodies must be effected, not by fire indeed, but by reasoning and true induction, with experiments to aid; and by a comparison with other bodies, and a reduction to simple natures and their forms, which meet and mix in the compound. In a word, we must pass from Vulcan to Minerva if we intend to bring to light the true textures and configurations of bodies on which all the occult and, as they are called, specific properties and virtues of things depend, and from which, too, the rule of every powerful alteration and transformation is derived. (II VII)

Bacon calls his method "induction." For twentieth century readers this can be confusing because in epistemological literature the term "induction" has become firmly associated with inference from the particular to the general, i.e., with any kind of generalization from particulars. But Bacon was highly critical of the process of drawing a general conclusion, (e.g. "All roses are red,") after having enumerated all cases of observed roses and having noticed that they have all been red. This is part of the Aristotelian hasty anticipation of nature which he castigates. At the very least Bacon says (ALNA, p. 145) one should not attempt any such generalization without having made a search for roses which are not red.

But his methods of induction, methods for interpreting nature, go further than this. We are to interpret nature and this means making inferences from what is present to view to the inner processes and structures of things. Mere generalization from observation will never take us beyond the level of the readily observable. Bacon's methods thus instruct us to construct for ourselves tools which will supplement our capacities for sensory observation, of memory, and reasoning; we are to think about constructing instruments and procedures which will correct for the distorting biases, to which we are prone, and which will augment our powers of observation. By proceeding methodically, even those of modest intellectual capacity should be able to make progress. The method comes in two parts. The first is an orderly presentation of existing observational knowledge on a given topic, followed by an orderly sequence of observation and recording designed to supplement this where necessary. Baconian induction is not a generalization procedure based on passive observation, but a procedure for theory building based on selective and directed observation. It incorporates the idea that there will be a continual interplay between theory and observation, since theoretical developments will allow for the formation of, and give rise to, new questions.

If, for example, we were to make inquiries concerning heat, we should arrange our observations in three tables: A Table of Essence and Presence, where we list examples, occasions when things are or become hot, and other phenomena involving heat; a Table of Absence in Proximity which we construct by looking for examples where there are situations very similar to those in the first list except that heat is absent; and a Table of Comparison where we note how changes in the degree of heat vary in relation to other properties. But even these tables should not be constructed at random. Bacon spends a long time advising us about the kinds of observations that it would be useful to make and for what purpose. To make our tables too long would be to make them unwieldy. They need to contain the kind of observations most likely to be useful. So, for example, observations made using measuring instruments are frequently more useful than mere qualitative judgments.

It helps to bear in mind the purpose for which these tables are to be used. Their initial use is to screen out false hypotheses, generalizations which we might tend to make on the basis of unreflective extension of past experience, but to which we can find counter-examples. This is what the Table of Absence in Proximity sets us looking for – exceptions to the generalizations we might make on the basis of the Table of Essence and Presence. The Table of Comparison further screens those conjuctions which survive for being accidental, or not directly causal, connections. If we cannot vary B by varying A or vice versa, even if they do seem always to occur together, we should not look on either one as the form of the other but should look for some other explanation for both of them and for their co-occurrence.

After forming an initial hypothesis on the basis of these tables, we should then set out to design experiments to test it, framing questions that we want to put to nature and designing experiments which will force a response one way or the other. It is at this point that Bacon would urge us to see if we cannot devise a crucial experiment, one whose outcome will decide clearly for or against a hypothesis. To do this we must be able to use the hypothesis to predict what would be the outcome of the experiment if the hypothesis were correct and to be able to predict what would be the outcome if some other, possibly competing hypothesis, were correct. A classic exemplification of this part of the method occurred a century later when Newton argued (in his *Opticks*) that if colored light were simple, and white light composite, then it should be the case that when he passed white light through a prism, obtaining a spectrum, and then allowed just the red to go on through a second prism, then there should be no spectrum produced by the second prism; whereas if red light were not simple or if a spectrum is merely an effect produced by the prism in response to any light, one would expect a spectrum to be produced by the second prism. When the experiment is tried, he reported, no spectrum is found; and from this he concluded that red light is simple, whereas white is composite.

Bacon gives examples of the many ways in which we can improve our capacity for extracting information from nature. He groups these under three heads – aids to the senses, aids to the intellect, and aids to practice. Aids to the senses of course include instruments, such as microscopes. But they also include the theoretical work of determining what observation to expect if a particular micro process or micro structure is present. The tables are one of the aids to the intellect. There are other procedures we can adopt to counteract the intellect's known weaknesses, or bad habits. Crucial experiments are important in this regard. We are instructed to look for these, not to rest content with pleasing hypotheses, as we are all too prone to do. Aids to practice include further methodological study (pointing out how one can or should proceed in a particular kind of inquiry), the making of measurements and the development of instrumentation, and the collection of practically useful general procedures (modes of action which are currently within our power and the sorts of effects they have).

Bacon's method, we have seen, was recommended as a way of reaching the sort of knowledge he wished humans to seek. It was also tied to a conception of certain obstacles which lie in the path of those who wish to advance knowledge of the natural world. Bacon believed that induction, properly carried out, would not only advance us in the direction of the right goal, it would help us over the obstacles which are likely to stall progress. His characterization of these obstacles made them out to be illusory objects which humans were commonly tempted to mistake for the genuine objects of knowledge. This characterization had an additional function; not only did it further recommend the method, but packed into the accounts of the false objects, the "Idols," were criticisms of the alternative and competing conceptions of knowledge which Bacon needed to supplant if his project were to win support. The very choice of the word "Idols" to label what was to be avoided and overcome, was designed to support Bacon's method and his goal by connecting them both to a network of already established religious and philosophical associations. This network deserves a close examination.

7 Idols and Ideas

The word "form" marks a pivotal concept both in Bacon's philosophy and in Plato's. The two concepts are quite distinct, but not unrelated and it is important to understand both the differences and the relations between them. In brief the difference is this: Plato's Forms (or Ideas) are standards against which to judge the success or failure, the worth or otherwise, of human efforts. When a craftsman is given an instrument (e.g. a shuttle) to make, modify or repair, his mind must grasp the Form of that instrument, something which will not be embodied in any reliable way in any physical thing. All existing shuttles may be poorly designed and badly executed and will in any case not reveal in their sensible appearance the full range of shuttles' possibilities.

Bacon's forms are laws governing the behavior of natural objects. They must be grasped by a craftsman not in order to assess his performance but in order to recognize the potentialities and limitations of his materials. Just as the sensible appearance of an artifact does not reveal its Form, so the sensible appearance of a natural object does not reveal its form. To discover a Platonic Form requires thinking about the rôle a thing is ideally to play in our lives; to discover a Baconian form requires subjecting the natural object to a systematic series of tests and contrivances until it reveals the hidden springs of its action. It is oversimplified, but nevertheless instructive to say that a Platonic Form is what designers seek if they believe there *must* be a better way to, e.g. conceive a mouse trap; and a Baconian form is what designers seek if they believe that existing mouse traps could be improved by adopting better materials or designs.

One large step, in the transformation of the Platonic notion of Form into the notion which Bacon used, occurred while Plato was still living. Aristotle was the first of a succession of philosophers who rejected Plato's notion because his Forms were "separated" from the material world. Plato was open to this criticism to the extent that he sought to use his notion of Form in the explanation of the natural world. It makes sense to say that the ideal Form of an artifact is, and can be, embodied nowhere in the natural world; that only says we can always make improvements on any existing example of that artifact. To say the same about a principle, which is supposed to explain why things behave as they do, only makes sense if it is read as an appeal to something mysterious transcending nature.

When Christianity took over elements of Plato's thought, however, it also took over a later Platonist adaptation of Plato's notion which located the Forms in the mind of God. Plato's notion provided Christianity with a unitary source of both the principles which governed the natural world and the principles by which human conduct (especially its moral aspects) were to be judged. Thus when Bacon joins the succession of those who rejected Plato's Forms, he sees Plato's error as that of dragging natural philosophy in the direction of theology.

> But it is manifest that Plato, in his opinion of ideas, as one that had a wit of elevation situate as upon a cliff, did descry *that forms were the true object of knowledge*; but lost the real fruit of his opinion, by considering of forms as absolutely abstracted from matter, and not confined and determined by matter; and so turning his opinion upon theology, wherewith all his natural philosophy is infected. (ALNA, p. 110)

Aristotle and the Hellenistic schools, which dominated philosophy after Aristotle's death, were too thoroughly naturalistic to accept Plato's notion. Aristotle himself appealed to a notion of "form" as something integral to – indeed constituting – the very being of a natural object. Bacon, we have seen, advances what is in effect a revisionary Aristotelian position by reinterpreting "form" in terms of universal law.

Plato and Bacon thus advance different versions of the claim that what we have to concentrate on, if we are to achieve worthwhile knowledge, are not objects which strike our senses, but objects discerned only with the subtle and disciplined use of the mind. Both men emphasized that seizing on a genuine object of knowledge was difficult and that what most people fancied were objects of knowledge were in fact illusions. Plato, we have seen, represented the intellectual condition of the majority of people by placing them in the depths of a cave preoccupied with the shadows cast by poor images of the Forms, absorbed in a play of worthless shadows, which he called "*eidōla*" (images, phantoms, fantasies).

Bacon went further than Plato to the extent that he offered a classification of the various false ideas which obscure and interfere with our grasping the true objects of knowledge. Although urging us to seek knowledge that was morally neutral, Bacon was not above playing on the way Christian thought had used Plato's idiom to locate the ultimate explanation for the natural world in the mind of God.

Christianity had moreover adopted the Greek word, *eidôlon*, which Plato used to convey the benighted state of "the many" in his cave, to convey the benighted state of heathen who were mistaken about the true God and worshipped Idols. "There is a great difference between the Idols of the human mind and the Ideas of the divine. That is to say, between certain empty dogmas, and the true signatures and marks set upon the works of creation as they are found in nature" (I XXIII). These Idols are classified into four groups: Idols of the Tribe, the Cave, the Market Place, and the Theater.

Idols of the Tribe have their foundation in human nature: "The human understanding is like a false mirror, which, receiving rays irregularly, distorts and discolours the nature of things by mingling its own nature with it" (I XLI). In particular, humans have a tendency to presume that the world is orderly and regular and tend to see more order and regularity than there really is. To this tendency Bacon ascribes, for example, the belief that all celestial bodies move in perfect circles. He notes that people also have a tendency to form an opinion and then see everything around them as confirming that belief, completely ignoring what another person may see as glaring counter-examples. Beliefs, once established, are hard to dislodge. As he notes, "the human understanding is no dry light, but receives an infusion from the will and affections" (I XLIX). We are prone to wishful thinking, and to reading purposes into the world. We have a natural tendency to generalize and abstract too quickly, leading to the "anticipation of nature" rather than the interpretation of nature. On the contrary, we should pay more attention to observing particularities, but there is a crucial problem which is that for this we must use our senses and they are not adequate to the task (as the skeptics had pointed out). It is to remedy the defects of the senses that we need instruments and experimental methods.

Idols of the Cave have their foundation in the biology, psychology and socio-historical location of the individual. The opinions we form are determined in large measure by our education, our individual life histories and the cultural milieu in which we find ourselves. As a result people differ in their thought styles. Some tend to analyze and distinguish where others note resemblances and put together large pictures; some revere the past, whereas others value novelty above all, and so on. To conform to any of these tendencies exclusively would be a mistake, in Bacon's view. They should be alternated so that our understanding can become both penetrating and comprehensive, both open to development and respectful of the learning to be derived from the past. By extension one might persuade him to agree that if there are both masculine and feminine thought styles these too should be alternated, and neither pursued single mindedly.

> And generally let every student of nature take this as a rule: that whatever his mind seizes upon and dwells upon with particular satisfaction is to be held in suspicion, and that so much the more care is to be taken in dealing with such questions to keep the understanding even and clear. (I LVIII)

There is an element of asceticism prescribed for the natural philosopher. The quest is not for what is pleasing, but for the knowledge of how the world is. To this end personal preferences must be put aside, for they will only tend to distort one's vision. The goal, after all, is not *individual* enlightenment, but knowledge usable by many people, so it is important to overcome individual biases. For this reason Bacon envisions the new natural philosophy as essentially a social enterprise, the product of cooperative inquiry conducted by people prepared to give and accept criticism.

Idols of the Market Place have their foundation in language and the use of words. "Words plainly force and overrule the understanding, and throw all into confusion, and lead men away into numberless empty controversies and idle fancies" (I XLIII). These Bacon regards as being by far the most troublesome Idols. People believe that they have power over words and determine what they mean. But Bacon notes that words also shape and determine the paths that our thought can follow. Attempts to advance in a discussion often end in disputes over the meanings of words. This suggests that we should possibly start, as in geometry, by setting out definitions of our terms and agreeing upon them. But definitions too have to be couched in words. Moreover, in the case of inquiry into material things, part of what we hope to discover is how best to set up a systematic nomenclature in a given area (for plants, chemical substances, etc.). Words can lead us into two kinds of errors: (1) by getting us to take seriously things which do not exist (the word is there and in use so we presume that it stands for something) e.g. the Prime Mover, the Element of Fire, Fortune; (2) by being ambiguous or very imprecise they can lead us to class together things which really have nothing in common.

Finally, there are the *Idols of the Theater*, which have their foundation in the philosophical systems handed down as dogma. Our thinking is colored by the tradition in which we are educated, by the canon of texts which are held up as authoritative and with which we are required to have acquaintance if we wish to claim the right to speak with authority in a chosen discipline. In this respect Bacon's time was no different from our own. Bacon insists the theoretical views we inherit from traditional authorities are not innate, but derived from the "playbooks of philosophical systems and the perverted rules of demonstration" (I LXI). From the founding of the universities of Paris and Oxford in the thirteenth century, the Western philosophical tradition had reproduced itself through a process of reading works of ancient authors, together with commentaries on them provided by equally illustrious figures such as St Thomas Aquinas, the writing of new commentaries and the disputation of contested points of detail. These formal disputations were conducted according to well-recognized rules, rules which were in their turn derived from Aristotle's treatment of logic and rhetoric. This set of practices is what Bacon, Descartes, Locke, and others writing in the seventeenth century are referring to when they talk of the philosophy of the Schools. It is the philosophy done in the universities (Schools). By distancing himself from these recognized philosophic positions, and by the way in which he did so, Bacon located himself on the intellectual map of Elizabethan England. But it must be remembered that this was not just an intellectual map; philosophy and theology were, at this time when Catholic and Protestant forces were fighting for religious and political control of Northern Europe, intensely political disciplines.

Instead of writing yet another play of Idols, Bacon wanted to walk out of the theater; he was not going to construct another, rival philosophical system. His purpose was to convince people that the goal of natural philosophy is not that of building speculative systems, but acquiring practically applicable understanding of the way the world works. The cause of natural philosophy is not, in his view, served by conducting disputations, but by going out into the world and conducting systematic investigations. In other words, he wishes to depart from the Scholastic conception of the way in which philosophy should be conducted, instead proposing a method by which knowledge, firmly founded in observation and experience, can be gradually built up.

As Bacon says (I XXXV), since his disagreement with tradition is not over the quality of the reasoning but over the goal toward which it was directed and the methods by which it was thought appropriate to reach knowledge of the natural world, he is not in a position to enter into detailed argument against individual positions within the tradition. Because Bacon wanted to effect a fundamental philosophical reorientation, he did not engage any of the established systems in detailed argument; he was not going to enter the disputation game.

To attempt refutations in this case would be merely inconsistent with what I have already said, for since we agree neither upon principles nor upon demonstrations, there is no place for argument. And this is so far well, inasmuch as it leaves the honour of the ancients untouched. For they are no wise disparaged – the question between them and me being only as to the way. For as the saying is, the lame man who keeps the right road outstrips the runner who takes a wrong one. Nay, it is obvious that when a man runs the wrong way, the more active and swift he is, the further he will go astray. (I LXI)

This is particularly true because he applies a standard to past methods – the criterion of truth is fruitfulness in works – which that tradition would not acknowledge. By this standard the tradition fails; it has had plenty of time to deliver, but has produced little.

But since this standard is derived from Bacon's conception of the goal of knowledge, not the traditional conception, its application will not make headway against those wishing to stand by tradition. Acceptance of Bacon's call to put the past aside and start again is premised on acceptance of his conception of the goal of knowledge and of the standard of success which follows from it. How, then, can Bacon hope to persuade anyone to follow up on his call for action? It comes back to having to convince people that a reorientation in their conception of the goal of knowledge is necessary. In the first book of the *Novum Organum* Bacon seeks to undermine the authority of accepted sources of knowledge, classifying and revealing them as Idols. This is a crucial stage, for once faith in these sources has been undermined we will be receptive to a method which promises to lead to genuine knowledge.

The metaphor Bacon used in presenting the Idols of the Tribe guides his thinking in a crucial way. The mind of man is a distorting mirror; it reflects what goes on in the world around it, but in a distorted fashion. Its images are therefore false images, or Idols. These distortions can never, he thinks, be wholly avoided, but it is possible to make corrections for them. If we first learn about the human mind and the kinds of distortion to which it is prone, then we will be in a position to construct correcting lenses to compensate for the distortion (just as we can construct spectacles to correct for defective vision once we have identified the defect). In the first book of the *Novum Organum* Bacon discusses the Idols, and in the second he outlines the method, Induction, which is designed to correct for these distortions. With this emphasis both on knowledge of our own mental capacities (especially our weaknesses and limitations) and the conception of a method designed to deploy these capacities to maximum possible advantage in the acquisition of knowledge of the natural world, we find part of the configuration of concerns which came to define epistemology in the modern age (for what has become known as "modernity"). We must first be acquainted with the scope and limitations of the system, whether it be the individual mind or public language, in which we can represent the world. We then have to consider the means available to us for distinguishing true from false, accurate from inaccurate representations.

2
Idols of the Tribe:
Perception and Prejudice

The Idols of the Tribe have their foundations in human nature itself, and in the tribe and race of men. For it is a false assertion that the sense of man is the measure of things. On the contrary, all perceptions as well of the sense as of the mind are according to the measure of the individual and not according to the measure of the universe. And the human understanding is like a false mirror, which receiving rays irregularly, distorts and discolours the nature of things by mingling its own nature with it.

Novum Organum I XLI

1 "Scientifically Objective Knowledge"

Francis Bacon was one of several people who helped in significant ways to put in place a conception of a form of authority, which we now recognize under the label "scientifically objective knowledge." Accompanying this conception is the belief that there is or could be a method, "the scientific method," which guarantees the objectivity, and hence the authority, of results obtained by following it. It is for its "objectivity" that scientific knowledge is now prized, and it is for their capacity to be "objective" in their investigations that scientists are held in high regard and their findings treated as authoritative. But what does this objectivity consist in, and why should it be held in such high regard? Is there really any method which will ensure the objectivity of results obtained by following its prescriptions?

Important light is shed on the first question by noting that the term which forms the contrast to "objective" is "subjective." Thus scientific knowledge is objective to the extent that it has been possible to eliminate from it all "distortions" introduced by "subjects," that is by those who would know, or would be "scientists." Objectivity requires first of all that people acknowledge that their view may be limited by their circumstances and skewed by their particular concerns; and secondly, it requires that they put aside those concerns and seek to transcend the limitations of their particular vantage points in an attempt to attain a view which will be equally correct for everyone.

> Objectivity consists in so fully realizing the countless intrusions of the self in everyday thought and the countless illusions which result – illusions of sense, language, point of view, value, etc. – that the preliminary step to every judgement is the effort to exclude the intrusive self. Realism, on the contrary, consists in ignoring the existence of self and hence regarding one's own perspective as immediately objective and absolute. Realism is this anthropocentric illusion, finality – in short, all those illusions which teem in the history of science. So long as thought has not become conscious of self, it is a prey to perpetual confusions between objective and subjective, between the real and the ostensible (Piaget (1929), p. 34).

Bacon's Idols are collectively a warning against being taken in by the illusions of what Piaget calls "realism." By raising our consciousness of these obstacles, Bacon contributes to a method for achieving greater objectivity. The Idols which represent the intrusions of the self and its particular concerns are associated with "the cave or den" which is Bacon's image for the mind of an individual, which is prone to collect prejudices and invidious preoccupations as well as secure understanding. Most of the influences which furnish caves with idols, e.g. education, conversation, prevailing opinions, etc., affect groups of individuals. Some, for example our intellectual heritage and language itself, are important enough to have their effects assigned to their own class, the Idols of the Theater and the Market Place. Some have their origins in what is universal in the human condition, in human nature itself. These are the Idols of the Tribe.

All human beings become aware of their surroundings by means of sense organs which are similar in everyone, even though there are individual differences of range and degree of sensitivity and sometimes damage to organs. Moreover, all humans by virtue of being both biological and social creatures have desires which influence their beliefs. "The human understanding is no dry light, but receives an infusion from the will and affections. . ." We consequently give more credence to what we would like to be true (I XLIX), and tend to notice evidence which supports our favored beliefs while overlooking what would count against them (I XLVI). We are, moreover, all prone to suppose the world is more orderly than is justified by our experience (I XLV), to over-generalize from a few striking examples (I XLVII), to mistake the resulting abstractions for reality itself (I LI), going so far as to fancy that we can conceive the limits of endless processes and finding ourselves ensnared in the problems of the infinite (I XLVIII).

But does, or could, objectivity require putting aside our humanity in an attempt to transcend once and for all the limitations of the human condition? Would true objectivity consist in attaining knowledge from a non-human perspective, from what for a human would be no perspective at all (a conception which Thomas Nagel recently called "the view from nowhere")? Is the knowledge we seek "absolute" in the sense of "unconditioned"? Is this what Bacon was requiring when he said that the Idols of the Tribe should be put aside?

Bacon certainly does not suggest that all Idols can be overthrown in a single purge; the account of the Idols which he gives appears designed to help us recognize obstacles to sound understanding *as they are encountered*. His motive for seeking understanding is human (perhaps too human), viz. that we should find ways to improve the material conditions of human beings. Whatever Bacon contributed to our notion of scientific objectivity, it did not include the impulse to transcend altogether the limitations of the human condition. This impulse originated elsewhere and created an important tension within our concept of objectivity.

The issues revolve around one apparently inevitable limitation imposed by our nature, the fact that we respond to influences from the physical environment through identifiable sense organs. The senses are a source of vital information about the natural world but because of their limited capacities they set limits on the knowledge we can acquire. The complexity of the issues involved is due in part to this dual rôle which the senses can play in any dispute about knowledge and understanding. But in the seventeenth century this was *only* a part, for the concept of objectivity emerged from a struggle for intellectual authority in a historical context where a largely political struggle over religious authority had been going on for nearly a century. And the struggle was further complicated by the way protagonists borrowed resources from disputes which had taken place in the ancient world.

These are the main threads of this tangled tale: Bacon, as we have observed, is an early contributor to a movement to reform the way people try to understand the natural world. The tradition which at the time held authority, i.e., prevailed in the universities and had the sanction of the Church in Rome, derived from the work of Aristotle. Aristotle was a younger contemporary and close associate of Plato. His thought will be considered in some detail later; for the present it is enough to identify him as the established authority figure whose influence was seen as standing in the way of Bacon's project as well as in the way of the methods and doctrines of such early modern scientific thinkers as Galileo and Descartes.

Many of those who contributed to the development of what we now recognize as modern science adhered instead to either or both a Copernican view of the heavens and a "corpuscularian" view of the fine structure of the material world. Copernicans held, against the authority both of Aristotle and of the senses, that the sun is the center of heavenly motions. Corpuscularians, although disagreeing quite substantially about specific details, held that the things we experience are in fact made up of small material particles and the way we experience them is a product of the action of these small particles on our sense organs. This general view of the constitution of nature had a pedigree even more ancient than the Aristotelian natural philosophy for it was advanced by Democritus of Abdera, a generation before Plato.

Any such view is committed to saying that our unaided senses do not disclose to us the full reality of physical objects. The knowledge that is sought by the new science is characteristically knowledge which the unaided senses cannot reveal, a knowledge of internal structures and processes. Such an outlook is an excellent example of an attempt to conceive nature from a standpoint not found in human experience, but it is certainly not the only route to such a conception. Christian philosophy can point to the perspective which God takes on the universe, and insist that humans can have adequate (objective) knowledge only to the extent that they can approach God and conceive things from his (unlimited, unconditioned) standpoint. Plato's Forms also represent an attempt to take such a standpoint.

The earliest reported repudiation of any such standpoint is attributed to Protagoras, a contemporary of Democritus and also a native of Abdera. When Bacon insists that "all perceptions as well of the sense as of the mind are according to the measure of the individual and not according to the measure of the universe," he is alluding to one of the few surviving quotations we have from Protagoras. Plato's *Theaetetus* (152a) is one place where Protagoras is quoted as saying, "Man is the measure of all things, of those which are, that they are and of those which are not, that they are not." Plato interprets this as the claim that there is no "truth" which transcends the perceptions and judgments of individual human beings; we cannot assess them "according to the measure of the universe." This is a doctrine which clearly subverts all claims to intellectual authority.

Although Protagoras' doctrine is not confined to sense perceptions, it does give such judgments sovereignty. Anyone, Democritus, Plato or, Bacon, who wishes to appeal to "the measure of the universe" has to insist that the judgments of the senses be subjected to higher authority. Bacon, as we saw in the first chapter, denied that worthwhile knowledge of the natural world could be attained merely by the use of our senses; they have to be used in conjunction with the intellect. To take sense perception at face value as yielding immediate knowledge of how things really are is to place one's faith in an Idol. Plato tended to be even more extreme in his rejection of the senses. While Democritus also said similar disparaging things about the senses, his general corpuscularian view left him in some doubt as to whether it was possible for humans to attain any knowledge whatsoever. We can see a tension in the surviving fragments of Democritus' writing. With his bold claim about how the universe is in itself, independently of how it appears to us, Democritus also expressed grave doubts about the possibility of our knowing anything, including presumably his own general view of the natural world.

In the generation, which followed Aristotle's death, Democritus' natural philosophy was taken up, and his skepticism toned down, by Epicurus, who founded a school which lasted into the Christian era. It was through the writings of Epicurus and the Roman Epicurean, Lucretius, that the seventeenth century knew of the ancient forebears of corpuscularianism. This presented a problem, for Epicurus also taught an ethics based on pleasure, and in medieval philosophy this had been caricatured as a morally licentious hedonism. Seventeenth century corpuscularians had to use their ancient sources with care. Bacon, for example, chose to express his limited approval of this ancient approach to understanding nature by referring not to the Epicureans, but to "the school of Democritus" (I LI).

Corpuscularians also had to fend off the accusation that their doctrines led to skepticism. Anyone who wants to supplant an established view has to work to subvert its authority. Arguments which target specific doctrines can frequently be generalized and used on much wider targets. Opponents will frequently defend their positions by arguing that attacks on their doctrines destroy too much. Moreover efforts to question the authority of sense experience in order to clear the way for their view of the natural world, made the seventeenth century corpuscularians sound like the ancient skeptics whose arguments frequently were targeted on the senses. Skepticism can be every bit as subversive of intellectual authority as Protagoras' doctrine of relativism. Relativism holds that every person's judgment can claim to be valid; skepticism holds that no person's judgment can claim to be valid. Both can function as forms of intellectual anarchism and in the seventeenth century it was commonly assumed they would both lead to licentious hedonism.

But skepticism can also be co-opted by authoritarian tendencies. If no individuals can claim authority for their judgments, then those in authority can claim that in continuing to hold onto their positions, they offer continuity and stability. And if they can claim some independent source of authority, so much the better. Moves like this had been made in the sixteenth century in the disputes about religious authority. Ancient skeptical arguments were revived to undermine the claims of individuals to know the truths of religion on the basis of what their consciences told them. If one's conscience could not be trusted, then proper humility dictated that one submit to the authority of the Church, which by God's special grace appears to have access to the truths of religion. Skepticism thus cuts along more than one line.

Those who pressed the case for reform of natural philosophy had to undermine the unexamined deliverances of the senses, as well as the doctrines of Aristotle, without appearing to contribute to a general climate of skepticism, which would undermine all intellectual authority including that of the views which they wished to establish. In this complex situation the framework which supports our concept of "scientifically objective knowledge" was forged with a number of tensions which have yet to be satisfactorily resolved. Important elements which contributed to the process have their origin in the ancient world, but as we will see many of these elements underwent transformations as they were drawn into seventeenth-century and later contexts.

2 Subversive Philosophy

We have observed on the one hand an impulse to rise above the human condition to a level where the Idols of the Tribe do not obstruct the view and there to lay claim once and for all to intellectual authority. One question is whether the view would unfold onto Plato's

Forms, Democritus' tiny particles, or something else. Other questions are whether we are able to ascend high enough to escape the Idols of the Tribe without having to secure some non-human route to knowledge or understanding, and whether we need to aspire to such lofty heights to improve our perspective in worthwhile ways.

On the other hand we have observed contrary impulses to deny either the need for, or the possibility of, achieving a view of things more comprehensive than that provided by our particular experiences. The latter kind of impulse subverts claims to authority and there is little doubt that the way Protagoras' outlook undermined Plato's hopes to establish political authority on a secure intellectual basis is what brought Plato to confront Protagoras' position. Two of Plato's crucial arguments focus on where Protagoras' doctrine leaves Protagoras' own authority. How can Protagoras offer his services as (what nowadays we would describe as) a freelance consultant, if his judgment has no greater validity than anyone else's (*Theaetetus*, 161e, 179b)? And how can Protagoras advance his "Man is the measure of all things" doctrine as an authoritative statement, if to accept it is to accept that no statement is more authoritative than any statement to the contrary (*Theaetetus*, 170a–171d)? These arguments reveal respects in which Protagoras' position is difficult to maintain, but they do not establish what Plato needs, the possibility of there being authoritative judgments.

Plato's examination of Protagoras includes some speculation about other beliefs one might have to hold, e.g. about the natural world and our place in it, in order to sustain Protagoras' position. He associates with Protagoras certain doctrines attributed to Heraclitus to the effect that everything is changing all the time (*Theaetetus*, 160d–e). Heraclitus' doctrine, that everything "is flowing" or "in flux," bears no immediately obvious relation to Protagoras' claim that "Man is the measure." But when Plato discusses the doctrine of flux in the *Theaetetus* he does not treat it as confined to the effects of changes in things themselves. The examples he uses to illustrate the Heraclitean thesis either do not involve changes in things, but only in the perspective from which they are examined (six dice are more if compared to four, but less if compared to twelve, *Theaetetus*, 154c), or they involve change only in other things (Socrates ceases to be large and becomes small, compared to Theaetetus, when the latter grows up, *Theaetetus*, 155b–c).

Since Plato regarded Protagoras as committed to treating judgment as equivalent to what appears to our senses, Heraclitus' doctrine allows Plato to represent the extent to which Protagoras must regard human judgment as an interaction between several things. Protagoras' challenge to all intellectual authority is then seen as arising out of this view of our situation in the natural world. If judgment is a relational affair depending for its outcome on contributions from all the things related, can any of these relations be preferred to any other? The dice are from different perspectives many and few, and thus change from being many to being few as they are differently regarded. What would give one perspective authority over another?

Conversely, Plato has Socrates argue, since things appear differently to different people, if Protagoras is right and things are truly as they appear to different people, they must undergo constant change. Here Plato's argument rests on the assumption that we almost always find ourselves in situations analogous to that of two people to whom the summer wind feels very different because one is leaving a hot bath house while the other is just entering it (cp. 152b). That is, he assumes that agreement between the judgments that people make will be relatively uncommon and so makes his point only by exaggerating the extent to which the different relations, in which people stand to things, actually give rise to conflicting judgments.

The point of connecting Protagoras' doctrine to the world view associated with Heraclitus appears to have been to reduce Protagoras' claim, that everything literally is as it appears to be to any human, to the claim that nothing is determinately anything. Much the same conclusion could have been reached by appealing to Democritus' view of the natural world and our place in it. What is crucial to the argument is that our perceptions and judgments arise in complex interactions of unstable phenomena and the argument did not require details which were specific to Heraclitus.

Democritus is remembered as a figure in the history of early science for his advocacy of atomism, a version of corpuscularianism which holds that there is empty space (a void) between particles and a limit to the divisibility of material particles. Indivisible corpuscles are referred to as atoms (*atomos* = not able to be cut). Democritus used this view to interpret all natural phenomena including human perception, but he did not, it seems, advance it as a source of hypotheses to be tested. Whatever empirical evidence he might have been able to adduce in its favor would not, by modern standards, have been very impressive. There is, moreover, evidence that Democritus wanted to dispense with the authority of the senses and rely on that of the intellect, referring to knowledge based on the former as "bastard" and that based on the latter as "legitimate" (Sextus Empiricus, *Adversus Mathematicos* VII, 139). Although he also appears to have had some misgivings about this since Galen quotes him as saying on behalf of the senses, "Wretched mind, do you take your assurances from us and then overthrow us? Our overthrow is your downfall" (*On Medical Experience*, p. 114).

Democritus' devaluation of the senses had its source in his atomist interpretation of our sense experience, for his view represents it as events in which the clusters of particles which constitute our bodies, interact with the various clusters which constitute our environment. The outcome of such events is portrayed as depending as much on the condition of the perceiver and on the context in which the object of perception appears, as on the condition of the perceived object itself. Aristotle reports that Democritus concluded "either nothing is true, or it is unclear to us," and suggested the fact that we perceive things differently on different occasions is what led to this conclusion (*Metaphysics* 1009b7). This is very similar to the picture of our perceptual interaction with the world, which Plato drew from Heraclitus, except for the embellishment provided by thinking of atoms and the void.

Tradition has it, however, that Democritus dissociated himself from Protagoras' position, arguing as Plato did that the doctrine can be turned on itself (Sextus Empiricus, *Adversus Mathematicos* VII, 389). He was sufficiently firmly convinced of his view of the natural world to insist that because the tiny particles did not appear to anyone, the world really is not at all the way it appears to anyone. We may establish conventions (*nomoi*) on what general terms to apply to our individual experiences, but these conventions have nothing to do with the way things really are. "By convention sweet, by convention bitter, by convention hot, by convention cold, by convention color: but in reality atoms and void," he is quoted as saying (Galen, *On Medical Experience*, p. 114; Sextus Empiricus, *Adversus Mathematicos* VII, 135). It was this aspect of ancient atomism that many seventeenth century mechanists sought to rehabilitate while glossing over the problems which Democritus himself saw for the very possibility of human knowledge – problems which led him to the pessimistic conclusion, as Cicero reports, that truth lies buried in an abyss (*Academica*, 1.44, 2.32).

Looking at the natural world from the perspective of Democritean atomism one might very well be overwhelmed by the seemingly chaotic character of our sensory interaction with our environment. But one need not, as a consequence, deny the fact that we have somehow managed to establish enough conventions to be able to communicate to one another. Similarly, when Plato linked Protagoras' doctrine to the world view derived from Heraclitus he did not prove that there is insufficient commonality in our perceptual experiences for various groups of us to be able to establish common languages. Within a language community, moreover, there are standards of correct and incorrect speech which include standards for accepting some descriptive claims as true and rejecting others as false. The seat of authority for these community standards is diffuse and difficult to locate, but there are nevertheless standards, or conventions, which are neither the measures of the individual nor the measures of the universe.

However, the problem which Plato pressed on Protagoras then reappears at the level of the various human communities, some constituting discrete cultures, some constituted by special professional, religious or economic interests. The picture of individuals plagued by conflicting judgments to the point where the very possibility of communication seems threatened may not answer to our everyday experience. But the picture of communities and cultures at odds in this way is not at all remote. People living and working in similar circumstances and contexts may share sufficient interests, affections and ways of thinking to sustain conventionally based standards of correctness. Against such standards it may well be clear whether someone is deciding impartially and objectively, but when conflict with another community occurs the question arises, "How, if standards of correctness are different in these two communities, can this conflict be judged impartially and objectively?"

Protagoras' name may be used to mark a thoroughly negative response to this question. A Protagorean relativist will say, "No, there is no such authority because the judgments sanctioned by any such community are as correct as any conflicting judgments sanctioned by any other." Democritus' name may be used to mark a less thoroughly negative response. A Democritean will say, "No, there is no such authority because the judgments sanctioned by any such community are as incorrect as those sanctioned by any other, except in matters where it is possible to judge by the measure of the universe." In the late twentieth century the Democritean will probably have modern natural science in mind when speaking of matters where it is possible to judge by the measure of the universe, and will hold that science has a special authority based on methods which not only generate knowledge but also render its institutionally sanctioned judgments both impartial and objective. The Protagorean (relativist or "postmodernist") will, however, be unwilling to recognize this special authority and will treat the judgments which issue from the community of scientists as no better than those which issue from any other community.

The locus of the issues has changed but there are nevertheless features common to present debates about the authority of claims to knowledge and the ancient disputes in which Plato, Protagoras and Democritus and their followers were embroiled. The issue is nothing less than whether a criterion of truth, a source of authority can be located in individuals or in specially constituted institutions. In the sixteenth and seventeenth centuries this was also an issue of central concern to philosophy, only it had been brought to center stage by the schisms which occurred after Luther (Diet of Worms, 1521) challenged the authority of the Pope and the Church in Rome.

3 From Ancient Skepticism to Modern Philosophy

Richard Popkin (Popkin, 1964) has shown how an exchange between Erasmus and Luther set the stage for the epistemological debates of the seventeenth century. He also stresses the importance of a historical accident in shaping these debates. The exchange between Erasmus and Luther, which raised deep questions about the criterion of truth, was followed closely by the rediscovery of the works of Sextus Empiricus, the only writings from the long skeptical tradition in ancient Greece to survive substantially intact.

Luther denied that the Pope could claim to be the only authority in religious matters. Instead, he insisted that what conscience is compelled to believe on reading scripture is true. Luther was challenging the traditionally accepted standard of religious truth along with the authority of those able to claim knowledge of that truth. This challenge was not just a doctrinal matter internal to the existing framework of theological debate. It opened up the whole question of how to justify or defeat a claim concerning the criterion of religious truth. Erasmus (*De Libero Arbitrio*, 1524) responded by offering a skeptical defense of faith. Erasmus had no regard for complex theological disputes and thought they could get nowhere, preferring instead "the views of the sceptics wherever the inviolable authority of Scripture and the decision of the Church permit – a Church to which at all times I willingly submit my own view, whether I attain what she prescribes to or not" (Winter, 1961, p. 6). Luther's riposte was to the effect that skepticism is incompatible with Christianity (Winter, 1961, p. 102). If Christians cannot be certain of what they affirm in their beliefs, they are not Christians, for their salvation must lie in the genuineness of their beliefs. Certain knowledge based on one's own inner convictions could be the only ground of religious faith.

Clearly both of these positions contain difficulties. Whilst Luther's response raises genuine problems for the position held by Erasmus, his own is vulnerable, for it comes very close to Protagoras' position. The difference is that Luther assumed that each individual will in studying the scripture arrive at the one, genuine Christian religion (Winter, 1961, p. 103). But the fact is (as his critics pointed out) people do not agree on their readings of the scriptures. This being so, either Luther should go with Protagoras and say that every reading is right, or he must offer some further criterion of genuine religious knowledge. How is one to tell who is right when different people arrive at differing convictions on the basis of their reading of scripture? Such questions were extensively exploited by subsequent writers from both Catholic and Protestant sides. It was into this situation that Sextus' writings were inserted.

The term "skeptic" (searcher) was not in use before the Christian era, but once in use it was, with justification, applied to a number of philosophers who had flourished during the previous four or five centuries. Democritus, as we have seen, could be said to have read skeptical conclusions off his picture of the natural world and of our position in it. A younger contemporary of Aristotle, Pyrrho of Elis, gave his name three centuries later, to the brand of skepticism which Sextus represented, "Pyrrhonism." What little we know of Pyrrho suggests that his pessimism about the possibility of establishing the authority of any judgment rested, as did that of Democritus, on a picture of the world, one in which "things are equally indifferent, unmeasurable and inarbitrable" (Eusebius in Long and Sedley, 1987, 1F). But as we have already observed, to defend the claim that we cannot know anything about the world by deriving it as a conclusion from a view of the nature of the world, is a flawed strategy; the conclusion of the argument undermines its own premise.

A more stable skepticism evolved, oddly enough, in the Academy in Athens, the school which Plato had founded. There, within a few generations of Plato's death, the members came to be known as "those who suspend judgment about everything." The Academics sought to suspend judgment out of a sense of loyalty to what they took to be the spirit which Socrates exemplified in Plato's early dialogues. In these dialogues Socrates is not made to advance any explicit doctrine and the discussions characteristically end in *aporia* or puzzlement (literally, lack of provisions). It was the character of Socrates rather than the doctrines of Plato which held the imaginations of the Academics. The Pyrrhonists, founded by a disaffected Academic named Aenesidemus, recommended suspending judgment as a way of life which enabled those who practised it to live unperturbed, free of the ordinary troubles of life. Pyrrho was chosen as a figurehead for this revivalist movement not because of the subtlety of his skepticism, but because of the exemplary nature of his life and character. Skepticism was first and foremost a way to conduct oneself.

The Academics achieved a stable skepticism by being careful to avoid committing themselves to knowing anything; that included avoiding the claim that they knew of their own inability to know anything (Cicero, *Academica* 1.44). This sounds easy, but the Academics recognized that we are naturally prone to commit ourselves and that it takes hard work to suspend judgment. To succeed they cultivated the practice of pitting reasons against one another. Wherever there appeared to be strong reasons for believing something, they sought equally strong reasons for believing the opposite.

The different ways in which belief was pitted against belief, reason against reason, were drawn together from Academic sources and organized into "ten modes" by Aenesidemus. These were expounded by Sextus Empiricus, who lived in the second century AD, and in virtue of the timing of the rediscovery of his works, they became the source of standard problems to be tackled by seventeenth century writers on epistemology. The ten modes reveal the extent to which ancient skepticism, like relativism, was rooted in conflicts of judgment, perception and belief, conflicts which were taken to imply that no perceptions, judgments or beliefs could be taken as more authoritative than any others (see esp. Sextus Empiricus, *Outlines of Pyrrhonism*, 1.31.). The net effect of skepticism was, like the relativism of Protagoras, to subvert intellectual authority; and the overall deployment of its strategy of pitting reason against reason echoed the arguments for relativism.

Different species of animal have different bodily constitutions and are, not surprisingly, observed to be attracted and repelled by different things (mode one). The same is true of different races of human beings, and even of different individuals (mode two). Different sensory modes of the same individual provide conflicting information (mode three), and the same sensory mode provides information which conflicts with what it provides when it is in a different physical condition (mode four). Similar conflicts are based on the relative location of the sense organ and its object (mode five) and on physical influences, which can be exerted on a perceptual interaction by the presence or absence of other objects in the perceptual field (mode six). Objects affect us differently if present in different quantities or configurations – there are differences, in other words, which do not depend on some feature of our relationship to the object (mode seven). The very fact that things are relative to one another means that we must suspend judgment about how they are in any unqualified sense (mode eight). Things affect us differently depending on how frequently we encounter them (mode nine). Finally, different conduct and lifestyles are encouraged and prohibited in different societies because of different customs (mode ten). (ibid., 1.31–1.163)

This catalog of the features which constitute the differences in (to use a currently popular metaphor) the perspectives of human beings, is meant to show the would-be Pyrrhonist how to set one opinion against another, so that none could be regarded as authoritative. But do we not form opinions in order to determine how we should conduct ourselves? Do we not need to believe in order to act and thereby to live? In response to those who held that everything that was X was equally also not X, Aristotle (with doctrines of Heraclitus and Protagoras in mind) had asked why they didn't walk into a well or over a cliff, since this would be as good (or safe) a thing to do as it was not good (or unsafe) (*Metaphysics* 1008b 16).

The response to the challenge of how to live as a skeptic, which had been developed in the Academy, and to which the Pyrrhonists subscribed, was to let one's conduct be guided by appearances (*phainomena*) without committing oneself to the truth (or authority) of those appearances. Appearances are whatever are presented to our minds minus any commitment to them one way or another; they trigger natural impulses to act, which we should rely on and not presume to be able to look out for our welfare better than nature can. Just do what seems best in response to what the circumstances seem to be and seem to require. If we measure commitment (what is taken to be true) not by what people say, but by what they do, the distance between this position and that of Protagoras is not very significant. To Protagoras what appears true to a person is true for that person. For the skeptic (Academic or Pyrrhonist) what appears to a person to be what should be acted upon, is for that person what should be acted upon.

In advising us to be guided by appearances the ancient skeptics did not consider what appears to us to be something we can know; they comprehensively denied that we can know anything. At the same time the existence of something other than appearances – what as it were lies behind appearances and does the appearing – was never questioned by them. They took it for granted that something appears to us and denied that we could say anything with authority about it.

The insertion of these doctrines into the debate between Catholics and Protestants, clearly placed them in a context significantly different from that in which they had been developed. The new issues in the new context were over religious knowledge and moral authority, based in scripture, rather than knowledge of the natural world, based in sensation. Catholics nevertheless found in the armory of the ancient skeptics a battery of powerful techniques for undermining Protestant claims to knowledge. But since these were to be used to uphold the authority of the Catholic Church, they would not want to draw the conclusion that what appears to a person to be what should be acted upon, is for that person what should be acted upon.

The strategy developed by Catholic writers of the Counter Reformation was, following that already adopted by Erasmus, to use the skeptical arguments to destroy all claims to knowledge and then instead of appealing to natural impulses as a source of action and commitment, appealing to faith. Christian faith, simple piety, is the extra source of commitment which was absent from the context of Greek debate, but which had been cultivated over the intervening centuries. This strategy was employed for example by Montaigne and by La Mothe Le Vayer, who is quoted by Popkin (1964, p. 96) as saying,

> The soul of a Christian Skeptic is like a field cleared and cleansed of bad plants, such as the dangerous axioms and infinity of learned persons, which then receives the new drops of divine grace much more happily than it would do if it were still occupied and filled with the vain presumption of knowing everything with certainty and doubting nothing (*Prose Chagrine*, in *Oeuvres*, vol. IX, p. 359).

Christian skeptics would leave their doubts at the foot of the altar and accept what faith obliges them to believe.

As result of the adoption of this type of skeptical defense of fideism, those, whether Catholic or Protestant, who wished to urge the cause of natural philosophy found themselves obliged to seek a way to counter the battery of skeptical arguments that could be mounted on the basis of the ten modes recorded by Sextus. A tactic which came naturally to humanist scholars was to see if it was not possible to mine recently recovered ancient texts for responses to ancient skepticism which could be adapted to fit the new context. The name of one ancient philosopher, Epicurus, had already been involved in the confrontation between Luther and Erasmus. In his rejection of Erasmus' criticisms Luther accused Erasmus of Epicurean sympathies, indeed of "swilling Epicurus by the gallons" (Winter, 1961, p. 104). The use of Epicurus' name here did not reflect any detailed understanding of his philosophy, but functioned as an abusive epithet based on the medieval view of Epicureanism as equivalent to immersion in sensual living, the philosophy of those who are slaves to lust. Erasmus' response was to try to disarm this attack by looking more seriously at Epicurus' position, arguing that general condemnation of it was unjustified. Erasmus appreciated that Epicurus himself would have rejected base, sensually indulgent pleasures, as they result only in later physical infirmity and discomfort. Erasmus uses his re-reading of Epicurus' position as a way of arguing that a life devoted to the righteous pursuit of virtue does not require the denial of pleasure, but amounts to pursuit of the highest pleasures (Jones, 1989, p. 164).

It was, however, Gassendi, encouraged by a group of like-minded French philosophers, who undertook an extensive study and rehabilitation of Epicureanism (*Animadversiones in decimum librum Diogeneis Laertii*, 1649). He saw in it the basis of an anti-dogmatic response to the inconclusive and frequently violent religious debates (Jones, 1989 ch. 7), and also as providing the most fruitful hypothesis under which to advance natural philosophy. The epistemological position which he worked toward came to be known as "mitigated scepticism" (Popkin, 1964, ch. VII), and was developed further by Mersenne and Hume. But many who disagreed with Gassendi's position benefitted from his careful rehabilitation of Epicurean philosophy.

4 Democritus and the School of Epicurus

It was close to a century after Democritus' death that Epicurus adopted Democritean natural philosophy as the basis of a moral outlook. Epicurus subscribed to the atomism of Democritus but worked to allay the accompanying suspicion which it generated about the senses. In a letter, which survives, (to Herodotus, 68–9 in Diogenes Laertius, *Lives of Eminent Philosophers*) Epicurus insists that sensible properties of bodies, while not part of nature in their own right, are nevertheless not to be dismissed as non-beings. Epicurus, moreover, took to heart the threat, which Democritus expressed on behalf of the senses, viz. that the mind can reject their authority only at its peril. One of a list of key doctrines attributed to Epicurus argues, "If you fight against all sensations, you will not have a standard against which to judge even those of them you say are mistaken" (*Key Doctrines*, 23 in Diogenes Laertius).

It is not, however, obvious that the claim that the senses are not to be trusted is subject to the same sort of self-refutation which threatens

Protagoras' relativism. If skeptics about the senses were presented with the challenge, "Do you not have to rely on your senses in order to cast doubt on them?" they could reply that the testimony of the senses is like that of different messengers, liable to support conflicting interpretations. Now one does not have to rely on one out of a group of messengers in order to know that the group as a whole does not tell a consistent story. If two people offer conflicting testimony, reason tells us that both cannot be telling the truth (and possibly neither is) without our needing to accept the testimony of either one.

It was possibly with this argument in mind that Epicurus and his followers insisted that the senses could not conflict with one another (Diogenes Laertius 10.31–2; Lucretius 4.469–501). Sensory experience at different times or at the same time through different senses is simply what it is; it embodies no messages capable of standing in conflict with one another. In effect the Epicureans here adopted a position similar in form to that of Protagoras. Everything (strictly) present to a given mode of sensing (seeing, hearing, etc.) is true for that mode, just as for Protagoras every judgment is true for the person making it. Our eyes might suggest that it is cold outside, but this is actually the mind judging something which is strictly present to the eyes (an opaque white layer) to be suggestive of something (frost and hence cold) which can be strictly present only to the sense of touch. It should be observed, however, just how small a distance the Epicureans travelled with Protagoras before parting company. Most of the judgments we make on the basis of sense experience are not authoritative, only those which report exactly what is presented to the senses can be counted as true.

To accord even this much authority to the senses and not seem to be departing from the spirit of Democritus, Epicurus and his followers argued from the physical account of sense perception given by the atomist doctrine. According to this doctrine every body is a conglomeration of atoms which are vibrating so that the body is constantly giving off thin layers of atoms. The relative position of the atoms in these layers hardly changes as they travel outward, preserving in their configuration a matrix of information about the body from which they originated. These layers of atoms (which Epicurus refers to both as "imprints" (or "blows," *tupoi*) and "images" ("idols," *eidōla*) strike human sense organs and a series of them gives rise to a "presentation" (*phantasia*) to the soul, of the body from which they originated (Letter to Herodotus, 46–50, in Diogenes Laertius). Looked at in this way, what the sense organs receive is simply natural influences. If we make mistaken judgments on the basis of these influences, that is not the fault of what happens in or to the senses, but is the fault of the soul which does not deal sufficiently carefully with its resources.

The claim that whatever presentation the senses receive at any time is true, turns out not to be the claim that we cannot fail in making certain simple judgments, but rather the claim that we are provided with something completely reliable on which to base judgments, something which cannot possibly mislead us if we treat it as we should. An analogous claim would be that every photograph can be relied upon regardless of its perspective, the conditions under which it was exposed, or the amount of retouching it has undergone, providing we are cautious about the inferences we are tempted to draw from it. But no photograph is in or of itself misleading – the camera never lies (cp. Long and Sedley, 1987, pp 85–6).

As a response to the problem which Epicurus inherited from Democritus, the attempt to separate what is presented to our minds from the response our minds make to it, represents an astute maneuver. At the same time as the senses are offered as part of what Epicurus held was our "yardstick" (*kanôn*) for measuring the truth, we are encouraged to suspend the beliefs that we ordinarily base on our sense experience, beliefs which stand in the way of accepting the atomist picture. We can see why this strategy should have attracted some seventeenth century mechanists. But there is still some way to go to get from the truth of our sense presentations to the truth of atomism.

Epicurus held that there are two additional criteria which humans have for judging truth. One was "feeling," e.g. of pleasure and pain, which served as a guide to action. The other was "preconception" (*prolêpsis*, more literally "pregrasping" or "prehension"). There is no hint in Epicureanism of any tendency to the vulgar pragmatism which holds that a thought can lay claim to truth to the extent that it makes us feel good to accept it. So the doctrine of atoms and the void could not have been supposed to be judged by the criterion of feeling. This leaves preconception. Could it secure knowledge of the truth of the atomist view of the world?

The notion of preconception as introduced by Epicurus (Cicero, *De Natura Deorum*, 1.43–4) constituted an acknowledgment that to recognize or judge something we must already possess concepts or notions under which to place it. That is we must have concepts corresponding to general terms such as "man," "animal," "colour," "place," etc. Something like this is required if we are to connect the separate kinds of information provided by the different senses and so judge, for example, that we are seeing and touching a cat. The

Epicureans also rested the use of common language on preconceptions (Diogenes Laertius, 10.33).

The formation of this essential cognitive equipment has to take place at a stage which is prior to that at which judgments are made, assent is given, or opinions are formed. Not all conceptions need be formed prior to these other mental activities, but these activities will be limited to those notions that have already been formed. The acquisition of the required preconceptions was regarded as a natural development during the early years of life, prompted by what is evident in sense experience. It is not clear, however, that there is anything in experience which could be responsible for forming the preconceptions necessary to come to believe that the world is composed of atoms or that motion is unintelligible without a void. The latter of these was the premise on which Epicurus rested his argument for the existence of the void (to Herodotus 39–40 in Diogenes Laertius).

Given the significant similarities between the Epicurean picture of the natural world and that of modern (post-sixteenth century) science, we might expect the intellectual heirs of Democritus to have sought to support their doctrine by amassing what empirical evidence they could. But what we find is a mixture of dogmatic assumptions and arguments based on disputable analyses of concepts. It should, however, be emphasized that the primary function of a world view in antiquity was not to generate hypothetical explanations of natural phenomena which were then subjected to tests. Its function was to support a moral outlook and make intelligible a way of conducting oneself. The Epicurean natural world is one in which blind forces combine to produce, quite without purpose, the world we experience, a world which is indifferent to our welfare. In the face of such a world, the best humans can do is to live out their lives with as little distress and as much enjoyment as they can manage. To convey this attitude toward life, it was enough to get people to understand the basic picture of their position in the universe. The picture is not, as it was for Bacon or Descartes, part of a promise of increased power and material benefits and for this reason it was not required to pass severe empirical tests.

The Epicurean attitude toward improving their cognitive position *vis-à-vis* the world around them was like this: We have opinions, some of which are attested by what is self-evident (in sense experience.) If our opinions are not attested by what is self-evident, we should wait until they are attested, until, for example, we can view the object from nearby (Diogenes Laertius 10.34). Regarding matters such as the nature of celestial objects and events, where it is not possible for us to obtain a view from nearby, the least we can do is refrain from believing anything which directly conflicts with (or which is "contested by") what is self-evident. Among the possible uncontested accounts of such phenomena, we should not rule any out; we may, for all we know, be confronted by a state of affairs which is over-determined, making more than one of the apparently competing explanations correct (Letter to Pythocles, 85–8, in Diogenes Laertius). Officially the atomist view of the world around us was supposed to be attested by experience, even though it purported to describe affairs too small to experience favorably in the way suggested by the expression "nearby".

What the Epicureans did not emphasize was the contrast which appears in Plato and was taken up and developed by Plato's one-time student and later colleague, Aristotle – the contrast between experience (*empeiria*) and understanding (*epistêmê*). Understanding involves the ability to provide explanations, and this theoretical knowledge, not experience, was the form of knowledge which Plato and Aristotle privileged and regarded as the goal of the philosopher. By not making this contrast the Epicureans left room for less stringent conceptions of knowledge, a space which was exploited by their seventeenth century counterparts seeking a mitigated skepticism. (It should also be observed that when the conception of knowledge is altered, the possible criteria of truth will change correspondingly, and thus skeptical arguments which work against one conception of knowledge may not be effective against another.)

However, for the seventeenth century corpuscularians, unlike the Epicureans, detailed accounts of nature mattered, because they wanted knowledge which would enable them to manipulate situations in the world. Their goal was not just a general world view, which provided the basis for a general attitude toward life and how best to live it. For example, Bacon urges that the knowledge sought be practically applicable. This means that it must withstand empirical tests before being counted as correct, but he also proposes that success in "works," being able to do things we were not able to do before, is a criterion of truth. This meant that corpuscularians needed to preserve something like Aristotle's distinction between *empeiria* and *epistêmê*. They needed to distinguish between everyday experience and an understanding based on principles, which could explain the connection between the action of hidden causes and observed behavior, and thus needed to be able to give some account of how these principles could be known.

They followed the Epicureans in distinguishing what is immediately present to each sense (an onion-like smell), which could be treated as authoritative, and the judgments we habitually make on the basis of such presentations (someone is cooking onions), which are not always to be relied upon. They also, in various ways, sought to take over and adapt the Epicurean "preconceptions" as notions or concepts which the mind possesses naturally, realizing that a corpuscularian world view could not even be claimed to be understandable without recourse to these. But they were left with the problem of how to bridge the gulf between what the senses reliably deliver (knowledge according to the measure of man) and the knowledge sought by natural philosophers (knowledge according to the measure of the universe).

5 The Latter-day "School of Democritus"

The seventeenth century Corpuscularian imagination was not entirely inspired by ancient sources. The microscope (invented in 1590 and developed gradually during the seventeenth century) provided evidence that there are levels of internal structure in material things which are not visible to the naked eye. A considerable body of experience with machinery had been built up during the late middle ages, including the development of mechanical clocks. The Strasbourg Cathedral clock is frequently mentioned in philosophical writing of this period; it was an elaborate mechanism which not only chimed on the hour and on the quarters, but did so with a display of moving figures (see Stewart, 1979, p. vi.). It was used (by both Descartes and Locke) as an analogy which illustrates what we need to do in order to understand natural phenomena: instead of marveling like rustics at the wondrous effects, we must try to discern the inner mechanism which produces the observable phenomena. Of course the inner mechanisms of nature are too small to be observed themselves, but suppose you know something about clockwork mechanisms and, although not allowed to look inside a clock, are able to make careful observations of its external manifestations. Might you not discover the design of the hidden mechanism and prove your success by building a replica?

There is an obvious difficulty about discovering exactly the design of the mechanism, which is that there might be more than one way to engineer a given effect, so two people might come up with two different mechanisms each of which reproduces all the externally observable effects. How would it be possible to determine which, if either, had hit on the actual mechanism? (For Descartes' response to this problem, see Haldane and Ross, 1955, I 300.) If, moreover, you did not even know anything about the types of parts and materials available to the original inventor you would not have any way of limiting the possibilities – is this a hairspring, pendulum, electric or electronic clock? Bacon's position was analogous to one who did not know whether he was dealing with a mechanical clock or an electronic reproduction of such a clock. Descartes' position is analogous to that of one who assumes in advance that it is a mechanical clock. He is thereby in a better position to come up with hypothetical mechanisms, but if his initial assumption is incorrect and never questioned he may be permanently on the wrong track.

The difference between the assumptions made by Bacon and Descartes is important because it governs the attitudes that can be taken toward sense perception as a source of knowledge about the natural world. Bacon regarded all "world views" as Idols (of the Theater), and he treated Democritean atomism as no different from any other "world view." For he did not think that we could know in advance of experimental inquiry how things will look from the point of view of the universe. His approach clearly assumes that natural phenomena have unobvious explanations based on unobservable structures, and that knowledge of these is possible, although he is not committed in advance to any more determinate picture. From this standpoint the senses would only be a source of illusion if we presumed that the world really is as we perceive it to be and that there is no other perspective on it. Once this Idol (of the Tribe) is put aside, there is no need to discard the senses or to treat them as systematically misleading. It is clear, after all, that our senses provide our only immediate physical contact with the world. The problem of how to use them to get at the kind of information we want is entirely practical.

But from an *a priori* conviction that microscopic mechanical interactions are how the world really operates, the senses clearly do not supply us with representations that are in any way adequate. Things are not really colored, or warm, don't really give off smells or sounds; this is simply how they appear to us. In the terminology which Locke introduced, and which has become standard, these are secondary qualities. Primary qualities (for Locke: bulk, figure, extension, texture, motion of parts, number; *Essay* II. viii, 14–17) are the qualities that things really possess and hence the terms in which all explanations of what we observe should be given.

This distinction is thoroughly Democritean, except that Democritus designated a different list of qualities as primary. There were three, and translated literally from the Greek they come out as "rhythm," "contact," and "turning." This list was somewhat obscure even in Greek. Aristotle felt constrained to gloss it using further Greek words which mean, "shape," "arrangement," and "orientation" (*Metaphysics* 985b13–19). The point is that when Democritus insisted that things were only *by convention*, colored, sweet or bitter, hot or cold, he believed that there were atoms and void which were *really* shaped, arranged and oriented (or which, if you prefer, vibrated, collided and rotated). This is how things are according to the measure of the universe.

It is also in the spirit of Democritus to accord, as Locke does, a second-class reality to secondary qualities. Aristotle had a list of qualities, inherited from previous natural philosophy, the hot, cold, wet and dry, which he regarded as basic for the explanations of natural phenomena. He did not, however, treat other qualities as somehow less real than these. He criticized Democritus for holding that the respects in which things really differed were all to be found on the atomist list of primary qualities, when it was clear that there were many more respects in which things differed from one another and which (as he might have said using a later vocabulary) cannot be "reduced" to Democritus' favored three (*Metaphysics* 1042b11–25). Those who, following Gassendi and Descartes, drew more heavily on the Epicurean framework than did Bacon, inherited this reductionist outlook and its accompanying epistemological problems.

"Reductionism" is still a common impulse among philosophers who accord the achievements of modern science a special authority. Current science, for such reductionists, is our best account of what we (or at least our bodies) and our environment really are. The list of explanatory basics which science now uses is, however, by no means the same as Locke's. Indeed, as a package of basic explanatory concepts, Locke's list (which is essentially the same as Descartes') seems not only incomplete but crude and imprecise. For a time it was left to Newton's theory of mechanics to make the notion of bulk and movement of parts precise. Recent developments in the theory of sub-atomic particles have, however, left these notions radically transformed and very difficult for a lay person to comprehend without first mastering some complex mathematics.

In 1929 it was still possible to contrast the two conceptions in terms of visual images as the physicist Eddington did:

> I have settled down to the task of writing these lectures and have drawn up my chairs to my two tables. Two tables! Yes; there are duplicates of every object about me... One of them... is a commonplace object of

the environment which I call the world... It has extension; it is comparatively permanent; it is coloured; above all it is substantial... Table No. 2 is my scientific table... It does not belong to the world previously mentioned – that world which spontaneously appears around me when I open my eyes... It is part of a world which in much more devious ways has forced itself on my attention. My scientific table is mostly emptiness. Sparsely scattered in that emptiness are numerous electric charges rushing about with great speed; but their combined bulk amounts to less than a billionth of the bulk of the table itself. (Eddington, 1929, pp. xi-xii)

Already, as Eddington wrote, the terms in which the (quantum) theory of these electric charges was framed, had rendered this visual image little more than a conceptual crutch. We have the benefit of hindsight, which can draw on the history of science since the seventeenth century. The basic conceptual framework for physics has been fundamentally revised at least twice since the seventeenth century. We can see as a consequence, that the attempt to base an epistemology for science on a specific conception of how the world is, along with the attempt to secure within that epistemology the validation of that conception, is doomed to failure. Bacon was right to think that nature can not be anticipated to that extent. (What rôle that leaves for philosophy, specifically metaphysics, other than to expose what Bacon called the Idols of the Theater, will be considered in the next chapter.)

Does this mean we should avoid any attempt to distinguish between sensory experience which is indicative of the character of what is producing the experience and that which is not? Are the arguments which Locke, and before him Galileo, used, wholly fallacious? One might argue that the explanatory use which science made of Lockean primary qualities was not where their true significance lay. The importance of the distinction was to emphasize the difference between relative and non-relative characteristics of perceived objects. Locke, for example, asks us to acknowledge that because an object has the power to make us feel pain, it does not follow that pain is a quality of that object, and then invites us to regard warmth, odor and color in the same way as powers in objects to cause sensations in us (*Essay*, II. viii. 18). Sixty-five years before Locke published his *Essay*, Galileo argued (pp. 274ff.) that tickling is not a property of a feather, for to tickle it must be applied to the sensitive arm of a living human being, rather than to the marble arm of a statue. In a similar way warmth, color, etc. are not in bodies because they require sense organs to be realized.

This distinction, the argument continues, was an essential part of abandoning the cult of the Idols of the Tribe and taking up a properly scientific attitude toward the world. Our perceptual experience as Bacon's image suggests, "distorts and discolours the nature of things by mingling its own nature with it." Is there not reason to think that Locke's primary qualities can be possessed by things independently of being perceived by us, whereas his secondary qualities, as powers to cause sensations, clearly cannot be identified without reference to the presence of perceivers having sense organs of specific kinds? Why, for example, are we tempted to believe that bodies really do move (vibrate) in such a way as to set up motions (waves) in the air, but only appear to us to give off sounds? Is it that we can imagine the vibrations and the waves occurring in the absence of an ear to hear the sound, just as we can imagine there being no tickling sensation when Galileo's feather is applied to the marble arm of a statue? If so, what is the basis for this?

One suggestion comes from noting that Locke's list of primary qualities is remarkably similar to a list given by Aristotle of the "objects" (Locke would have said "qualities") which can be perceived by more than one sensory modality. Aristotle's list is "movement," "rest," "figure," "magnitude," "number," and "unity" (*On the Soul* 425a16). ("Magnitude" or "size" includes some of what Locke means by "extension" and "bulk"). The deaf and blind can perceive these "objects" as they still possess modes of perception which enable them to tell, e.g. whether a thing is moving or at rest, and they can, if nothing else, feel how many and what size things are.

Now one can argue against Aristotle that the same quality is not present to two different sensory modalities; the Epicureans would certainly have had to argue this to maintain their thesis that the senses can never conflict with one another. Shape (or figure) judged visually is a very different experience from shape judged by tactile experience. But the two experiences confirm one another with such consistency that a single concept emerges from a fusion of the two kinds of experience, one which, because of the alternative experiential routes (seeing and touching), is less dependent on us and seems less liable to have its nature distorted by mingling with the nature of our sensory experience.

This line of thought suggests why Locke's list of primary qualities is a better candidate for the measure of the universe than his list of secondary qualities. But it does little to sustain the claim that secondary qualities are not really in things. To the extent that colors, for example, can be reliably correlated with other experiences, are we not prepared to take them as indicative of real differences in things? The argument that colors are not real features of things because they do not appear to a blind person (or to a statue) should carry no weight. Movement cannot be detected by a creature (a plant) which is incapable of perceptually tracking an object. We cannot detect the sonar pulses (air vibrations) by which bats navigate. No one creature is a measure of all the differences in the universe. The confusion is to think that the measure of the universe can be found in any sensed quality; instead, it is made by careful correlation of detectable differences, however those differences are detected. This is why Locke's primary qualities have some privilege; as objects accessible to more than one sense, they are the product of such correlation.

It may be said that this attempt to restore secondary qualities to nature misses the point. Our experiences of color are, to be sure, indicative of real differences in the natural world, but our experiences are not part of that world. This is indeed part of what is implied by Locke's distinction and it marks a very important feature of the way we have thought about ourselves and about knowledge since the seventeenth century. An aspect of our experience (that which Locke classified as its secondary qualities), has come to be regarded as being intimately bound up with what we are and to be regarded both as a paradigm of what can be known and also as very difficult to locate in the natural world. What our bodies undergo (the impact of air vibrations, complex molecules and electromagnetic radiation) when we have experiences of colors, smells and sounds, is easy to locate, but what happens in our minds is more problematic. Somewhere on the way to the present age part of our experience lost its place in the natural world.

6 *Idols, Ideas, and Cartesian Epistemology*

The story of how our experiences of the secondary qualities of things along with our mental activities (reasoning, imagining, feeling, desiring) came to be located beyond the margins of the natural world is closely bound up with a shift in the use of Plato's word *"idea,"* which took place during the seventeenth century. Plato, we noted in the first chapter, used two words which had to do with the visual aspects of things, one *"ideai"* to label the highest grade objects of our minds, the other *"eidôla"* to label the lowest grade. *Ideai* are what we must make arduous intellectual efforts to grasp; *eidôla* are what our senses and imagination supply to us without effort and which are liable to hinder our efforts to grasp *ideai*. Epicurus used the term *"eidôla"* to label the perceptible physical effects which things make on us, effects which, if apprehended in a series, present something (a *"phantasia"*) to our minds.

The two Greek roots were drafted into theological service before they gave rise to the modern English words, "ideas" and "idols." Under Platonic influence early Christian theology came to identify ideas with the objects of God's perfect knowledge; "idols" served as a term for graven images of false gods. During the early seventeenth century (see entries for "idea" and "idol" in the *Oxford English Dictionary*; see also *Descartes' Conversation with Burman*, [26]) the two words were both used for images in general and for whatever is present to our minds. "Idea" in this use would suggest that what was present was satisfactorily conceived (by analogy with the use of "idea" for the objects of God's knowledge). "Idol," particularly as Bacon used the term, combined both Plato's and the subsequent religious use of cognate words to suggest a benighted state of ignorance and delusion.

The use of "idol" as a synonym (with negative connotations) for "idea" did not survive much past Bacon. Adaptations of Epicurean strategies for advocating corpuscularianism without total skepticism took the form of relabelling *eidôla* and *phantasiai* – things which are present to the mind in sensation and which cannot in themselves be false – as "ideas." This relabelling is indicative of the crucial cognitive role that these were to play in the so-called "way of ideas" and its strategies for overcoming skepticism and Aristotelianism. We cannot, after all, be wrong about the characteristics of what is present to our minds; we may be wrong about what to anticipate or infer from what is present to us; but about what is present, we can pronounce on with the degree of confidence and certainty that God must possess when he surveys his Ideas. The migration of Plato's Ideas into the mind of God and the conception of God's knowledge as a paradigm for human knowledge thus eventually results in a conception of knowledge and its potential grounding which is radically different from Plato's.

Plato had noted (*Theaetetus* 152c) that perception is free from falsehood, "as if it were knowledge." But he makes nothing of this. An argument later in the dialogue (168b–d) makes it plain that for Plato the cognitive interest in perception lay precisely in what could be inferred or anticipated from perception, not in the qualities of the experience which were immediately present. The thought of a person saying, "I do not know what to make of this, but at least I know (have knowledge that) I am presented with the color red," would have struck Plato and his contemporaries as a feeble attempt at a joke. If Plato were confronted by a skeptic who denied the possibility of achieving *epistêmê* (understanding) about anything, the move of pointing out that one cannot be wrong about certain qualities of what is present to the mind would not gain him much, since *epistêmê* is supposed to involve the ability to explain why, and reports of what is present to one's mind do nothing to establish this ability.

However, the challenge confronting reform-minded seventeenth century natural philosophers was much more radical. They faced the up-hill task of dislodging entrenched Aristotelianism, but their efforts to use their own intellectual resources against an authority structure grounded in tradition were exposed to Pyrrhonist arguments honed by Catholic forces of the Counter Reformation. These arguments were designed to show that no one can, on the basis of their own faculties, make an undeniably authoritative statement about anything and had been used on Luther's claim that inner conviction provided a criterion for religious truth. The fact that the epistemological battle had already been joined on the territory of religious knowledge rather than that of knowledge of nature or of society had an important bearing on its focus, for although religious knowledge is not directly sense based, conviction can be treated as analogous to inner perception.

Descartes took up this challenge in his *Meditations on First Philosophy* (Haldane and Ross, 1955, I 144-9). The project he undertook there was threefold: to undermine Aristotelian metaphysics, to put in place the basic framework of a new, mechanistic metaphysics, and to show that he was entitled, Pyrrhonist arguments not withstanding, to claim to know the correctness of this position, thereby showing how knowledge in general is possible for human beings. His strategy was to build on the methods of the Christian skeptics, first to purge the mind of traditional beliefs, but then to try to beat the skeptics at their own game by showing that this can provide a tool for refining (Luther's criterion of) inner conviction to the point where it will no longer, at least in the realm of natural philosophy, face the problems of conflicting opinion.

Descartes begins with a standard skeptical move, noting that there are conflicts amongst the opinions he has accumulated through experience and education. They clearly cannot all be right and he has as yet no criterion for sorting the true from the false, but he notes that most of these opinions have been based directly or indirectly on sense experience. So he turns to consider the reliability of the senses. His subsequent retreat in the face of doubt comes in three distinct waves. In the first he acknowledges that he has trusted what he learned through the senses, but is aware that sometimes the senses have been deceptive and it would be wise not to trust them entirely. At this point the wave of doubt recedes before the thought that there may be specially favorable circumstances where the senses simply cannot fail us. Epicurus, recall, regarded sense perception as one of the criteria that constituted his "yardstick" of truth; what is presented by the senses is the natural effect on us of things around us and consequently is never deceptive if properly used. But this criterion had to be used in favorable circumstances. Descartes' next move is therefore to consider the reliability of sensory information in favorable circumstances – can he at least be sure that he is sitting by the fire?

At this point, where the advance of skeptical doubt stalled over the thought that some of our perceptual judgments can be made in such favorable circumstances as to guarantee their truth, Descartes recalls that he is prone to sleep and in his dreams has experiences indistinguishable from those of his waking moments. He argues that however favorable the circumstances appear to be for making a true judgment on the basis of an immediately present sense experience, there is nothing in that experience which will distinguish it from a dream experience and so nothing that will assure him that he is not dreaming. The skeptical momentum is thus resumed and carries Descartes as far as the thought that he may only have imagined that he has a body, eyes, head and hands, the things about which he is most confident his sense perception cannot deceive him.

The momentum of the second wave of doubt has spent itself as Descartes reaches the thought that judgments about the truth of the basic principles of geometry and arithmetic can be relied upon whether one is awake or asleep, since their truth does not depend on the existence of material things; these are truths grasped by the intellect independent of any evidence from the senses. The last wave begins with the thought that God is powerful enough to have supplied Descartes with experiences, but at the same time brought it about that none of the earth, heaven, bodies and places, which are represented in his experiences, exist. This wave washes past the point about the simple truths of mathematics when Descartes realizes he might even be deceived when he adds two and three or counts the sides of a square.

To allow anyone to be constantly deceived in this way would, however, be contrary to the goodness of God, but Descartes is not yet in a position to appeal to any of the traditional attributes of God; he is not even in a position to appeal to the existence of God. To keep up the skeptical momentum he resorts to the hypothesis of a powerful and deceitful demon who has created in Descartes illusions of "the heaven, earth, colours, figures, sounds and all other external things." Now everything Descartes has believed is held hostage by this hypothesis until he can establish the existence of a benevolent God, who would not allow him to be deceived in this way.

There remains, Descartes observes, at least one thing untouched by the waves of doubt, one thing about which he cannot be deceived. This is the fact that he thinks – since only a being who thinks could be deceived about everything else – and therefore exists, at least so long as he thinks ("*Cogito ergo sum*"). It is here that Descartes finds his fixed point, the foundation on which he will erect his philosophy. It also provides his criterion of truth; truth is reached by willfully doubting until one reaches the point where one cannot doubt. Those things which cannot, when one thinks about them, be doubted – those things about which the will must submit to intellect – must be granted to be true. However, even to use this as a general criterion of truth depends on establishing the falsity of the evil genius hypothesis, since an evil genius might just have given us insufficient powers of doubt.

Moreover the proofs of the existence of a benevolent God, which will ultimately rescue Descartes from the "deep water" of doubt into which he has fallen (Haldane and Ross, 1955, I 149), require that he be able to rely on his own reasoning not to deceive him. Descartes works to establish his own existence, but what he does not doubt and does not trouble to prove is his own mental competence. Each of the three waves of doubt push Descartes near to confronting the thought that would prematurely end his project, the possibility that he is not fit to use his judgment or trust his reason.

The first occurs as the first wave of doubt recedes in the face of the question, is it not the case that our sense experience of our own bodies is so reliable that to doubt that "I am here, seated by the fire, attired in a dressing grown...that these hands and this body are mine" would place one among the senseless, the insane (Haldane and Ross, 1955, I 145)? The second occurs when dream experiences are cited. Does the possibility that one is dreaming raise only the doubt that one's present experience is indistinguishable from experience with a completely different origin? Should it not also be asked whether one's judgment is functioning normally when one is dreaming? The third occurs in the shadow of the thought that God is powerful enough to render the whole of experience an illusion. Two plus three is supposed to add up to five, even in dreams, but "...sometimes I imagine that others deceive themselves in the things which they think they know best, how do I know that I am not deceived every time that I add two and three. . ."? (Haldane and Ross, 1955, I 147) A benevolent God would not allow Descartes to be so deceived, but while the hypothesis of the evil demon is in place, what prevents Descartes from deceiving himself? What prevents him from deceiving himself about the proofs by which he will convince himself of the existence of a benevolent God, a God who will then be his proof against massive deception?

The question of whether one is competent to judge (is not insane, befuddled or unable to concentrate) is not a question which can be raised and then fruitfully pursued from the standpoint which Descartes takes up. To question one's sanity is to question one's ability to carry out the kind of inquiry on which Descartes is embarked. Reassurance on this question has to come in the first instance from other people, as they assess the appropriateness of one's responses to what is around one on the basis of their perspectives of that environment and their expectations of what are appropriate responses. Descartes is conducting his inquiry without assuming that there are other perspectives on the objects of his experience, which are comparable to his own perspective. There is only his own (subjective) experience and the (objective) view of an omniscient God. Epistemic salvation is a matter between the individual (the would-be knower) and God.

Descartes is consistent in this. At the very end of the *Meditations*, assured by the existence of a benevolent God that he is not massively deceived, he is now prepared to rely on at least one salient difference between dream (deceptive) and waking experiences. The former cannot be connected with one another or with the course of our (individual) lives; the standard is based on other perspectives occupied by the same self. If, during what otherwise appear to be waking moments, there is a phenomenon which cannot be connected to the rest of Descartes' experience (a man who suddenly appears and then suddenly disappears), Descartes would conclude that his brain (part of his body), not his mind, is malfunctioning.

Many subsequent philosophers, who discarded Descartes' doctrine that the mind and the body are distinct substances (kinds of reality), continued to assume this epistemic dualism which made the intellect sovereign and gave it indisputable authority over its (subjective) kingdom of ideas. The reason the "subjective" aspects of our experience lost their place in the natural world was that they were needed to furnish this autonomous mental realm.

7 Cartesian Epistemology and Stoicism

Descartes' skeptical strategy, once in place, sets the agenda for a great deal of subsequent philosophy. The paradigm of knowing becomes the relationship in which we as individuals stand to what is present to our conscious awareness. Few find Descartes' arguments for the existence of a benevolent God as convincing as the skeptical steps which preceded them. Consequently a characteristic problem for "Cartesian epistemology" becomes the possibility of our having knowledge of the physical world beyond our minds, that is of the "external" world which appears to be represented in our experience.

This is not a significant problem for the ancients, and to see clearly the respects in which Cartesian epistemology is a new departure, it is useful to identify some of the ancient elements in Descartes' strategy and the quite different ways these elements were deployed in the ancient disputes. For example, the phenomenon of dreams, on which Descartes mounts his second wave of doubt, was also used by the ancient skeptics, but to a much less radical effect. To appreciate this we need to identify one more position in the ancient disputes.

We have so far identified two of the movements which came to prominence in Athens after the death of Aristotle and which lasted well into the Christian era. There is on the one hand Epicureanism and on the other hand skepticism, which until the first century BC was identified with the Academy in Athens and then dispersed more widely through the Pyrrhonist movement. A third movement, Stoicism, had during this period a higher public profile than the other two, but contributed less to the formation of the framework of modern epistemology. Nevertheless, Stoicism exerted an important influence on the ancient doctrines and arguments which did find their way into more recent philosophy.

When Descartes' first wave of doubt ends with the thought that there are sense perceptions which simply cannot be doubted, he is pausing at a point where the Epicureans and Stoics were in broad agreement. Both held that sense experience could function as a criterion of truth. The Epicureans, we have seen, thought of perception as separable into the reception of influences, which impress us from outside, and the judgments we make in response to those influences. The former provided the criterion of truth; it could not mislead. Descartes follows the Epicureans to the extent that he treats what is present to his consciousness as containing at its core an element which cannot but be true and if not misused, cannot mislead.

The Stoics rejected the Epicurean claim that there was something in sense perception which cannot mislead us. Nothing which is present in sense experience (i.e., a *phantasia*), can be treated as a bare object; a presentation is always a presentation of something's being the case and hence capable of misleading. The *phantasia* of a partly submerged oar is the presentation of something bent and hence misrepresents the object from which it originated (Sextus Empiricus, *Adversus Mathematics* 7.245–6). In the seventeenth century Spinoza took issue in a similar way with Descartes' attempt to locate an element of incorrigible truth in ideas, accusing Descartes of inappropriately treating ideas as pictures on a panel (*Ethics*, Book II, note to Prop. XLIX). (Compare the expository device, cited from Long and Sedley (1987) above in section 4, of associating the Epicurean position with the claim that "the camera never lies." Analytic philosophers in this century have similarly disputed whether all perception must be the perception of something's being the case.)

Where Epicurean natural philosophy portrayed human sense experience as based on the passive reception of influences, Stoic natural philosophy underwrote a picture of humans as thoroughly active: light stretches the air, creating a cone with its tip at the pupil of the eye and its base at the object, so that seeing is like probing with a walking stick (Diogenes Laertius 7. 157). The Stoics held that sense perception could be a criterion of truth because if we take care and in our sensory activity have properly grasped (*kataleptikê*) certain presentations (*phantasiai*), these presentations were guaranteed to yield the truth. Not surprisingly the skeptics in the Academy opposed the Stoic doctrine of "properly grasped presentations," and one of the arguments which they used against it was the argument from dreaming, taken up by Descartes. But when the Academics appealed to the phenomena of dreams, it was in the company of several arguments designed to show that there might be indistinguishable presentations of distinct objects.

The Stoics held that the correct response to the occasions when the senses prove deceptive is to improve our habits of discrimination. Hardly any adult is fooled by the appearance of a partly submerged oar; the presence of a body in water is an indication not to take this appearance at face value. But, the Academics objected, could there not be two things, e.g. two eggs, twin children, dreaming and waking experiences which, however hard one tried, could not be distinguished, because in fact there were no discriminable differences between them? The Stoics insisted that just as a mother learns to distinguish between her twin children, we can learn to discriminate between any two distinct things, because there always will be something we can use to tell them apart.

This dispute eventually reduced to an unresolvable stand-off over conflicting fundamental assumptions about reality, the Stoics holding that different things were always marked by discriminable differences, the skeptics that distinct indiscriminable things were a real possibility. What was not at issue in this dispute was whether we had eyes, a head, hands, or a body at all. Descartes' use of the argument from dreams carries him well past the point reached by any ancient skeptic.

In the light of the way Descartes fails to engage the question of his own mental competence to apply his methods, it is interesting to note that the Stoics identified the ignorant as insane. This appears harsh and inappropriate, but it followed from a widely held attitude in Greek philosophy and Greek culture generally, that to know oneself was the first and perhaps most difficult task for someone who aspired to wisdom. "They [the Stoics] also say that every inferior man is insane, since he has ignorance of himself and of his concerns, and this is insanity (*mania*)" (Stobaeus, in Long and Sedley, (1987), 41I). The Stoics, recall, accepted that sense experience could be deceptive, but placed responsibility on the perceiver to recognize the deception and take steps that would yield a non-deceptive presentation. This might simply require getting a better view; it might require developing more finely attuned abilities to discriminate. People who misjudged what was before their eyes did so in part because they needed a better appreciation of their own position in the natural world, not because they misused presentations which in and of themselves were true (as they were for Epicurus and later for Descartes).

Moreover for the Stoics, a person's epistemic situation (both what that person is aware of and the abilities of that person to discriminate and to reason) was a significant part of that person's moral character. The fragment from Stobaeus, quoted above, continues, "Ignorance is the vice opposite to moderation, and this is insanity because in its relative disposition it makes our impulses unstable and fluttering. Hence they give this outline of insanity – fluttering ignorance." Ignorance for a Stoic is not simply failing to represent things as they are; it is an unsteadiness in response to the buffeting which judgment receives from impressions and impulses. Like skepticism and Epicureanism, Stoicism was first and foremost a way of conducting oneself, but unlike the former two schools, it did not encourage suspension of judgment or withdrawal from public life. The point of knowing, of having sound habits of discrimination, was to have sound habits of choice. The aim was to acquire a perfectly stable disposition, which will enable one to choose and judge correctly in either private or public (political) affairs.

The stability of these dispositions of choice was secured in the same way that one secured one's epistemic situation, by a correct appreciation of one's position in relation to nature. Unlike the Epicurean world of blind forces indifferent to our welfare, the Stoic world was fashioned and held together by an immanent intelligence. Our lives from part of the design with which this intelligence works. It consequently is concerned for our welfare and the correctness or otherwise of our judgments and choices can be assessed by whether they accord with or conflict with its comprehensive design. In such a world humans are called upon to discover their place(s) and to work to develop the capacities which will enable them to perform their function(s) well. From this perspective knowledge, or understanding, and rational capacities develop together.

Spinoza, critical of Cartesian philosophy, but persuaded of the general correctness of the mechanistic approach to natural philosophy, formulated what amounted to a Stoic counterpart to Descartes' position, (with, however, the important difference that Spinoza's immanent deity was, unlike the Stoics', indifferent to our welfare, while the benevolence of Descartes' transcendent God is crucial to Cartesian epistemology). As already mentioned, Spinoza denied that something incorrigible can be isolated within our ideas. Ideas are not mere presences but present what is the case in some way or other. Spinoza does not suggest that truth can be determined by inspection of an isolated something immediately present to consciousness. Since knowledge can only be gradually improved, truth similarly is something which is not an all or nothing affair; it is judged by the overall coherence of the totality of our beliefs about the world and of our place in it and by the adequacy of those beliefs for understanding that world and our relation to it. Since complete adequacy would require understanding of the whole system of the world, it is a goal we can only work toward, but never fully attain.

The goal of knowledge under this conception, however, is not domination of nature, but freedom from being determined by external forces, from having to be passive in relation to them. Enlightenment is active self-determination. This kind of position was an undercurrent in the seventeenth and eighteenth centuries, but surfaced in a variety of forms (from German idealism to American pragmatism) during the past two centuries. To sustain this position in any of its forms involves rejecting in some way or other Descartes' conception of the self and self-knowledge. It could be argued that Descartes begins like the Greeks with self-knowledge. But he presumes such knowledge to be possible without an understanding of one's relations to the rest of the natural world. The only relation that is important to Descartes is his relation to God and acknowledgment of his dependence on a benevolent God.

Descartes does urge that disciplined activity on our part is required if we are to have a hope of acquiring any kind of knowledge. Our rational faculty needs to be developed through use. The doubt which disentangles the intellect and its ideas from distortions and confusions introduced by its associations with the body is something we must actively undertake. Nevertheless Descartes, and therefore epistemology in the Cartesian tradition, starts from a presumed separation between subject and object and the basic epistemological problem is framed as an encounter between a self-contained subject (intellect, understanding) and an independently given object (whether the involuntarily changing content of consciousness or the external world). The alternative involves rejecting the Cartesian starting point in a self-contained, perfectly rational knowing subject whose knowledge is founded on passively perceived presentations to consciousness. It has to insist instead that the distinction between subject and object is not given, but is something which is the product of an ongoing process of disentangling one from the other and that part of this disentanglement involves recognizing respects in which previous thought or practices have failed to be conducted properly.

8 Theory, Practice, and Experiment

Epistemological questions in the ancient world were not separated from questions of how we should conduct our lives. In the seventeenth century questions of moral conduct lay within the domain of religious authority and it was expedient for those like Bacon and Descartes who wished to clear a space for a new approach to natural philosophy to set such questions carefully and visibly to one side. In the third section of the *Discourse on Method* (Haldane and Ross, 1955, I 95–8), for example, Descartes sets to one side questions of conduct and determines to adopt a moral and religious code based on the prevailing laws and customs of his country. The radical solvent of doubt was not meant to touch any practical question. As he says just prior to introducing the hypothesis of the evil demon, "For I am assured that there can be neither peril nor error in this course, and that I cannot at present yield too much to distrust, since I am not considering the question of action, but only of knowledge". (Haldane and Ross, 1955, I 148) But the suspension of practical questions is not, and cannot be, entirely innocent. To suspend interest in acting prior to taking up questions of knowledge shapes the questions which will be raised and the attitude adopted to the objects of knowledge. Suspending practical involvement in the world is to withdraw from it and consequently to remove oneself and one's epistemic position from among the objects of investigation.

This separation of practical from cognitive concerns makes a significant difference to the effect of skepticism. Both ancient and modern skepticism have the net effect of subverting claims by individuals or groups to special authority for their knowledge claims. But when knowledge claims have been disconnected from moral commitments, skepticism becomes compatible with a strong voluntary decision to accept something or to act on behalf of some cause. This was already made clear by the Christian skeptics of the Counter Reformation. Because such commitments are not claimed to have rational grounding they do not need to be justified and one may acknowledge no obligation to listen to the claims of competing commitments.

The ancient skeptics would have treated commitment which came without any attempt at rational justification as a form of madness. Their response to the commitments of others took the form of rational engagement, not the resistance of a deaf ear. But deafness lay, perhaps, at a deeper level. If ancient skeptics were to engage you with the aim of finding an equally good argument against any commitment for which you offer a reason, would they be offering you any better hearing than a modern skeptic? Can either hear of the possibility that by putting their differences together instead of playing them off against one another, humans stand to achieve something that will enrich rather than impoverish one another?

The real (i.e., religious) politics of the need to make this separation of natural from moral philosophy in the seventeenth century context are clear. But the very radical separation which Descartes achieved, a separation which distinctively marks off Cartesian epistemology from ancient epistemology, has continued to shape not only our philosophic tradition, but also the conception of science on which many of our institutions have been based. The dominant conception has been that science is a quest for truth, for objective knowledge, and as such is not and should not be concerned with practical, political or moral issues that might arise as a result of making its knowledge available for application. It is this conception which many, including scientists such as those who formed the Union of Concerned Scientists, are now questioning. To provide a philosophical basis for this questioning requires us to move outside the framework of Cartesian epistemology to re-ask questions about the extent to which we can hope to depose the Idols of the Tribe.

In important respects Descartes carried out a purge of practical concerns from his philosophy far more thoroughly than did Bacon and this accounts for the obvious way in which Descartes has not taken us in the direction in which Bacon set out. But even if we do not succeed in setting the Idols aside when we suspend our practical concerns, Descartes' method makes it appear that Bacon's Idols can be purged in one session of methodical doubt. The method is carried out under the assumptions that the mind is both better known than, and can exist independently of, anything in the physical world. Moreover it is the intellect, not the senses, which alone is able to grasp the true nature of things, even of material things.

Thus the mind, when focussing on its own ideas as when engaged in mathematics, delivers fully objective knowledge. Our reason is not only God-given, it is a respect in which we fully resemble God. To the extent that we learn to see by its light we transcend the conditions of our human standpoint. Cartesian ideas, when clearly and distinctly perceived are, in and of themselves, neutral presentations of content to consciousness; they are not colored or distorted by judgment or desire. To judge, to desire or to will are separate mental acts performed on the basis of the attitude we decide to adopt to our ideas. The prejudices and biases that constitute the Idols, even those of the Tribe, are portrayed as easily put aside.

In another respect Descartes' radical separation of theoretical inquiry from practical involvement in the world shaped his account of perception in a way which left his epistemology hostage to the orientation of the Greek sources from which he drew. He was consequently unable to appreciate the force of Bacon's call for experimental investigation of nature. It is the Greek attitude of disdain for getting involved in practical labor that Bacon regards as having been detrimental to the cause of natural philosophy. The focus on sense perception in Cartesian epistemology, a focus which has continued through the twentieth century, together with its lack of concern with practical application, made it ill suited to be the epistemology of the kind of natural science that Bacon envisioned. Science, nevertheless, particularly in the nineteenth and twentieth centuries, developed down the path which Bacon pointed out.

The whole idea of experimental investigation was to develop means of probing the natural world that would overcome the limitations of our sense perception. This was to be done, as Bacon already suggested, not principally by sharpening our perceptions, but by putting questions to nature in such a way that perception has a minimal role to play. In other words we devise and construct controlled situations, ones where things are simpler than those to be found in the natural environment. This is why laboratories and expensive equipment are necessary. As technology develops so do our means of setting up new, controlled situations. The "observational" base of experimental science is increasingly not a matter of relying on the sense perceptions of individual observing conscious subjects. This point was already made in 1934 by Bachelard in his critical discussion of Descartes' epistemology (Bachelard, 1984, pp. 171–2).

In the second Meditation Descartes, by focussing attention on a piece of wax, argues that the senses, and hence sensory qualities, do not contribute to knowledge of the nature of wax. This is argued by noting that its sensory qualities, color, shape, fragrance and consistency change as the wax is brought near the fire and melts. Since the wax is the same stuff throughout, none of the particular sensed qualities, which it can lose whilst remaining the same wax, can be used in an account of what that wax is. On this Cartesian account a largely passive sensory observation is accompanied by a wholly intellectual contemplation of the observation process.

Bachelard contrasts this with the way in which scientists might now think it appropriate to investigate the properties of a piece of wax. They would first carefully prepare the object of study in the light of the kind of inquiry they were conducting. The wax would be purified; that is, it would be the product of a series of manipulations which serve to fix its chemical identity; it would in other words be an artificial product identified by its method of preparation. If it is to be studied by X-ray diffraction techniques it must have been cooled under carefully controlled conditions to ensure that the surface molecules are suitably aligned, and so on. This object is not "given" in pure sensory perception, nor is its nature grasped in any pure intellectual contemplation. The active manipulation, coupled with the scientific understanding of the effects of that manipulation, all contribute to determining or preparing the object for scientific study. Bachelard coins the word "phenomeno-technique" to contrast this base of experimental science with sense perception and passive observation.

Over the past ten years much more philosophic attention has been devoted to considering experimentation and the nature of the experimental base of science. These studies have revealed the complexity of experimental procedures and of the interplay between theories and experimental constructions. The claim on behalf of modern science would be that its public institutions of peer review and the demand for independent repetition of experimental results are effective counterbalances to the various tendencies which generated what Bacon called the Idols of the Tribe. This is clearly the kind of corrective which Bacon himself envisioned. In *New Atlantis*, he describes in some detail the organization of the House of Salomon, the scientific research organization of his utopia. Here all stages of investigation are carried out by teams and are subjected to the critical review of others (ALNA, pp. 288ff.).

There are two questions to be raised about whether public institutions of this kind can claim to secure objectivity for scientific knowledge, and in particular whether they secure its value neutrality. First, it is clear from the writing of Bacon and of more modern philosophers of science, such as Popper, Harré and Bachelard that they perceive the quest for objective knowledge as dictating a code of ethics to the scientist. If the goal is objective knowledge then investigators must put aside personal concerns and interests, must be open to criticism and must look strenuously for evidence that might show their theories to be incorrect. In the interests of objectivity they should share their results and methods with others. To this extent there is not just a personal ethic required but an ethos of cooperative endeavor and common concern required within the scientific community. This ethos was apparent, for example, amongst physicists prior to the Second World War but appears to some extent to have broken down since then under pressures of professionalism and commercialism. The validity of continued claims to objectivity on behalf of science depends on whether the institutions of science can secure objectivity in the absence of the recognition of any corresponding ethic on the part of individuals engaged in it.

Do the tendencies which create Bacon's Idols operate only at the level of individuals? Can they not also operate at the level of institutions? For example, suppose we grant that it is a general human failing not to notice flaws in one's own theories or to believe those theories which fit in best with one's prejudices rather than those which accord better with the evidence. If these failings were manifested in sufficiently different ways in different individuals, then it would be not unreasonable to suppose that the various biases should cancel each other out, so that what would be left standing as agreed by a sufficiently wide segment of the scientific community would have a good claim to objectivity. If, on the other hand, institutions themselves can introduce biases or impart specific sets of values in enough of those who participate in them, then they cannot be implicitly relied upon but must themselves be the objects of critical scrutiny from time to time. Since the issues here concern the relation of the individual to the wider human community, further discussion of this question will be postponed to chapter 5.

3
Idols of the Theater: *Metaphysics and the Aim of Inquiry*

Those who have handled sciences have been either men of experiment or men of dogmas. The men of experiment are like the ant, they only collect and use; the reasoners resemble spiders, who make cobwebs out of their own substance. But the bee takes a middle course; it gathers its materials from the flowers of the garden and field, but transforms and digests it by a power of its own.

Novum Organum I XCV

1 Metaphysics

Idols of the Theater include the philosophical systems, spun by rational philosopher-spiders out of their own substance (I LXIII), cobwebs woven by reasoning and demonstration which ensnare the mind. They also include the "deformed and monstrous" speculations dreamt by Empiric philosopher-ants, whose imaginations feed obsessively on a narrow range of experiments (I LXIV). But since these Idols are fabrications, since they arise not from innate impulses and weaknesses but are consciously developed, they are easier to cast down than other Idols (I LXI). But did Bacon think it possible to engage in natural philosophy without presupposing a general view of the nature of reality and did he regard it as advisable not to attempt to articulate that general view?

Undertaking to systematize such general views has come to be known as "metaphysics." When Aristotle outlined a program for achieving understanding of natural phenomena he recognized that his account of what understanding consists in rested upon important assumptions about Being (*ousia*). For example, if we are seeking to understand why natural objects have the qualities they do and behave in the ways that they do, we are already presuming that the world has in it individual objects which are relatively permanent, which have qualities and which either act or undergo change. Aristotle assigned to a separate discipline, which he called "First (or Primary) Philosophy," (*Metaphysics* 1026a30) the task of investigating Being or Reality along with related concepts and principles. This discipline came to be called "metaphysics" because, in a traditional ordering of Aristotle's works used in ancient times, his treatise on the subject came after ("*meta*") his treatise on nature ("*physis*").

Aristotle's treatise on First Philosophy included his criticisms of the claims about Being or Reality embodied in Plato's doctrine of Forms or Ideas. According to Plato only the Forms are real and knowable; the natural world which we experience consists of mere appearances, of transitory and imperfect realizations of the eternal and perfect Forms. This doctrine came to typify a conception of metaphysics as concerned with a Reality beyond (above, behind, or in some way transcending) the natural world. Having rejected "separate" (or transcendent) Forms, Aristotle was prepared to accord full reality to natural objects; and metaphysics, as he conceived it, was concerned with questions and principles which apply to nature. *Epistêmê* for Aristotle rested on the ability to define things (definitions, he insisted, were not merely verbal (*Metaphysics* 1030a9), on a vitally important distinction between things which are what they are in virtue of themselves and things which are what they are only accidentally, on the difference between (immanent) form and matter. These are among the topics which Aristotle treats when he addresses the question of what Being or Reality is.

Bacon rejected Plato's transcendent Forms; Plato's was a case of the corrupting influence of superstition mixed with theology (*Novum Organum* I LXV). Bacon's opposition to Aristotle did not rest on Aristotle's attempt to give a systematic account of Being or Reality, but on what Bacon saw as the logical straight-jacket which Aristotelian philosophy placed on understanding; Aristotle's natural philosophy, Bacon held, had been hopelessly corrupted by logic (I LXIII). Although metaphysics does not necessarily invoke a reality which wholly transcends experience, there is, nevertheless, some reason to think Bacon would have advised against engaging in any kind of metaphysics. For metaphysics traditionally proceeds speculatively in a posture of repose, by-passing the experimental efforts on which Bacon insisted; and it tries to decide issues *a priori*, prior that is to experience, a procedure which Bacon repudiated.

Outright rejections of all metaphysics became characteristic of empiricist philosophy and indeed Bacon has frequently been cast in the rôle of founding father to this line of modern philosophy. Empiricists insist that all knowledge must ultimately be derived from and relate to the empirical world, the world of which we have experience, and they consequently treat as metaphysical any claim whose truth or falsity could not in principle be settled by appeal to experience. Thus, for example, we find Hume in the eighteenth century:

> If we take in our hand any volume; of divinity or school metaphysics, for instance; let us ask, *Does it contain any abstract reasoning concerning quantity or number?* No. *Does it contain any experimental reasoning concerning matter of fact and existence?* No. Commit it then to the flames; for it can contain nothing but sophistry and illusion. (*Enquiry* XII, Pt. iii)

And again, early in this century the logical positivists: "In the domain of *metaphysics*, including all philosophy of value and normative theory, logical analysis yields the negative result *that the alleged statements in this domain are entirely meaningless*" (Rudolf Carnap, 1959, (1932), pp. 60–1).

But if we avoid systematizing a general view of the nature of reality, does that mean we do not have such a view, or that our investigations are unaffected by whatever view we may hold? Bacon's method of "Induction," it should be noted, presupposes that observed material bodies are composed of smaller material parts whose action is responsible for what we observe. Hume's arguments presuppose that experience is a linear sequence of distinct and independent existents and the logical positivists rest their case on very similar assumptions about the history of the physical world – that it consists of sequences of mutually independent events – as well as about experience. Can the truth or falsity of these assumptions be in principle settled by appeal to experience? Could these assumptions not give rise to Idols; are they not more likely to do so if left implicit rather than made explicit? Does not the spirit of Bacon's method oblige us to be as explicit as we can about such assumptions? Does it not admonish us only to refrain from bowing down before our systems as though they presented the one true reality?

Bacon does not suggest that there might be any value in system building. He is preoccupied with insisting that systems, which had already been built, were obstacles to carrying out his program of reform, and among the chief authors of these obstacles were Plato and Aristotle. In Bacon's image these are two of the dramatic styles which appear on stage at the Philosophical Theater, where one can see things "more as one would wish them to be" than as they are in reality

Metaphysics and the Aim of Inquiry

(I LXII). Because he did not want to set up one more rival system, Bacon abstained from the enterprise of making his assumptions about reality explicit and systematic. Had he made a principle of his abstinence, however, subsequent events would have proved the principle misguided. Changes in the conception of knowledge, in the objective we have when we inquire about the natural world – changes of the sort Bacon had initiated – are inseparable from changes in the way we think about the object of our inquiries, reality. Developments which took place at the level it would be appropriate to call "metaphysical," came to threaten Bacon's whole project; what Bacon took for granted became highly questionable.

It is generally characteristic of metaphysics that what is felt at one period to be in need of explicit defense will fail to include something a later period finds problematic, and what one period can treat as defensible, a later period will reject altogether. Aristotle and Plato defended different versions of the principle that to understand events requires grasping the end (*telos*), purpose or "that for the sake of which" events develop as they do. Their conception of reality was structured in important ways by concepts derived from that of design and underwrote the place of "teleology" (the study of ends) in their respective epistemologies. Bacon led the campaign to remove all teleology from the study of nature.

Plato, Aristotle and Bacon all in different ways took for granted the relationship between human beings and the natural world and between human beings and the things they aspired to understand. From the time of Descartes these relationships became problematic, until, as the work of Kant made clear, any systematic picture of reality must include a satisfactory account of the place of human beings in that reality.

It is salutary to be reminded of the way speculative system building can generate Idols. Bacon's advice to beware of the Idols of the Theater needs, however, to be balanced by the thought that if we place our assumptions on stage, the spectacle may not only beguile but also instruct. To make out a case for this requires a review of some of the history of what appeared on the stage of the Philosophical Theater both before and after Bacon.

2 Aristotle's Speculative Knowledge

The first chapter of the work we now know as Aristotle's *Metaphysics* reveals that, like Plato, Aristotle assumed that the central questions about knowledge concern what it is that qualifies a person to claim expertise. He adopts a contrast, which Plato had used in the *Gorgias* (465), between trial and error experience (*empeiria*) on the one hand and *technê* and *epistêmê* on the other. What distinguishes the master builder from the ordinary workers is his ability to explain why his way of proceeding is correct. This is why being able to teach what one knows is the mark of possessing a *technê*. People who have only experience can try to provide similar experience for learners; but they cannot communicate any principles.

Aristotle, however, goes on (*Ethics* VI 3–4) to distinguish between *technê* and *epistêmê*, whereas Plato made no sharp or explicit distinction between them. Although both *technê* and *epistêmê* involve the use of rational principles, the former uses them in generating products, whereas the latter uses them to generate "demonstrations" of why something is the way it is. People who possess Aristotelian *epistêmê* concerning a natural phenomenon should be able to explain it. They would not, however, be called upon to explain the bearing of what they know in terms of the benefits which will accrue to someone or something if the goal is achieved – as they would under Plato's conception in which *epistêmê* and *technê* are not sharply distinguished.

A Platonic Form, such as that of the shuttle (mentioned in *Cratylus* 389b), guides a producer in designing and repairing products. No material shuttle can reliably guide designers or repairers; they have to know what a shuttle is for in order to recognize how it should be. That is, they have to grasp something abstract, something which is not evident in the physical appearance of any existing shuttle. Thus it was important for Plato to stress the way that all productive activity, which is guided by rational thought, strains to transcend the material world. Aristotle, however, appears to be far more interested in the explanation of natural activity than in the guidance of productive activity. He regarded the ability to provide demonstrations as the highest use of the mind, and this is something which involves no intervention in the world. For someone with only that interest, separate Forms are indeed quite pointless.

It is precisely against the notion of demonstration that Bacon reacts most strongly: "But vicious demonstrations are as the strongholds and defenses of idols; and those we have in logic do little else than make the world the bondslave of human thought, and human thought the bondslave of words." (I LXIX) To understand what a demonstration is, it is necessary to appreciate what Aristotle thought about the form which explanations should take. If something of the form A is B (the moon is eclipsed, *Posterior Analytics* 90a6–24) is to be explained, we need to find a term linked to both A and B, so that A is C and C is B (thus: "the moon is positioned so that the earth blocks the sun's light" and "being positioned so that the earth blocks the sun's light is what an eclipse [of the moon] is"). The term C then functions as the middle term of a syllogism, A is C, C is B, therefore A is B. This is why emphasis on demonstration brings with it an emphasis on formal (syllogistic) logic.

The statements "A is C" and "C is B" constituting the above explanation may themselves need explaining, so that further middle terms must be sought to mediate between "A" and "C" or "C" and "B." Aristotle believed, nevertheless, that we would eventually come to the point where there would be no further need to seek middle terms to complete an explanation. The statements linking terms would be "immediate" and self-explanatory. Complete demonstrative understanding of a truth (one cannot after all explain what is not true) of the form A is B consists in the ability to deduce this truth from true, immediate and self-explanatory starting points (*archai*, *Posterior Analytics* 71b26–72a24). Getting from observed truths to the ultimate starting points of explanation, however, is not a matter of either deduction or demonstration. Aristotle referred to this process as *epagôgê*, which is commonly translated "induction." Like Bacon's use of "Induction" (see chapter 1.6) this invites confusion with the modern use of the term to label the inference which supports a generalization by citing as many instances (without there being a counter instance) as possible.

Apart from comparing *epagôgê*, as the process of coming to recognize starting points or first principles, to the process of acquiring concepts through sense perception (*Posterior Analytics* 99b14–100b19), Aristotle's account is decidedly vague. Enough is said in various places to make it plain, however, that *epagôgê* has more in common with abstraction, with finding a unity in a variety of particulars, or with settling on an explanation for some phenomenon, than with supporting a generalization by citing instances. It has in fact a great deal in common with what Bacon called "Induction," enough for the function and scope of this process to be a real issue in Bacon's criticisms of Aristotelian methodology.

The overall picture Aristotle leaves of the process of understanding is of a clockwise movement starting from the bottom of Figure 3.1. Bacon's complaints about demonstration focus on the left-hand movement from the bottom to the top. What makes it plausible to think that we can reach starting points that are self-explanatory is the feeling that when we have said precisely what, for

Figure 3.1

- First principles
- Deduction via middle terms in syllogisms
- Observed phenomena
- Epagôgê – induction

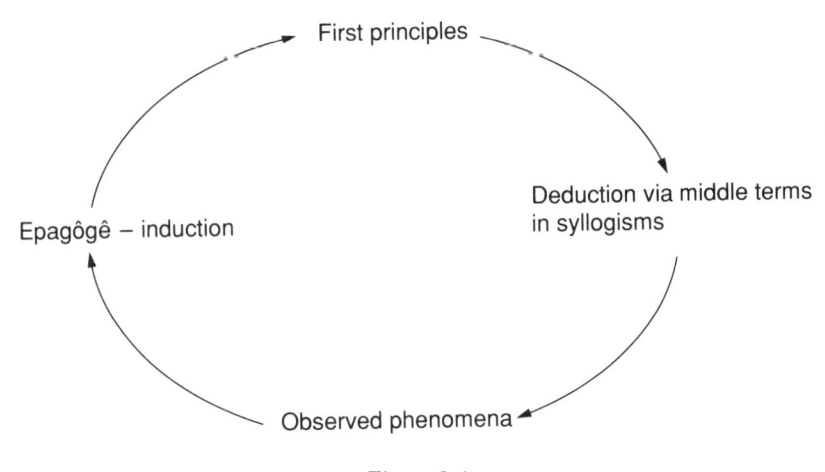

Figure 3.1

example, an eclipse of the moon is – given a definition of what it is for the moon to be eclipsed – there will be nothing more to say.

Definitions (such as that of an eclipse) appear, however, to operate purely on a verbal level, hence Bacon's complaint about thought becoming the bondslave of words. Aristotle did not, to be sure, intend that the definitions occurring in demonstrations should be merely verbal. A definition of what it is for there to be an eclipse of the moon is an account of the being or essence of such an event. Such accounts can be correct or incorrect, they do not merely record conventions over the use of words. But how are such accounts of essence, and the knowledge of the natures of things, which they convey, to be reached? This is where Aristotelian procedure is, in Bacon's view, wholly inadequate, so that the net effect is to have erected a speculative system which is little more than a web of words supplied with conventional definitions – mistakenly thought to be accounts of essence – given specious authority by being linked together through demonstrations.

A sign that Aristotle did not conceive his principles as conventions is his insistence that premisses of a demonstration (and ultimately the first principles) must be more intelligible and explanatory than the conclusions which they serve to explain. This did not mean that they had to satisfy us by *appearing to us* to be more intelligible and explanatory, they had to be so according to nature (*Posterior Analytics* 71b33–72a5). In other words, to claim understanding of the natural world we have to transcend our particular experience and view things from the standpoint of nature. Here Bacon would not disagree. His complaint was that Aristotle, or at least those who represented Aristotle's natural philosophy in Bacon's day, had failed to comply with this standard (Bacon's criticisms, it should be remembered, were in the first instance leveled against the practice of the self-proclaimed Aristotelians of his day). Aristotelians were guilty of anticipating nature (making hasty generalizations from a few observations) and giving them the status of first principles when they had no legitimate basis for claiming to know that they were true let alone primary or intelligible from the standpoint of nature.

A difficulty, which had been extensively debated in connection with astronomy in Bacon's day, was how to know that the principles used in an explanation are in fact true. Ptolemy's earth-centered mathematical model of the universe and Copernicus' sun-centered model fit with planetary observations almost equally well (and neither perfectly). Both could be used to explain those observations, yet they could not both be true. How was one to choose between them? In general, several theoretical explanatory hypotheses may be created to account for a given range of phenomena; merely "saving the phenomena" (demonstrating them from one's chosen hypotheses) is not sufficient assurance, therefore, that such hypotheses are true.

Bacon insisted that it is not possible to leap in one step from observations to first principles and essences. The essences, or forms, of natural things are not open to view, are not outwardly displayed but, being hidden, must be gradually and methodically revealed. The problem in Bacon's view was not just that the Aristotelian procedure might yield false or inadequate principles, but that it enshrined these principles, making them extremely difficult to displace. The reliance on logic and reasoning to construct explanation, regardless of pious intentions to the contrary, serves only to entrench the received use of words (the Idols of the Market Place). A procedure which relies solely on the method of constructing rational arguments from first principles, where there is no adequate basis for calling those principles into question, will always need to work within a fixed linguistic frame and cannot hope to overturn the Idols supported by accepted practice. It is the lack of constraint on explanatory principles in speculative systems that enables them to function dogmatically and without warrant.

Thus it appears that Bacon's complaint is not against philosophical systems as such, but against a particular conception of the way theory functions, which leads to the premature ossification of systems. By requiring knowledge to yield practical results Bacon places additional constraints on the principles used in explanations: they must be such that they can be used as the basis for action to produce new effects or prevent undesirable ones, and practical failures must be taken as indications of theoretical inadequacy: "Truth, therefore, and utility are here the very same things; and works themselves are of greater value as pledges of truth than as contributing to the comforts of life" (I CXXIV).

Aristotle's notion of demonstration had no precedent in Plato's thought. Plato did not describe the form of communication which should be used by someone who is to convey his understanding. Like Bacon and Descartes he concentrated his attention on the methods that might be used to generate understanding. The word which Plato used for that method, whatever his current opinion about its nature happened to be, was "dialectic." Whereas Aristotle accepted that an activity called "dialectic" – an activity not at all unlike what Plato called "dialectic" – would contribute to the task of reaching the basic principles of a body of understanding (*Topics* 101a37–b4), he did not accord this activity anything like the dignity which Plato gave it. For Aristotle, it was much better to possess understanding than to grope toward it, and much more important to characterize the form that understanding will take when it is communicated to other people than to dwell on the activity by which understanding is reached.

Understanding as a human capacity or disposition is realized, for Aristotle, not in working to bring something about, not even working to bring new explanations to our notice, but in the contemplation of the explanations once they have been brought to notice. "Contemplation" translates "*theôrein*," a verb which is the source of both the English words "theater" and "theory" and which applies to the activity of spectators at a performance (it's Latin equivalent, "*spectare*," is the source of our words "spectator" and "speculation"). Here is another source of Bacon's animus against Aristotle. Bacon urges that the focus be placed on methods of discovery and on the active realization of human understanding in bringing about improvements in the material conditions of human life. The mere passive contemplation of explanations, the rôle of the spectator, the conception of the goal of knowledge linked to the construction of speculative systems, are all to be displaced by putting aside the Idols of the Theater.

3 Practical Knowledge and Explanation

In discussing our cognitive relationship to the Forms, Plato is as prone to cast knowers in the rôle of spectators as is Aristotle, when he describes the use to which epistêmê is to be put. But there is a very striking difference between the respective starting points and hence the overall orientation of Plato's thinking and that of Aristotle. Whereas the former approached understanding from the standpoint of the person who is to redesign something (the constitution of a city) by reference to what it ideally should be; the latter approached understanding from the standpoint of a close observer of the natural world, who might use his understanding of the normal course of natural development only to intervene to stop what might discourage its full flowering. The standards (Forms, *ideai*) guiding the application of Plato's understanding transcend anything found in the natural world; the standards (forms, *eidê*) guiding Aristotle's understanding are immanent in natural events. Aristotle's repudiation of Forms, which were regarded as "separate," expressed his sense of this difference in orientation.

In the Christianized versions of these two Greek philosophers, issues of transcendence and immanence were transposed into theological issues. It was not unnatural for Christian theologians, who came under the influence of Plato, to assimilate Plato's Forms to ideas in the mind of the transcendent, Christian God, and to assign to God himself a rôle not unlike that of the Form of the Good, that is as the ultimate source of the authority of individual Forms. This is one of the reasons why Platonists, who in the Renaissance neglected the virtue of *humilitas*, ended up flirting with heresy. Platonism invites one to aspire to knowledge of the Form of the Good (God) and of subordinate Forms (Ideas in the Mind of God), when it is not clear that a mere mortal can presume to be capable of such knowledge.

Both Plato and Aristotle were concerned with the political wisdom required of those who would rule a city well. Practical knowledge thus had, for them, primarily a moral/political orientation. But where Plato viewed this by analogy with the practical skills of craftsmen, Aristotle drew a sharp distinction. Human freedom was freedom from concern for the material necessities of biological life; it was freedom to engage in political activity or preferably in philosophical contemplation. Thus we find in Aristotle not only a contemplative paradigm of understanding, but also a disdain for practical material concerns, as beneath the dignity of a person living the life of a truly fulfilled human being.

Plato, having appealed to the form of practical knowledge displayed in crafts, drew the conclusion that there should be super craftsmen ("statesmen") to whom all other forms of expertise should be subordinate. The net effect of Plato's philosophy for the intellectual and social standing of practical material concerns was much the same as Aristotle's. It was precisely this relative devaluation of the practical-material that Bacon sought to reverse.

Aristotle did not share Plato's hope that all the different branches of human expertise could be organized under and assessed in terms of a single standard, embodied in a unifying Form like that of the Good. This is not to say that Aristotle had no interest in, and offered no philosophic resources for, guiding practical activity. But his interest was primarily in activity (*praxis*) such as participation in political affairs rather than in the productive efforts (*poiêseis*) which interested Francis Bacon. At the beginning of the *Nicomachean Ethics* Aristotle borrows Plato's example (*Republic* 601c) of the bridle to highlight a very Platonic point about the centrality of political concerns. The work of a bridle maker will answer to the *technê* possessed by the horseman. The horseman will in turn answer to the strategist (since the principal serious use the Greeks made of horses was in warfare) and the strategist to the politician (cp. *Euthydemus* 290d). Since other endeavors will be linked in this way to politics, politics is an activity which requires a comprehensive grasp of all human activities.

But rather than seeking to establish that comprehensive grasp on the basis of a notion that would take in everything, namely the Good itself, Aristotle dismisses Plato's Form of the Good. He does so on the ground that Plato's program rests on the unwarranted assumption that one is saying the same thing (and hence could do so in virtue of a single comprehensive standard) when "good" is applied in widely different contexts. Instead, Aristotle adopts a more limited basis: the good for human beings. When statesmen deliberate about legislation, they do not have to assess alternatives in terms of a standard for assessing how everything should be, they need refer only to what will promote the flourishing of their fellow citizens. This standard, moreover, is not to be found by turning the mind in the direction of a non-sensible, supernatural realm, but by consideration of that one segment of the natural world which is constituted by human beings and the way they live.

This position provided the Renaissance humanists with a model for urging the possibility of secular human statecraft, which had no theological pretensions. But it was also used by the Catholic Church –

once the Church's theological framework had come to be recast in an Aristotelian mould – as a basis for claiming jurisdiction over natural philosophy. This is because of the way in which Aristotle provides a foundation for his moral and political philosophy in an account of human nature, which is the same in form as knowledge of other natural things. The seamless treatment which Aristotle's natural philosophy is able to give to human nature along with the rest of nature is interesting in the light of the seemingly unbridgeable gap between human nature and the physical world which has appeared in modern times.

The line of reasoning which takes Aristotle from the question which should guide all political thinking, "What is the good for human beings?" to a question belonging to natural philosophy, is in part lifted from the first book of Plato's *Republic* (352d). It goes like this: If you want to know what is good *for* something, X (human beings, tennis rackets, kidneys), you have to know what a good X is. This is because what is good for X is what will preserve, restore or make it a better X. And to know what a good X is, you have to know what an X is (or know the nature of X). What an X is will be expressed in terms of what an X does or is characteristically called on to do. You do not know whether painting a tennis racket has left it better, worse or much the same, unless you have some idea of what is done with a tennis racket. You do not know whether a certain diet leaves a person's kidneys better, worse or much the same, unless you know what physiological function kidneys are called on to perform.

Knowing what an X characteristically does is also involved in distinguishing Xs from other things, which is indeed the foundation of any kind of knowledge of Xs. Knowing what is done with tennis rackets puts one in a position to tell them from squash rackets and table tennis bats. Knowing what kidneys do is what enables a person to identify the kidneys in an animal with an unfamiliar or unusual anatomy. It is easy to see how Aristotle could treat the basis for evaluating humans and what was good or bad for them, as a part of natural philosophy. All understanding of nature involves the grasp of something that permits evaluation.

Normative constraints on how society is best organized, how it is best to educate people to live with one another and which dispositions to encourage as human virtues, can be derived from Aristotle's claim that what is characteristic of human beings is to engage in activity which is guided by discourse (*logos*, *Nicomachean Ethics*, 1098a7) and to live in a kind of association, a *polis*, where this activity is facilitated (*Politics* 1253a7–17). Claims about what is required for humans to flourish have the same status as claims about what is required (diet, habitat, type of association with members of the same species) for camels, honey bees, or wolves to flourish. To understand any natural thing (animate or inanimate) is, for Aristotle, to grasp what that thing is, through an account of what it characteristically does (*Meteorology* 389b–390a24), and this grasp will automatically put a person in a position to identify good and bad examples of things of that kind and discover what is good and bad for it (as a thing of that kind).

Someone who has a grasp of this sort will be in a position to answer "why?" questions which relate procedures and activities to the end (*telos*) of developing and maintaining the capacities for the characteristic activities of different kinds of things. It thus constitutes the basis for understanding (*epistêmê*). Although Aristotle tends to assign a privileged position to understanding based on what have come to be called teleological explanations, he insisted that there are three other importantly different forms of explanations. Sometimes, indeed, what is being sought is an answer to the question, "To what purpose or function does X (walking, having multiple stomachs) contribute?" But what is sought may also be, "What started X (a war) or was responsible for bringing X to be (a statue)?"; sometimes, "What qualifies that stuff as an X (man, house)?"; sometimes even, "What is that made of?"

All four of these explanations answer questions which in Greek have a common form, "*dia ti* ?" which is literally "through what?" often in the sense of "Why?" And the answer in each case will be thought of as a "because" (*aitia*). Why do camels have multiple stomachs? (Because of the food they have to digest in their native habitat.) Why did that statue come to be? (Because Polyclitus made it.) Why does that piece of timber qualify as a lintel? (Because it is positioned over a doorway.) Through what did that cup come to be? (Because of clay, which was shaped and baked.) The word "*aitia*" was translated into Latin as "*causa*," so tradition came to refer to these kinds of explanation as Aristotle's "four causes" and we refer to them in order as the "final," "efficient," "formal," and "material" causes. We may raise all four questions about a single object, e.g a house, and the answers may all be, but will not necessarily be, distinct. Why did that house get built? Because (final cause) Jack wanted shelter for his family. Because Jack (efficient cause) built it. Why does that qualify as a house? Because (formal cause) of its capacity to shelter. Through what did that house get built? Because (material cause) of bricks and timber, which were arranged thus.

Aristotle used the four causes to define his relationship to natural philosophers who had preceded him, by noting which of the four causes they recognized. Of the four kinds of explanation which a person possessing Aristotelian *epistêmê* would be called upon to provide, Plato's Forms might plausibly be taken to provide final and formal explanations, although Aristotle would stress that *separate* Forms are unnecessary and unsuitable for this. Moreover, Forms which transcend the natural world cannot, Aristotle argued, explain why things happen in the natural world (provide efficient causes, *Metaphysics* 990b1–8). For Aristotle, by contrast, the form of a natural body (a nature) is a principle of change or remaining the same (*Physics* 192b21–3). In the case of a living body it is the maintenance of this form in a body, which provides the "end" (final cause) that explains much of that body's actions. Forms of natural bodies also explain why a given lump of stuff constitutes a natural body of a given kind (formal cause). And the forms of less complex natural bodies help to identify the material of which more complex bodies are formed (material cause).

Although this framework applies without any fundamental difference to the forms of human bodies as well as to the forms of other natural bodies, there is one group of things not covered by this framework – artifacts. Every artifact is of course made of natural materials but insofar as it has a nature, that nature is confined to those materials; the form in virtue of which it is *an artifact* of that kind is not a nature (*Physics* 192b28–33). This might seem strange in view of the respects in which artifacts are prime examples of things which need to be understood in teleological terms, but although Aristotle insisted that natures must be understood teleologically, that is not what makes them natures. A nature is a source of change (or remaining the same) and no artifacts in Aristotle's experience contain their own motive principles (batteries were never included). Aristotle's distinction between natural and artificial things is a product of the technology with which he was familiar and would not be very important except that the distinction stands in the way of using artifacts and artificial situations in the study of nature. This is precisely what experimentation consists in and Bacon needed to work to undermine this distinction in order to gain acceptance for his experimental method.

Of the four causes Aristotle regarded those which referred to ends (*telê*, final causes) as the most important and he attempted to apply this pattern of explanation even to inanimate bodies (*Parts of Animals* 646b5–10). (Things could have ends without these ends needing to be the purposes of some conscious being.) For this reason his conception of the understanding of nature is frequently characterized without qualification as teleological. Thus for all the important respects in which Aristotle differed from Plato, there is one important respect in which he shared Plato's general orientation. A satisfactory explanation for Plato referred what was happening to an outcome regarded as good. This did not mean "good" in the sense that the person, who was working to bring about this outcome, had judged it to be good (or just happened to desire it), but that the person had judged it to be good from a comprehensive standpoint, a standpoint from which it could be seen how everything ought to be.

A satisfactory explanation, for Aristotle, similarly referred what was happening to an outcome regarded as good, although not good from the standpoint of the universe, but good from the standpoint of the things involved. (Camels have the peculiar anatomy, which we observe them to have, because it serves them well in the environment in which they live, *Parts of Animals* 674a30–b12.) But for both men the primary pattern of explanation was teleological, derived from the thinking in which objects and events are related to some state of affairs regarded as an end (*telos*) to be attained. For philosophers in the seventeenth and eighteenth centuries, debate about what is, from a comprehensive standpoint, good, would inevitably be debates into which theology had to enter. Final causes thus served these philosophers as an important reference point, for they frequently took their bearings by this issue and either rejected or attempted to rehabilitate teleological explanations.

4 *"Mechanism" and the Rejection of Teleology*

What perhaps most strongly characterizes the natural philosophy which Bacon heralded and which we now think of as marking the beginning of modern science is its rejection of teleological explanations, its refusal to look for final causes, or to see these as forming any part of the brief of natural philosophy. Because this attitude requires belief that an understanding of the natural world – one adequate to the end of improving the material conditions of human life – can be attained without reference to final causes, it carries with it a metaphysical as well as a methodological reorientation. The metaphysical shift, however, is not from one speculative theory to an opposed theory, but at a deeper level, at the level of what people will entertain as an appropriate attitude to take to the world when trying to understand it.

This shift was in an ironic way facilitated, as well as necessitated, by the Christian appropriation of Aristotelian and Platonic philosophy. Since questions about final causes had become questions about God's purposes and hence inherently theological questions, natural philosophy, if it was to secure autonomy from theology, needed to foreswear inquiry into final causes. On the other hand, to the extent that God's purposes have become the final causes of things and events in the created world, final causes have been taken out of the world and have become external to it. The over-riding purposes are those of God, not those of any of his creatures. It is therefore possible to frame a more limited project of inquiry, namely that of seeking to understand the world as it has been created, without asking why it is as it is or for what purpose things behave in the way that they do. This would be a project limited to asking about formal, efficient and material causes.

Thus, even though Bacon rejected Aristotle forcefully, we find him using Aristotelian terminology to explain the kind of knowledge he thinks natural philosophy should be seeking. Physics seeks knowledge of efficient and material causes. Metaphysics – Bacon here signals that he is using this term in his own special sense, (*Novum Organum* II IX) – seeks knowledge of forms. These forms are neither Plato's nor Aristotle's. They are to be found, Bacon insists, immersed in matter; they are not transcendent. But they are not linked to our ordinary classifications of kinds as Aristotle's forms would be. We are not looking for forms of naturally existing kinds of things but for basic principles and laws of action. The example that Bacon gives is of inquiring into the form of heat, suggesting that it is some sort of motion of material particles (see chapter 1.6, above). Further inquiry should say what sort of motion it is and give laws covering heat phenomena in general. Since the aim is not to be able merely to imitate nature but to be able to control it and to produce new kinds of things and new effects, inquiry cannot be limited to studying things as they naturally are, but has to use experiments to determine how they may be altered.

Bacon's project, mastery over nature, goes hand in hand with a removal of final causes from nature (I XLVIII; II II), and a separation of questions about what is good (questions of value) from questions about what is the case (questions of fact). To seek domination of nature with a view to improving the material well-being of humankind is already to presume that the question of what constitutes human well-being can be settled antecedently to, or independently from, natural philosophy; at any rate it will not be continuous with natural philosophy. It is further to presume that humankind has a right to require nature to serve its purposes. This presumption will seem more justified if one views the world as not containing any other beings with purposes, than if one views it as full of creatures each of which strives toward its own good.

The conception of the material world as, very roughly speaking, a large machine, consisting entirely of matter in motion, and the adoption of domination and control of the material world as the goal of knowledge, although not mutually entailing, are mutually reinforcing (this comes out more strongly in Descartes' philosophy). It also means that as the pretensions of metaphysics come to be limited in relation to natural philosophy; the status of knowledge of humankind and its relation to the world is left problematic. Bacon, for example, recognized that as part of the project of natural philosophy it would be possible to treat human beings as objects of a knowledge which aimed at their domination. But he held that one should not seek this kind of knowledge (see chapter 1.5). This gives the division between natural and human science a purely moral status. Descartes, on the other hand, opens up an alternative route to knowledge of human beings, thus creating an epistemological division between human and natural sciences (one which in his case corresponds to a highly problematic seam in the fabric of reality itself).

Descartes' philosophy undermines the Aristotelian distinction between natural body and artifact more thoroughly than does Bacon's. Bacon argued that the sort of knowledge sought by the natural philosopher as potential master over nature can only be acquired by learning from attempts at such mastery and by contriving artificial situations to force nature to reveal her secrets. Descartes did not approach from this epistemological direction but argued from a metaphysical direction, insisting that animals and human *bodies* are machines, automata (Haldane and Ross, 1955, I 116). As such they are no different in kind from clocks and other mechanisms that humans construct. He says for example that is it possible to describe "the earth and all the visible world, as if it were simply a machine in which there [is] nothing to consider but [the] figure and movements [of its parts]" (HR I 289). Past philosophy is faulted for not adopting this "mechanic's" (what we would call "engineer's") approach to knowledge (*Conversation with Burman* [73]).

The mechanical philosophy which Descartes proposed is thus both a metaphysical view – the view of the world as a large machine which can be understood wholly in terms of the shapes and movements of its material parts – and a view of the kind of knowledge to be sought

– the kind of knowledge that enables a mechanic to build, understand, and design machines. This "engineering" conception of knowledge can be contrasted with the earlier conceptions of knowledge as accurate description of natural processes based on detailed but passive observation and of understanding as confined to sorting out which observed phenomena offer explanations for other observed phenomena. From Descartes' point of view it is therefore obvious that we can learn about the natural world by studying mechanical artifacts. For example, the study of pumps makes it possible to recognize the heart as a pump and to use this as a basis for demonstrating that and how blood circulates in creatures which have hearts. (This explanation was advanced by Harvey although Descartes (Haldane and Ross, 1955, I 110ff.), preferred a different explanation of circulation based on heating the blood.) Descartes and a number of his contemporaries were fascinated by mechanical devices and devoted time to designing automated models of human and animals (for illustrations, see Adam and Tannery (1912), 11, pp. 212–15, 669).

This difference between the ways in which Bacon and Descartes sought to undermine the epistemological significance of the Aristotelian distinction between natural object and artifact reflects the wider disagreement between them. Descartes is confident that the universe is a machine, analogous to a clock (see chapter 2.5 above), and is explicable therefore in terms of motions, shapes, and positions. This makes his natural philosophy inseparable from a clearly articulated metaphysics and his epistemology must account for the possibility of acquiring this metaphysical knowledge. Bacon, whilst sympathetic to the mechanist view, does not see the universe in wholly mechanistic terms. He was also influenced by the alchemical treatises, which were very popular at that time.

Bacon in fact relegates the study of mechanical causes (material and efficient causes) to physics whilst insisting that the natural philosophy should not stop at this. The natural philosopher should aspire to a knowledge of forms (conceived as laws of action) and this inquiry forms that part of the domain of "metaphysic" which is relevant to the study of nature. (The other part, "the inquisition of Final Causes is barren, and like a virgin consecrated to God produces nothing" (*de Augmentis* III v.)) Effects produced as a result of acquisition of this kind of knowledge would be magical rather than mechanical (*Novum Organum* II IX). Magical here means that a quantitatively great effect is produced by a relatively small cause. An example available to Bacon is the explosive power of gunpowder. Nuclear power stations would be a twentieth century realization of this dream of (natural) magic.

Bacon and Descartes share the view that the kind of knowledge sought must involve looking into the internal structures of things. The way to understand the observable behavior of things is by determining how they are composed out of simpler parts. But for Bacon the character of the simple components and/or simple forces is something which cannot be known in advance. This is knowable only at the end of inquiry. Descartes emphatically does not share Bacon's belief that the most general laws of nature are to be discovered by a gradual ascent from experiments and observations through the formulation of intermediate, less fundamental laws. He believed that this knowledge could be attained by methods similar to those used in mathematics, not by experimental methods. The claim, for example, that animals and human bodies are just complex machines is not a conclusion reached by experimental methods but a principle accepted prior to experimental investigation which is used to guide and justify certain lines of inquiry.

Bacon rejected mechanism precisely because it involved imposing principles which are accepted prior to inquiry – what later came to be known as "*a priori* principles." To appeal to such principles is to assume that it is possible to have a *priori* knowledge of laws governing the natural world but this would be to repeat the mistakes of the ancient philosophies. To see anything other than the flickering images on the walls of Plato's cave requires finding ways for nature to reveal itself (Bacon would say "herself") directly to us. This, Bacon believed, was possible only by posing carefully framed questions taking the form of well-designed experiments and systematically tabulated data. Method has two aims: to counter general human tendencies to form and be taken in by Idols, and to bring us to interact in more revealing ways with our object of study, the natural world. Bacon does not suggest that the human mind can ever be wholly purged of Idols. His method involved putting us on our guard against them and providing a method of preventing, as far as possible, their formation.

Descartes did not accept Bacon's view that the mind of man is by nature a distorting mirror. He believed that it is a clouded, but non-distorting mirror. The images in the minds of most people are confused, blurred, but not false. The key to knowledge, the way out of Plato's cave, is thus to provide a method of rendering ideas clear and distinct. These differing attitudes to the mirror metaphor reveal important differences in the way Bacon and Descartes conceive knowledge.

5 The Foundations of Cartesian Method

Descartes believed that he had found a method for rendering ideas clear and distinct in his mathematical work and thought that this method could be generalized over all fields of knowledge. He presents this method of solving mathematical, and by extension physical, problems as a rediscovery of the ancient analysis-synthesis method of solving geometrical problems. This method – given a canonical formulation by Pappus (Alexandria, fourth century AD) but also a source of Plato's conception of dialectic (fourth century BC) – involved a technique for trying to prove a given proposition by assuming it true and then working backwards (by "analysis") to determine what more fundamental results would have to hold in order to produce that result. One works backwards until one comes to first principles accepted as true. That is to say the proposition is either seen to rest on recognized principles or to contradict something which follows from such principles. If the former, one then reasons forward ("synthesis") showing that the result really does follow from these principles.

The process here is comparable to the cycle which takes us from observed phenomena through induction to first principles and back to observed phenomena, but where a candidate theorem takes the place of observed phenomena and analysis takes the place of *epagôgê*-induction (figure 3.2; CP. figure 3.1, p.90).

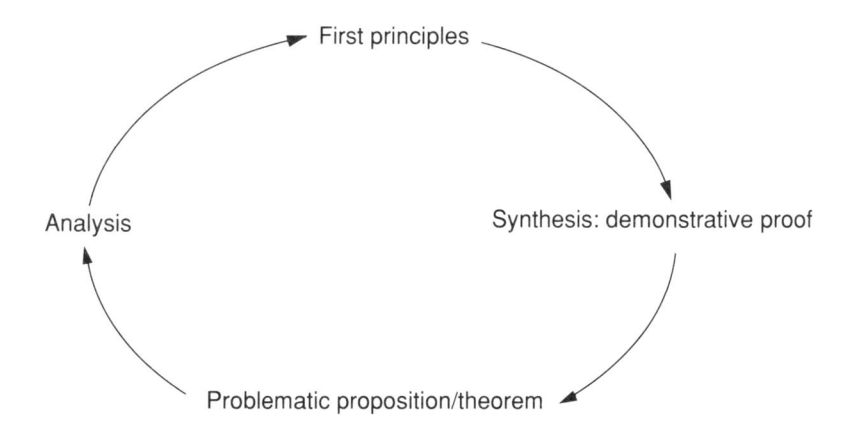

Figure 3.2

The movement downward on the right was indeed frequently conceived as reasoning from causes to their effects, but the movement upward on the left was conceived as a way of reducing the content of the problematic proposition to elements which were antecedently accepted as the foundations of geometrical understanding. This upward movement was therefore not conceived as a technique for discovering what the first principles are, but rather for discovering which principles, already accepted, the problematic proposition might rest upon. This difference has an important bearing on Descartes' method.

The use which Descartes made of geometry as a paradigm of rational method was thoroughly traditional. The revolutionary effect of his conception arose from the fact that he used a radically reformed geometry – Cartesian or analytic geometry – in which algebraic and geometrical techniques were, for the first time, effectively integrated. The basic idea is simply that any point in a plane can be indexed by two numbers (x,y) each specifying the distance of that point from a given point, the origin, as measured along two lines which intersect at the origin. This is a generalization of the idea of fixing one's position on the earth's surface by determining one's longitude (distance east or west of Greenwich, England) and latitude (distance north or south of the equator). The idea is already implicit in the grids to be found on navigation maps produced by Mercator in 1569 and after. Just as a sailor could plot a course as a sequence of such pairs, so the geometers can define the curves they study by using equations which fix the relation between x and y coordinates that must hold for all points on the curve. For example, $y = x^2$ defines a parabola (figure 3.3).

Descartes' method for solving geometrical problems involved finding the equations which define the lines or curves involved in the problem and setting up systems of simultaneous equations. To do this the problem must first be analyzed to determine exactly what magnitudes are involved and what relationships there are between them.

> If, then, we wish to solve some problem, we should first of all consider it solved, and give names to all the lines – the unknown ones as well as the others – which seem necessary in order to construct it. Then, without considering any difference between the known and the unknown lines, we should go through the problem in the order which most naturally shows the mutual dependency between these lines, until we have found a means of expressing a single quantity in two ways. This will be called an equation, for the terms of one of the two ways [of expressing the quantity] are equal to those of the other. And we must

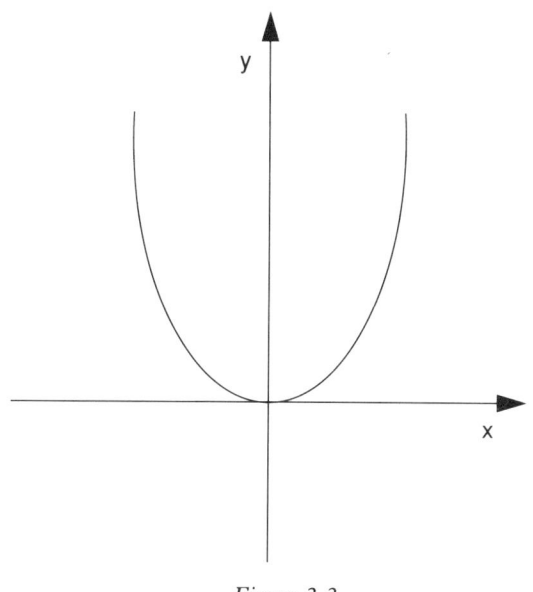

[Figure: parabola on x-y axes]

Figure 3.3

find as many such equations as we assume there to be unknown lines. (*Discourse on Method, Optics, Geometry and Meteorology*, p. 179)

Here the method of analysis-synthesis is converted into the method of finding an algebraic representation of the problem (a set of equations) and then using the method of solving simultaneous equations. The equations give us a clear and distinct idea of the situation which is less clearly and perhaps misleadingly represented by a diagram. Once we have the algebraic analysis we can either solve our problem, or will be able to see that it is insoluble because we have insufficient information to give an equation for each unknown.

Descartes' more general methodological prescriptions are derived from this procedure. They are that we pursue inquiries in a systematic fashion, and analyze the phenomena under investigation to determine what are the fundamental questions which must be answered in order to begin to provide answers to more complex questions about these phenomena. Each phenomenon must be analyzed into its various aspects; the independent variables involved must be identified and the mode of dependence of other variables on these must be determined, measurements must be made and equations set up. As a result Descartes can say:

All knowledge whatsoever, other than that which consists in the simple and naked intuition of single independent objects, is a matter of the comparison of two things or more with each other. In fact practically the whole task set the human reason consists in preparing for this operation; for when it is open and simple we need no aid from art, but are bound to rely on the light of nature alone, in beholding the truth which comparison gives us. (Haldane and Ross, 1955, I 55)

Forms and essences are no longer the objects of knowledge; Descartes' mathematical method is linked to a shift of the focus of attention onto knowledge of relations. Even in geometry the definition of a circle now has the form of an equation $(x-a)^2 + (y-b)^2 = r^2$ which specifies the relation which must hold between x and y coordinates for them to be the coordinates on the circumference of a circle whose center is (a,b) and whose radius is r. Method is the art of so ordering our inquiry that illuminating comparisons can be made, but it is the "light of nature," our innate faculty of rational intuition, which makes those comparisons and yields the insight.

Cartesian science is thus mathematical as well as mechanist and reductive in the sense that scientific understanding results from a procedure of analyzing in terms of, and thereby reducing phenomena to, what were antecedently accepted as the elements of all things. The complex variety of observable phenomena is presumed to be a consequence of the operation of the simple mechanical constituents of the material objects involved under the governance of a few mathematically formulatable fundamental principles (the laws of mechanics). All knowledge conforms to the pattern of classical geometrical knowledge, where knowledge of the elements – the axioms – which govern the simple figures (straight line and circle) suffice for knowledge of the complex properties of complex figures. Descartes did not, of course, suggest that classical geometry had an adequate grasp of the necessary elements.

It is a consequence of adopting this model that knowledge has to have a foundation. In effect the theory of knowledge has to split into two parts, giving accounts of (1) how we acquire knowledge of complex phenomena (how we render confused ideas clear and distinct) given that we have a knowledge of first principles, and (2) how we acquire knowledge of the first principles, the foundations. Descartes' discussion of method really addresses (1) but not (2) and thus the methodological cycle through analysis, first principles and synthesis is not at all the same in function as the cycle through induction (*epagôgê*), first principles and demonstration. For Descartes, the analytic method presupposes that we already have knowledge of first principles, it will not deliver this knowledge. Bacon insists that the first principles must be reached by the long term application of his method of induction; there is thus no scope for the procedure of (1), and the split between (1) and (2) does not arise in his account of method.

Descartes' originality as a philosopher lies in the way in which he sought (2) given the methodological distinction between (1) and (2). The problem was not entirely new. Plato had already posed it when he argued that the work of geometers is incomplete until a dialectician finds in the Form of the Good a foundation for the principles used in geometry (*Republic* 511). The Christian appropriation of Plato's philosophy, most notably by St Augustine, assigned to God a rôle comparable to the rôle Plato assigned to the Form of the Good. Descartes says on a number of occasions that he is returning to an Augustinian position, rejecting the Aristotelianism of Aquinas which was at that time the orthodox position of the Catholic Church and of the universities of Paris and Oxford. We thus find Descartes insisting that the atheist mathematician cannot really have true knowledge because he is ignorant of the foundation of geometrical principles (Haldane and Ross, 1955, II 39). Knowledge of the existence of a benevolent God (and of the mode of our dependence on him) is the necessary foundation for all objective knowledge.

The danger of taking this Augustinian path is that it promises to leave the whole of mathematics and natural philosophy under religious authority. Unless individuals can presume to claim knowledge of the existence of a benevolent God, as opposed to faith in him, they are not going to be able to claim the ability to acquire scientific knowledge. Moreover, to establish his mathematical physics Descartes needed to overturn the whole framework of Aristotelian physics, and so it was vital that he be able to establish his right to challenge this framework, still sanctioned by the Catholic Church. He therefore needed, in other words, to establish that all individuals, in so far as they are rational, have the capacity to acquire knowledge for themselves, by the right use of reason – the use specified in the principles of Descartes' method.

Descartes' strategy was to show that his method is self-validating; i.e., that it can itself be deployed to reveal and secure the foundations of mathematical and scientific knowledge. This is done by deploying the method in a quest for self-knowledge. Like Bacon, Descartes sees that the acquisition of knowledge is a matter of establishing a relation between a knowing subject and the object of knowledge. Any method for acquiring knowledge must take into account characteristics of the knowing subject. Bacon draws on generalizations about human nature, based on experience both for the purpose of discrediting currently accepted "knowledge" (as reverence for Idols) and to determine what distortions a method needs to seek to correct. This is consistent with Bacon's overall conception of experience and observation as the source of knowledge and of his conception of knowledge itself as something lodged in society as the product of a cooperative effort. Bacon's route could never secure Descartes' first principles.

For Descartes' project to succeed it is necessary that there be a non-inductive route to knowledge of the human being as a rational inquirer. This Descartes found in the presumed privilege of people's knowledge of their own thoughts. This is not gained by observation, but by a much more immediate sort of experience. His strategy is thus not only to turn method back on itself, but also to turn his own thoughts back on themselves – i.e., to use a reflective, meditative turning inward to accomplish both the skeptical task of undermining the claims of traditional authorities and the task of securing a foundation for his own knowledge claims. Moreover, in the process he refutes those skeptics who insisted that such knowledge was impossible.

This inward journey is designed to show that individual human beings can come to knowledge of their intellectual selves and that as they do so they will find within themselves the idea of a benevolent, non-deceiving God, the mark of their creator, the mark which assures them of the existence of an objective order and of the objective validity of their rational faculties, thereby conferring on them the capacity for acquiring an accurate representation of the world. The order is not imposed from without, but is found within. The foundation and starting point of Cartesian knowledge is, for all individuals, within themselves, in their experience of that certainty which they must have of their own existence, and in the idea of a perfect, infinite Being which they find within themselves. This idea represents a Being so perfect that its source could only lie in a Being which is as perfect as what its represents (*Meditation* 3); the very essence of the Being represented in this idea entails his existence (*Meditation* 5).

6 *The Metaphysics of Representation*

It is not uncommon to portray the changes that took place in philosophy during the seventeenth century as a shift in which knowledge replaced Being (or Reality) as the central concern of philosophy. In other words metaphysics, as it had been conceived since Aristotle, ceased to be first philosophy and epistemology took its place. A careful look, however, reveals that a series of changes took place in the way people conceived what they were after when they undertook to investigate the natural world. The epistemology, which moved into the spotlight during the course of the seventeenth century, had not by any means been waiting in the shadows for two thousand years. Moreover, the questions about knowledge which came to preoccupy philosophers were shaped by assumptions about the nature of reality, not all of which were tied directly to the new ways of conceiving the goal of inquiry.

What counted as scientific knowledge (*epistêmê*) of nature was for Aristotle knowledge of forms which give us the ability to provide, above all, formal and final explanations of what we observe around us. For Bacon knowledge of forms consisted in a grasp not of ends and capacities of kinds of things, but of the laws of natural action, of how things work and of how to do things, that extend our mastery over the natural world. The claim that the object of our endeavors to know or understand nature has the form of a law came to be canonical, but knowledge of laws did not take the form which Bacon anticipated. Descartes accepted that increased mastery over nature would be a *consequence* of our having knowledge, but did not treat knowledge as *consisting in* the possession of practical abilities. Instead Descartes emphasized, what Bacon underestimated, the possibility that the laws of natural action could be represented in mathematical formulae and in general he held that knowledge of the physical world consists in holding an idea which clearly and accurately represents it.

Called upon to explain why people fail to achieve *epistêmê*, Aristotle could say little more than that they either lack the mental ability or have neglected to inquire. Bacon recognized weaknesses in the cognitive constitution of humans, which make them prone to embrace "Idols" instead of truth, and he sought public procedures which would help to unmask and remove such obstacles to truth. Descartes diagnosed error as the result of our over-hasty faculty of will, which accepts what appears in confused or obscure ideas instead of insisting on reliable ideas, i.e., those which are clear and distinct. It is significant that Descartes did not follow Bacon in using the term "idol." Descartes did not acknowledge that the mind has any strictly intellectual (as opposed to volitional) weakness; none of its contents needed to be discarded, only brought into the open and carefully distinguished.

This Cartesian account of error rests on the claim that any idea or thought can be entertained and considered whilst all judgment is suspended, "in willing, fearing, approving, denying, though I always perceive something as the subject of the action of my mind, yet by this action I always add something else to the idea which I have of that thing" (Haldane and Ross, 1955, I, 159). There is thus a core to every thought, an idea, which serves as its object (its content or subject matter) and which functions to differentiate one thought from another, e.g. one feeling (back pain) from another (headache), or one desire (for a hot cup of coffee) from another (for a refreshing swim). An idea, Descartes says, is "the form of any thought, that form by the immediate awareness of which I am conscious of the said thought" (Haldane and Ross, 1955, I, 54). An idea is an unproblematic presentation; there is no room to doubt what is immediately present to our minds. It is also typically a problematic representation (a presentation *of* something else) requiring careful scrutiny before we commit ourselves concerning its truth. For Descartes truth is accurate representation of a reality external to the mind, clear reflection without confusion. The standard of truth lies in God's own representation of things; this is an Augustinian Platonic element in Descartes' thought (see Augustine, *On Free Choice of the Will* II X-XV). To know some aspect of the material world is to view it in the way that God does.

This combination of the epistemic privilege of the idea as presentation with the epistemic problem of the idea as representation sets up an inevitable dualism. There are two kinds of knowledge, that grounded wholly in reflective self-consciousness, which apprehends what is immediately present to it, and that based on interpretation which takes ideas to refer beyond the subject (i.e., when sensations, and subsequently other ideas, are treated as representations of an extended world beyond the mind). In Descartes' philosophy this dualism is projected into a substantial dualism of mind and body. The mind is the realm where ideas appear, while bodies (extended, material things) constitute the system of mechanical interactions beyond the mental realm but represented in its ideas. As orders of reality (substantial) the two are entirely distinct (dualism).

This dualism is plagued by serious problems in that its epistemological foundation appears to preclude any coherent account of the interaction of its orders of reality. Mechanics can at most yield an understanding of the deterministic interactions of material objects. From its standpoint the action of a material body on an immaterial mind, as in sense perception, is unintelligible. But so is the spontaneous action of an immaterial mind on the material body, as when a person decides to get up and walk. Mechanical interactions are deterministic in that the configuration of the system of bodies at any one stage is wholly determined by the configurations at previous stages. The thinking subject, however, must be self-governing, free to transcend the influences of its previous stages, if its self-knowledge is to have the privileged status required by its foundational rôle (this becomes even more explicit in Kant's philosophy). The stage is thus set for the modern problem of how to reconcile (mental) freedom with (material) determinism.

For Descartes the mind can be relied upon to apprehend whatever is immediately present to it (its ideas), to tell whether it is dealing with clear and distinct (as opposed to obscure and confused) ideas, and to reason from the presence of one outstanding clear and distinct idea, to the existence of a benevolent God. From this stand point God's benevolence serves as a guarantee that Descartes' clear and distinct ideas are true representations of an extended world of material substance. Without God to underwrite our clear and distinct ideas, we would not even have the assurance that we have physical bodies. Only a malevolent demon would have created Descartes in such a manner that he could not rid himself of certain beliefs (those which are for him indubitable) when they are not true. But God does more than vouchsafe the truth of what is represented in our minds, because ultimately every feature of the world that is represented is a consequence of God's will.

The God of the *Meditations* has the aspect of a supreme dictator, bound by no laws or principles; he is supremely powerful and completely free. He acts as he chooses. He in effect creates the universe anew at every moment (Haldane and Ross, 1955, I 168; *Le Monde*, pp. 59ff); he could recreate it quite differently each time, if he chose, but he does not, for he is a benevolent, not a sadistic dictator. (Even the truths of mathematics and logic are within the omnipotence of Descartes' God, and hence expressions of his will; *Philosophical Letters*, pp. 11, 13–15, 151.) By resting all regularity in God's will, Descartes removes every last trace of final cause from the created universe; the universe is in itself radically contingent, contingent at each moment on its creator's will. The physical things and events which are represented in our ideas are therefore without any intrinsic connections to one another.

The *de facto* constancy of God's action is a condition of the possibility of our attaining genuine knowledge of this universe. He chooses to act with constancy and regularity. His universe is therefore, by his choice, law governed. Finite minds can only begin to comprehend the infinite with the help of general principles. For us, what is understandable, knowable, rational, is what can be subsumed under general principles. In itself the course of the universe is, according to Descartes, simply a series of mutually independent states. This it would have to be if God in sustaining the world is always free to choose the future course of events, if the acts by which he continually recreates the world are independent and not the outcome of a single act of creation. It is as much God's immediate action, and therefore as much a miracle, that the pattern of events should continue regularly as that the regularity should be broken.

In this way Descartes sets the stage for the empiricism of Hume and of early twentieth century analytic philosophy. The objective of scientific inquiry into nature comes to be focused upon laws, which are the product of God's legislation. As they do not have sources in the powers of created things, no further explanation of them can be required of natural philosophy. The success of Newton's theory of gravitation and the manner in which he presented it in his *Principia*, also contributed to this conception of a science firmly divorced from any metaphysical postulation of a reality beyond and yet constraining phenomena. For there (I pp. 5–6; II 546–7) Newton explicitly states (whatever other ambitions he may have harbored) that he is not speculating as to causes of gravity. He is merely giving a precise description of the laws of action for this force.

If, however, knowledge of the existence of God, of his constancy and his benevolence, is denied, we are left in a radically contingent universe in which all "knowledge" of general principles must be insecure because its possibility lacks any grounding in the nature of things in the world. Thus when Hume follows the Cartesian epistemological route, turning to inward reflection on the contents of his own mind, he fails to find there assurance of the existence of a benevolent God. He finds instead only a radically contingent succession of ideas and impressions – a sequence of representations which yield no representation of causal power, activity, or process. Indeed, Hume finds no basis for treating mental contents as representing anything beyond experience. Sensory impressions, which Hume's predecessors from Descartes onward took as obviously representing the action of external things on the mind, could only be accepted by Hume as original existences. Other mental contents, for which Hume used the term "ideas," served to represent impressions and had legitimacy as representations (as opposed to figments) only to the extent that they could be connected back to impressions.

The principle that all ideas must have their origin in impressions, was the basis of Hume's conclusion that there can be no ideas of power or agency. The notion of cause, in so far as it has any content, can refer only to regularities in the sequence of impressions. One kind of event (a ball is released from a high building) is regularly followed by another (its hitting the ground rather hard). To assert a causal connection is to assert no more than that the first kind of event will always be followed by an event of the second kind. But experience can never afford a rational ground for such a claim, which must always reach beyond its evidential base in past observation. There is nothing in past experience of the states of things and their successions which can underwrite assurance about future states.

Why have people believed otherwise? Because, Hume suggests, the experience of repeated successions of, for example, dropping things, and their hitting the ground, sets up a mental habit, an association of ideas (*Treatise* I III xiv). This connection which we become prone to make between ideas is projected onto the world – for although we have no foundation for our belief in a world beyond our experience, the structure and coherence found within our experience tempts us all to believe in an order of things which persist, although our experience of them is interrupted. Our habits of association are then projected onto this supposed independent order of persisting things and this leads us to suppose there are grounds in the objects of our experience for inferences to the future course of events – grounds which provide a rational justification of our expectations. In reality, Hume alleges, the expectation precedes the "inference," the transition from one idea to another; and there is no rational warrant for making the transition. Natural science can at most trade in fallible opinions and beliefs about natural laws, not in rationally guaranteed knowledge. It can legitimately hazard predictions about the future course of events, but cannot pretend to explain the succession of one event upon another. All speculative attempts to reach beyond experience to explain it are idle – indeed are incoherent.

Hume's attempts to cure us of aspirations, which he suggests lead only to sophisticated superstitions, appear to continue Bacon's efforts to drive the Idols of the Theater from the philosophical stage. "Nothing is more requisite for a true philosopher, than to restrain the intemperate desire of searching into causes; and having established any doctrine upon a sufficient number of experiments, [to] rest contented with that, when he sees a further examination would lead him into obscure and uncertain speculations" (*Treatise* I I iv). He thus dispenses altogether with the Platonic-Aristotelian distinction between experience and understanding, which made understanding a matter of knowing the causes or explanations of phenomena. *Understanding why* is dismissed in favor of *knowing that* and the criterion of knowing, as opposed merely to believing, is the strong kind of certainty which arises from recognizing that one cannot believe otherwise.

Theoretical claims about laws of nature will always be fallible; the rational man should thus learn to proportion his belief to the evidence (*Enquiry* I, X(i)) and epistemology should focus on methods for doing just this. These would be the methods of a non-Baconian induction, an induction founded on calculation of probabilities and the use of statistical evidence. But to what end would such "knowledge" be sought? Why should the rational man proportion his belief to the evidence? Hume has dismissed the classical goal of contemplative knowledge – understanding, explanations – as illusory. If explanations are not the goal, if the only possible goal is fallible knowledge of empirical regularities, for what reason would this be sought?

Hume does not entirely deny the practical utility of knowledge of empirical regularities. He acknowledges that human life, in so far as it involves purposive action, requires belief in such regularities. To undertake any course of action one needs to believe that the chosen means will bring about the desired end. To the extent that we are better at predicting the outcomes of our actions, to that extent we will be more effective at getting what we want. But purposive action also requires belief in our efficacy as agents. This means that there are grave problems facing those who try to take Hume's philosophy as a basis for the conduct of their everyday affairs. Hume himself certainly recognized the difficulty of trying to do so (*Treatise* I IV vii).

7 The Unavoidability of Metaphysics

If the anti-speculative thrust of Hume's philosophy is a legitimate continuation of Bacon's campaign against the Idols of the Theater, then Bacon turns out to have scripted yet another performance for the Philosophers' Theater. For the notions of power and agency were crucial characters in Bacon's plot which calls for humankind to increase its domination over nature. David Hume, on the other hand, restricts scientific man to the rôle of natural historian passively observing, recording and anticipating, but definitely not explaining. Moreover, without access to notions of agency and causality, the Baconian project of control over nature appears incoherent.

Can Hume really be said to have avoided, let alone banished, all Idols of the Theater? To the extent that all thought and all theorizing are confined to the experienced world, he banishes all speculation

Metaphysics and the Aim of Inquiry

about a "reality," which governs appearances, either beyond or within experience. But Hume's argument limiting the possibility of knowledge of the natural world rests crucially on assumptions which he takes over from Cartesian epistemology. These are (1) an account of what it is to have knowledge (it must be certain and rationally guaranteed) and (2) a model of experience, which takes the form of a succession of discrete mental representations. These, combined with Hume's empiricist insistence that all ideas and all knowledge must ultimately derive from experience, yield the conclusion that the only world view legitimately available to us is that of a contingent succession of events. This is an instance of the way in which no epistemology can be divorced from a metaphysics, in the sense of a set of assumptions about the general structure of that reality which is the object of knowledge. Metaphysical assumptions inherent in Cartesian epistemology, survive to infect the starting points and methods of Hume's epistemology and become constitutive of a conception of the object of which knowledge is to be sought.

If the resulting picture of the world seems unsatisfactory, we might, with the rationalists, supplement it by a metaphysics which reaches beyond what Hume's conception experience can justify and dogmatically proclaim our faith in its truth. Or we might adopt the posture of skeptics and lament our inability to have adequate knowledge of what we find ourselves strongly tempted to believe. Or we might, instead of advancing a metaphysics – whether in the fashion of dogmatists or of skeptics – try to refrain from further systematic philosophy. Now we will have avoided metaphysics only in the sense that once we have systematized the general account of knowledge based on Hume's conceptions, we have then chosen to rest content with the assumptions which it entails about that which we are trying to know. But this is to have done metaphysics at the same time as developing an epistemology and not to have avoided doing it.

For reasons like these Kant claimed that metaphysics is inevitable:

> There has always existed in the world and there will continue to exist, some kind of metaphysics, and with it the dialectic that is natural to pure reason. It is therefore the first and most important task of philosophy to deprive metaphysics, once and for all, of its injurious influence, by attacking its errors at their very source. (*Critique of Pure Reason* Bxxxi)

Kant was thus moved to take up the cudgels against the Idols of the Theater. Indeed, the second edition of the *Critique of Pure Reason* is

Metaphysics and the Aim of Inquiry

motto taken from the preface to Bacon's *Great Instauration* which ends with Bacon's exhortation to his reader not [to think] this Instauration of mine is a thing infinite and [beyond the power] of man, when it is in fact the true end and termination of infinite error."

But instead of mounting a purely negative campaign against speculative philosophy, Kant undertakes a "critical" inquiry which will determine both the extent to which we are entitled to accept principles which anticipate experience, and the source of the temptations to reach beyond experience. Kant appreciated not only the challenge which Hume mounted to the concept of causation but also the effect it would have on the traditional distinction between *knowing that* and *knowing why*, which Kant referred to as the difference between "historical knowledge" and "rational knowledge" (A836/B864). The distinction was prominent (as that between "historical and philosophical knowledge,") in the work of Christian Wolff, who had shaped the German philosophical tradition in which Kant had been raised (see Wolff, *Preliminary Discourse* I 3–7). Kant did not believe that Wolff's "dogmatic" methods could sustain the distinction in the face of Hume's criticism, and that was why his own "critical" philosophy was needed. "Those who reject both the method of Wolff and the procedure of a critique of pure reason can have no other aim than to shake off the fetters of *science* altogether, and thus to change work into play, certainty into opinion and philosophy into philodoxy" (*Critique of Pure Reason* Bxxxvii). Not only did Kant believe that the traditional distinction could be sustained, he believed it could be applied to the modern science which Bacon had prophesied and Newton accomplished.

Although the idea that we might establish *a priori* principles – principles in advance of all experience – is contrary to the spirit of Bacon's philosophy, Kant believed that he was making a fresh and legitimate application of the principles of Baconian science. The introduction to the second edition of the *Critique of Pure Reason* emphasizes the crucial Baconian theme – the need for active experimental investigation as the prerequisite for scientific knowledge. Science begins where natural history leaves off. The lesson of the revolution which Bacon initiated, is

> ...that reason has insight only into that which it produces after a plan of its own... Even physics, therefore, owes the beneficent revolution in its point of view entirely to the happy thought, that while reason must seek in nature, not fictitiously ascribe to it... it must adopt as its guide,

in so seeking, that which it has itself put into nature. It is thus that the study of nature has entered on the secure path of science, after having for so many centuries been nothing but a process of merely random groping. (Bxiii–xiv)

In applying this lesson to his own enterprise of "critical" metaphysics Kant does not propose a series of experiments to test metaphysical claims, but undertakes to make explicit the forms which the mind's own operations impose in order to represent nature (as well as the mind itself) to itself, and to inquire into the scope and limits of the legitimate employment of reason in pursuit of theoretical knowledge. It is in this sense that Kant's inquiry claims to be modelled on experimental, scientific inquiry: "What we are adopting as our new method of thought, [is] namely that we can know *a priori* of things only what we ourselves put into them" (Bxviii).

Before considering what Kant hoped to establish by means of this method, it is worth remarking on how this places him in relation to his predecessors other than Bacon. Kant does not move to discard the metaphysics of representation; for the most part he operates comfortably within that framework. (Where his predecessors use the word "idea," Kant uses a word "*Vorstellung*," the most natural translation of which is "representation.") But he does call into question one very important assumption, which that framework had carried with it, the assumption that the mind in knowing must be passive. That is to say the assumption that ideas (including sensory impressions) are presented to the mind, which takes them in and acts only to the extent of accepting or rejecting what they purport to represent. Any activity of the mind is associated with the imagination, which needs to be kept carefully in check, for the imagination generates fictions and whatever it contributes to a thought cannot be relied upon to represent its object correctly. Ideas must be purged of anything which our minds might have contributed to their character, for this will only obscure and confuse us about what they represent. All of this is rejected by the critical philosophy.

Kant recognizes that the source of experience lies in objects given to us through sensation. The only objects to which we stand in immediate relation (which are in Kant's language "intuitions") are given to us by means of sensibility (*Critique of Pure Reason* A 19/B33). But though sensibility is necessary, Kant does not accept that it is sufficient for us to have experience. Our experience has characteristics, which everyone from Descartes to Hume had taken for granted, but for which no account can be given if the mind functions only passively. For example, experience includes the awareness of plurality, one species of plurality being the succession of appearances. But to undergo passively a succession of experiences is not necessarily to experience a succession. Unless each influence which is felt is connected to the others and each represented in its relations to the others in the sequence, there will be no experience of a succession. Hearing a sequence of musical notes without relating one to another, forgetting each as soon as it is displaced by another, one could never hear a tune; one would simply, at each moment, hear a different note.

Thus, in addition to having a capacity for receiving representations we must have an ability to connect one representation to another or "synthesize" the multiplicity of appearances. (An appearance is an undetermined object of sensible intuition (A20/B34). The function of unifying the experience of a plurality of appearances is performed by judgment. In other words, judgment is not an act of acceptance or rejection of some representation which has been apprehended in experience; it is integrally involved in the synthesis of appearances which generates the representations. There can be no experience of any kind arising from intuitions if no judgments are made.

What Kant understands by knowledge, "a whole in which representations stand compared and connected," (A97) is not out of step with Descartes and Hume, who regard all knowledge as a matter of perceiving the relations between ideas. But the whole and its parts are not simply presented to consciousness; the mind must spontaneously integrate the elements it receives. Spontaneity does not have anything to do with arbitrariness in this context; the general forms which this spontaneity takes must be rigidly fixed in advance or experience as a whole will lack the unity which it characteristically has. There can be no knowledge of any kind arising from intuitions, if the forms of judgment are not determined *a priori*.

Kant appeals to logic for a categorization of the various kinds of judgments. From his list of forms he derives a list of maximally general concepts (categories) some combination of which must be involved in every thought. If we make these kinds of judgments, and are conscious of doing so, we must know what judgment we have made and be able to recognize how it would differ from some other kind of judgment. For example, we must be able to distinguish between the universal judgment "All men go bald," the particular "Some men go bald" and the singular "Aristotle went bald." Consequently, in as much as we are able to discriminate between various kinds of judgments, we must already possess the concepts (categories such as unity, plurality, negation, substance, cause, etc.) necessary for making these discriminations, even though we may not be able to give explicit accounts of them. The list of categories is complete and final in Kant's view because he assumes that logic provides a complete enumeration of the possible forms of judgment. These concepts cannot be derived from experience because it is only through them that empirically given objects can be objects of knowledge.

Categories are therefore *a priori* concepts which we necessarily find instantiated in experience because of their rôle in the forms imposed by the mind in making judgments. For example, it is inappropriate to expect the category of cause (as involving necessary determination) to be derived from experience. Rather, because it plays a rôle in constituting experience, it necessarily has application within the empirical realm. In particular, it is the concept of cause and of determinate causal order which is invoked to constitute the distinction between a sequence of perceptions of a static object, such as one might have on walking round the outside of a house, and a sequence of perceptions of something moving or changing, as when, standing on the curb, one watches a car pass by on the road. Both present a changing sequence of perceptions, but in the one case the change is referred to the motion of the observer, in the other it is referred to the motion of the object observed.

The difference is that in judging the house perceptions to be perceptions of a static object we thereby judge that the sequence of perceptions could have come in a different order – we might have walked round in the other direction, but in judging the car perceptions to be perceptions of a moving object we thereby judge that the order of perceptions was fixed by the order of events – they could not have been received in any other order because they were perceptions of states which occurred in a fixed order. In both cases the notion of causal determination is integral to our judgment that the perceptions are of things external to us and to the way in which we make the distinction between what is objectively given and what is dependent on the perceiving subject.

Possession of the concept of causality is thus argued to be a necessary condition of the possibility of self consciousness, i.e., of the very reflective awareness on which Hume relied in conducting his inquiry. A conscious being cannot think of itself if it cannot distinguish between the thought of a series of perceptual experiences as given to itself in a determinate order and the series being concatenated as it pleases. An event sequence can only be thought as presented to oneself in a determinate way if it is represented as one which could not have occurred in an order other than it occurred. It is thus incoherent to suppose we might have experience of a radically contingent world, if we also suppose that we can know the determinate order of the occurences which constitute that experience. This supposition is incompatible with the conditions of the possibility of knowledge.

In this way Kant suggests a totally new way of establishing the authority of *a priori* knowledge: we are justified in using certain concepts and in applying certain principles in advance of all experience, if we are able to show that without these concepts and principles the experience we have would be impossible. The force of this argument is, however, that *a priori* concepts and principles have necessary application only to objects presented as intuitions to our sensibility. In order for us to have experience our minds must represent that experience as *of* an order of events and things which are independent of us, but as this order is necessarily found only in objects as they appear to us, we cannot draw any conclusions about how things are in themselves.

The standpoint of "things in themselves" is the standpoint occupied by God in Descartes' philosophy and even after God could no longer be called upon to realize this view of things, it remained a crucial reference point for the metaphysics of representation. To call into question the intelligibility of this reference point would be to undermine that metaphysics completely and Kant does not do so. Unlike Hume – whose attack on certain familiar *a priori* concepts and principles was devastating but whose attitude to the standpoint of things in themselves was equivocal – Kant defended our right to *a priori* concepts and principles but was explicit both in acknowledging the intelligibility of the standpoint and in denying us access to it. Dogmatic metaphysics is constituted by its unexamined assumption that it can tell us how it is, indeed how it must be, from the standpoint of things in themselves. Critical metaphysics realizes it can have no access to this standpoint and is content to tell us what we are entitled to use *a priori*, if our experience is to be constituted as we find it.

8 The Demands of Practical Thought

Kant does not move to collapse the distinction between things as they appear to us and things as they are in themselves because the resulting framework would not satisfactorily locate the subject of experience. There are, to be sure, appearances which we identify with our selves, e.g. our bodies, and these constitute our empirical selves (the "empirical ego"). But the realm of appearances is governed totally by causal laws and all aspects of our empirical selves are therefore determined by empirical (empirically discoverable) causes. Being determined in this way is for Kant incompatible with being the sort of agent which can be held morally responsible. Hume had removed agency from the world by undermining the concept of power. Kant restored the concept of power, but that was not enough to restore fully the concept of agency which he required.

Kant links human freedom with active human reason. Hume portrays reason as a wholly passive faculty, unable to motivate any action, and portrays human freedom as simply the lack of external constraint which might interfere with humans acting as prompted by their own desires. Human freedom for Hume is compatible with being part of a regular and contingently predictable natural world. For Kant, human freedom is incompatible with being part of a knowable world, a world in which everything is causally determined. Human fulfillment requires more than lack of interference with the efforts of humans to satisfy their desires. There are, in addition to the motivational factors which can be assigned to the empirical self, motivations which can be assigned to reason; and these are not confined entirely to the sphere which we think of as moral. They also influence theoretical uses of the mind.

Given Kant's observations about the conditions of the possibility of experience, there is clearly a kind of agency involved in the synthesis of intuitions, which takes place through judgment, in constituting experience. But this aspect of the self ("the transcendental ego"), although "spontaneous," is not self-determining in the way required by Kant for genuine free agency. The transcendental ego operates according to universal and necessary principles; there is no scope for free choice. However, in addition to this activity, which Kant assigned to "understanding" (*Verstehen*), there is a further activity, which Kant assigns to "reason" (*Vernunft*). This active faculty drives and guides the quest for scientific knowledge and is inevitably a source of ideas (ideals) of things which can never be realized in the empirical world.

Kant uses the word "idea" with explicit acknowledgment to Plato (A313/B370 ff.). Just as Plato's Ideas provide goals which guide critical and creative activity and thus cannot be embodied in the empirical world, the ideas of reason which articulate the goals of reason cannot be located in the empirical world. Inquiry sets us off looking for chains of conditions; our reason totalizes the chain with the idea of something which is unconditioned, the place at which inquiry terminates.

Such ideas function as regulative ideals, they represent the respects in which we have not reached the end of inquiry.

It is part of the critique of reason, which Kant mounts, to caution us against being taken in by the illusion that such ideals are actually attainable, for to do so is to be led into contradictions. For example, if the tracing back of empirical causes were to come to an end, there would have to have been a first event, an uncaused event. But this is impossible if the principle that every event has a cause is to hold necessarily and universally within the empirical realm, and this principle itself was argued to be necessary. In response to these chronic tendencies, a critical metaphysics can only labor to expose the source of such illusions and prevent us from succumbing to the inevitable temptation to assign to our knowledge, a higher authority than it can possibly possess.

The project of critical, as opposed to dogmatic, metaphysics is thus conducted by Kant in the spirit of driving Idols off the stage of the Theater of Philosophy. To argue that we are, as a consequence of our cognitive constitution, prone to manufacture such Idols is to trace their lineage to one of the Idols which Bacon mentions (*Novum Organum* I XLVIII) among those of the Tribe: "The human understanding is unquiet; it cannot stop or rest and still presses onward, but in vain. Therefore it is that we cannot conceive of any end or limit to the world, but always as of necessity it occurs to us that there is something beyond." Kant shows why we are tempted into such errors: reason presents us with ideas corresponding to the goals (ends) it sets for our activities. These are ideas of ideals, of objects which could never be encountered in experience but which we interpret as legitimate representations of an actual, suprasensible reality; i.e., we mistake the ideal for the real. In so doing we make two mistakes. We overestimate the powers of speculative reason, and we thereby eliminate the possibility of comprehending the practical rôle of reason. Ideas embody the (non-naturally given) goals of the use of theoretical reason regarded as a form of human practice; they function as regulative ideals (A702/B730).

The empirical realm, governed as it is by deterministic laws, has a place neither for free moral agents, nor a place for free theoretical inquirers. Kant's solution is to regard the empirical realm as appearances, thereby securing a place for thinking beyond the confines of the empirical. The price is to remove the free, reasoning agent from the scope of what can be known. The upshot is similar to Descartes' in that the same important aspect of our humanity, our freedom, is located beyond the physical world, but dissimilar in not invoking a dualism of separate but equal realms of reality (substances) and in not regarding those respects, in which our mind functions autonomously, as transparently knowable, but as quite unknowable.

In many respects Kant's critical metaphysics provides the framework of Cartesian epistemology (and its accompanying metaphysics of representation) with a basis for engaging the Baconian project. The epistemologies of Descartes, Hume and Kant, in their different ways, all encounter the same stumbling block. The project of modern science, the Baconian project, needed to disclaim any pretensions to "moral knowledge" and any pretension to theorizing about final causes, or purposes. This was necessary to secure its autonomy from theology. A product of this strategy is a portrayal of the natural world, the object of scientific knowledge, from which final causes, purposes and values are absent.

This portrayal of the object of scientific knowledge is, as Kant reveals, a projection of the goal (objective) of scientific knowledge – it is the expression of its cognitive ideals. Kant's point is that to the extent that we mistake this way of conceiving things for total reality, we are taken in by an "illusion." We then find ourselves trapped because it is a conception of reality in which we cannot find ourselves. We cannot think ourselves to be without purposes, without values, to be fully determined and at the same time retain the supposition that we can acquire knowledge through our own spontaneous activity.

Kant's proposed solution requires a metaphysics in Plato's sense, one that is argued to be necessary in an Aristotelian spirit. That is to say, Kant argues that a systematic account of the structure inherent in the project of modern science requires a reality beyond the phenomenal realm, even though, unlike Plato's realm of Forms, it is a reality of which we can have no theoretical knowledge. Metaphysics is, then, not the positive science which systematizes knowledge of this reality; it is the science, which, although insisting on the existence of this reality, sets limits on our cognitive capacities. Nevertheless, Kant's solution remains firmly dualistic. Reason in its practical functions (which include governing the theoretical functions of reason) has not been re-inserted into the empirical world; it operates beyond it.

Kant's relocation of our place as agents subordinates the goal of Bacon's project, the material well-being of human beings, to higher, moral ends, but nevertheless strongly underwrites the idea of mankind as rightfully dominating nature.

> Now of man (and also of every rational creature in the world) as a moral being it can no longer be asked why (*quem in finem*) he exists...Only

> in man, and only in him as subject of morality, do we meet with the unconditioned legislation in respect of purposes, which therefore alone renders him capable of being a final purpose, to which the whole of nature is teleologically subordinated. [Kant's footnote:] This proves that happiness can only be a conditioned purpose and that it is only connected with it as a consequence, according to the measure of his harmony with that purpose regarded as the purpose of his being. (*Critique of Judgement* §84, pp. 285–6)

At the same time that these arguments legitimate the Baconian project, they undermine the claims of dogmatic theology, not merely in the realm of natural philosophy, but also in that of moral philosophy. Kant is in effect insisting that we can have no theoretical knowledge of ourselves as moral agents or of any non-natural reality which could provide a foundation for morality. But at the same time he argues for an *a priori* principle of morality which is neither groundless nor a mere product of human convention.

Empiricists, such as Hume, make a mistake similar to that of the speculative dogmatic rationalists, when they deny reason its practical rôle. Against empiricists Kant argues that the sensible world would not even be of speculative interest if there were not a higher, practical interest.

> Without men the whole creation would be a mere waste, in vain, and without final purpose. But it is not in reference to man's cognitive faculty (theoretical reason) that the being of everything else in the world gets its worth; he is not there merely that there may be someone to contemplate the world. For if the contemplation of the world only afforded a representation of things without any final purpose, no worth could accrue to its being from the mere fact that it is known; we must propose for it a final purpose, in reference to which its contemplation itself has worth. (*Critique of Judgement* §86, p. 293)

Bacon's outlook was not so radically secular that he would have found unwelcome this way of underwriting the aim of his project of securing mastery over nature by subordinating it to the notion of the supreme worth of humans as moral agents. And if persuaded to accept the concept of experience, which threatens the notion of agency, Bacon might well have acceded to the need to secure the notion of agency in a place not accessible to empirical inquiry. He professed, after all, not to desire knowledge that would allow some humans to manipulate or dominate others (see chapter 1.5, above). But he might have found Kant's concept of experience difficult to accept. The problem is that Kant equates the object of empirical knowledge with our conception of it; this is his "empirical realism." This is in effect to insist that we have to live our "illusion," for this is the only way we can represent (think) the empirical world. Knowledge of the forms of our representations then secures rationally guaranteed *a priori* knowledge of the most general scientific principles.

Bacon would not have been comfortable, as least initially, with Kant's hope of establishing the credentials of concepts and principles which are to be applied *a priori*. However, Bacon hardly raised his thoughts to the level of generality at which Kant's argument operates. Perhaps in the face of the threat posed by Hume, Bacon would have endorsed Kant's argument. But if Bacon is read as inclined to reject Kant and to insist that no such guarantees on *a priori* knowledge of any sort are possible, his subordination of theoretical to practical reason is more radical than could be acknowledged by any of the seventeenth or eighteenth century thinkers. For although they resisted the discursive framework of traditional philosophy, they did not succeed in breaking fully with its conception of theoretical knowledge. If Bacon's insistence on the unavailability of *a priori* first principles and on using practical success as the mark of truth is pushed rigorously, we would have to acknowledge that whatever conception of the object of knowledge guides inquiry, – whether it be speculative coherence, material well-being or whatever – it too must be regarded as revisable in the light of experience. To treat it otherwise would be to have created another Idol of the Theater.

By not being committed to knowledge as accurate representation, by insisting that the mind of man is a distorting mirror, Bacon might be read as disallowing (in advance) the strategy of reading the structure of the empirical world, the object of scientific knowledge, off the forms of our representations. (This would be true whether, like Hume, we read the contingency of the world off our fleeting impressions, or like Kant discover its governance by deterministic causal laws from the forms of our judgments.) Yet, we have argued that any epistemological project carries metaphysical commitments in the form of general assumptions about the structure of the object of knowledge. If this is correct, Bacon's project can be no exception. The problem with his project is that its commitments – to a strong sense of human agency and to a material world whose causal laws can be sufficiently well known to allow humans to dominate it in the service of their own interests – are hard to reconcile. If metaphysical presuppositions are required to be revisable (because not a source of genuine *a priori* knowledge of first principles) then, because they are linked to the definitions of epistemological projects, those projects too must be held to be subject to revision in the light of critical scrutiny.

By making theoretical reason subordinate to practical reason, Kant secures for the latter an absoluteness and objectivity which he denied to the former. Practical reason secures absolute moral standards and the moral vision of human domination over nature, which is inherent in the Baconian project. If all ideals are to be prevented from becoming Idols, however, the relation between practical and theoretical reason can neither be one of domination, nor of independence, but has to be one of interdependence. The values inherent in treating any kind of knowledge as authoritative and worthy of pursuit have to be able to find a place within the world which forms the objects of that knowledge, otherwise the project will be unable to offer any coherent account of itself, any convincing epistemology. The role of critical epistemology then is to work continually to reveal the metaphysical commitments inherent in existing knowledge projects and the practices which sustain them so that they do not take on the character of Idols falsely worshipped.

4
Idols of the Market Place:
Language and Representation

> *But the Idols of the Market Place are the most troublesome of all – idols which have crept into the understanding through the alliances of words and names. For men believe that their reason governs words; but it is also true that words react on the understanding; and this it is that has rendered philosophy and the sciences sophistical and inactive.*
>
> *Novum Organum* I LIX

1 The Tyranny of Words

The Idols of the Market Place are the most troublesome because the most difficult to avoid. To record and communicate knowledge we must use language, but we do not use language only for recording and communicating knowledge. It is a general purpose medium which sustains all manner of relations between human beings; it is a repository of culture, of myths and mystifications, as well as of knowledge. Early philosophers appreciated the confusion embodied in ordinary habits of speech and recommended taking deliberate steps to rise above it. Plato's method of dialectic proceeded from the assumption that people who understood what they were doing would be able to articulate accurate accounts (definitions) of the goals of their endeavors and of related key concepts. Aristotle accepted that understanding consisted in a grasp of "the what it is" of the thing that is understood and the communication of understanding would be based on definitions which conveyed a grasp of what things are. The philosophic tradition, which Bacon confronted, was both conscious of the inadequacies of ordinary speech and confident that it had accumulated enough precise definitions to rise above them.

But scholars, like other groups of people who have special concerns, refashion parts of language in ways which not only facilitate their transactions but also restrict the dimensions of question, explanation and dispute. Bacon, a lawyer by training, had first-hand experience of legal language and was conscious that to break with past systems of natural philosophy it would be necessary to break the hold of the technical language used in the Schools. He rebuked the learned for thinking that by giving verbal definitions they could cut through all the snares set by words. Since the process of definition cannot go on indefinitely, they must rely ultimately on the common understanding of some undefined terms. Furthermore, even a term which has been carefully defined, can in common use only be "applied according to the capacity of the vulgar" (*Novum Organum* I XLIII, LIX). No one person can control the use other speakers of the same language make of words of that language; linguistic habits once formed are hard to modify.

Bacon identifies (I LX) two distinct ways in which words can lead us into error; one is by giving us names for things which do not exist, the other is by words being ambiguous or very imprecise. The power of language to persuade people to believe in or take seriously things which they should not credit, can easily be proved by any group of conspirators capable of giving a convincing imitation of serious discourse. Other people can be drawn into the practice without realizing that crucial terms are not adequately connected to reality. The history of science since the seventeenth century contains numerous examples of students of nature who unwittingly convinced themselves of the reality of, for example, phlogiston, N-rays, the luminiferous aether, simply by linking these terms to phenomena in ways other people could easily learn. Introducing a term and having others agree on its use is clearly not sufficient to guarantee that the term stands for an object of scientific knowledge. This problem of determining under what conditions one is justified in believing that the terms of a scientific theory really do refer to entities in the physical world is one which continues to preoccupy philosophers of science (see, for example, Putnam, 1975, chapter 4).

Philosophers, we have seen, had long been sensitive to, if not wholly successful in combatting, the other source of error which Bacon cites, the fact that the use of words does not always trace the real distinctions between things. When words are imprecise we may be led to class together things which really have nothing of scientific significance in common. For example, if we class together all those flowers whose English common names indicate that they are some kind of

Language and Representation

rose – wild rose, christmas rose, rock rose, moss rose, etc. – we would not have collected together plants belonging to the same botanical family. Ambiguities can facilitate fallacious reasoning (the fallacy of equivocation), as in the syllogism "Man is the only rational animal; no woman is a man. Therefore, women are not rational." Here "man" is used first for the human species and then for just the male members of that species. Aristotelians recognized that the validity of their demonstrations (chapter 3.2) depended on the terms being used (at least within the context of the inference) with a single, precise meaning.

To avoid both kinds of error we need some way of ensuring that the terms we use really do refer to things and do so in ways which consistently follow real differences. If we could accomplish this on a wholesale basis, we would be able to create an ideal language for communicating scientific knowledge. Bacon did not believe such an ideal could be fully realized, although he clearly thought that significant improvements could be made over the language used in his day in the various systems of natural philosophy. Some later philosophers, most notably Leibniz in the late seventeenth century and the logical positivists early in the twentieth century, thought that it should be possible to create an ideal language for science and made attempts toward constructing one.

Even if we were to confine our aspirations to taking piecemeal steps to improve our language, there are two closely related questions which need to be addressed: (1) "How is knowledge conveyed by language?" and hence, (2) "How do, or should, the expressions of a language used for recording and communicating knowledge acquire their meaning?" Neither of these can be answered without reference to a third question, (3) "What does knowledge in general, or scientific knowledge in particular, consist in?" Recent philosophy has given a great deal of attention to the second question, assuming, without explicitly setting out, answers to the first and third. Bacon addresses the third question but does not address either of the questions about language. Nevertheless, by insisting that terms should have precise meanings Bacon contributed to a movement which shaped assumptions about how the first question should be answered and ultimately shaped assumptions about the nature of knowledge, which Bacon would not have found congenial. To understand this movement and Bacon's motives for contributing to it, it is necessary to appreciate how classical philosophy provided a habitat for a number of approaches to natural philosophy and the need, perceived by Bacon and others, to clear out what appeared to be slum neighborhoods.

2 Of Trees and Harmonies

The importance of definition in the work of Plato and Aristotle is based on the assumption that words embody understanding only when the rational connections between them, connections which hold in virtue of their meanings, reflect genuine connections between things in the world. Only if this is so will explanations, which involve connecting words together and making inferences, be satisfactory accounts of how things should be or accounts which say why things are as they are. The system of terms has to have a structure which in some way corresponds to the structure of the things for which the terms stand.

Because of the importance which he assigned to the ability to give accurate accounts (definitions) of certain key concepts, Plato was concerned to find a method that would yield such definitions. In several late dialogues (the *Phaedrus*, the *Sophist*, the *Statesman*, and the *Philebus*) we find attempts to develop "the method of division." First drafts of the method consist in advice to locate the object one wishes to define in its proper comprehensive kind (love, for example, is an attribute of the soul) and then repeatedly divide and subdivide that kind – not arbitrarily but according to its natural articulations – until one has isolated the object of the inquiry. Aristotle integrated the "method of division" into his influential account of how a finished body of understanding (*epistêmê*) should be constituted (see chapter 3.2). To counteract Plato's suggestion that somehow this method could be used to establish correct definitions, Aristotle insisted that this method could not establish definitions in the sense of "demonstrate" their correctness (*Posterior Analytics* 91b12ff.) although it had some value as a method for finding definitions (96b26–28). He clearly accepted the results as an important part of what constituted the understanding of something.

The kind of rational structure which is given prominence by Aristotle's conception of demonstrative *epistêmê* is that of a classificatory system – a hierarchy of kinds of things organized in terms of genus and species. A very general category (the highest genus) is divided into sub-categories, or species. These in turn become the genera which are subdivided into species, and so on. A definition, it must be stressed, was not thought to be merely an account of the meaning of a word, but an account of "the what it is" or "the what it would be to be" a thing of a certain kind. These are fairly literal translations of Aristotle's Greek; we can also say they are accounts of

Language and Representation 131

"the essence" of something which is a term we inherit from a word manufactured to translate Aristotle's Greek into Latin. To define an object or essence, and thereby give its name a precise and correct use, was to locate it in a classificatory system. Early in the Christian era this way of schematizing things was given a definitive icon in what is now known as the tree of Porphyry (who lived in the third century AD), on which the definition of man was displayed (see figure 4.1). Man is thus defined as a rational animal; rationality is that which differentiates him from all other animals.

Definitions (accounts of essence) such as this serve for Aristotle as the foundation for rationally demonstrable knowledge. One can show, for example, that it would be false to claim that some animals are

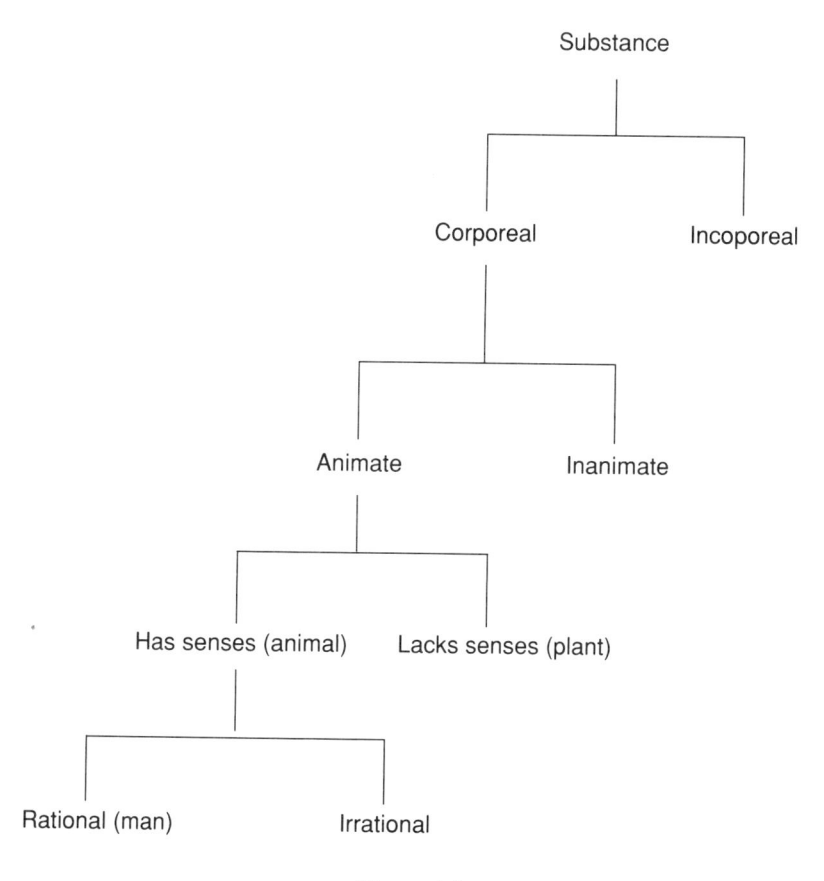

```
                    Substance
                   /         \
              Corporeal    Incoporeal
              /       \
         Animate    Inanimate
         /      \
  Has senses   Lacks senses
   (animal)      (plant)
    /    \
Rational  Irrational
 (man)
```

Figure 4.1

non-corporeal by noting that being corporeal is part of the definition of what it is to be an animal. This means that no animal can be incorporeal. Aristotle's syllogistic logic gives a complete catalog of the simple inferences that allow one to move around, and take advantage of knowledge embodied in, such classificatory systems. For example, moving up the tree we trace back the definitions:

> Men are animals.
> Animals are capable of sense perception.
> Therefore men are capable of sense perception.

Moving across the tree we note the exclusions:

> Men are animals.
> No animals are inanimate bodies
> Therefore no men are inanimate bodies

Plato, however, appears not to have been entirely satisfied by the method of division and a restatement of it in the *Philebus* includes the germ of an important elaboration. If Aristotle noticed this at all, he did not emphasize it, nor did subsequent Aristotelians. The additional requirement is that the forms, or species into which a kind, or genus, is divided should be interdependent, so that a grasp of any one of them is impossible without a grasp of all of them. In other words, the species into which a genus is divided should be internally related to one another; they should form a structured whole where the identity of each part is dependent on its relations to all the other parts. Plato illustrates this with a legend, which he attributed to the Egyptians, that it was someone named Thueth who divided the vocal sounds into vowels, semi-vowels, consonants and mutes and distinguished each down to individual sounds. "As he realized that none of us would ever learn about one of them in isolation from the rest, he concluded that this constituted a single bond that somehow made them a single unit, and he declared that a single *technê* of letters covered them" (*Philebus* 18c–d). This elaboration of his method opens the door to a number of important elements of a conception of knowledge which Plato had acquired in part from other sources, and to a conception of rationality which could not have rested entirely on the use which Aristotle made of division in the conception of demonstrative *epistêmê*.

The *Philebus* also advances the claim that to possess expertise about some matter involves the grasp of relationships between certain important parts or aspects of that thing (16c–17a). These relationships will, in better developed *technai*, be expressible in mathematical terms (55d–57e) and will provide the terms in which to give an account of how that thing should be. To take a very simple-minded example, a novice cook can by following a recipe combine four ounces of butter, four ounces of lard and twelve ounces of flour to make two pie crusts. More experienced cooks will recognize that what is important in pastry making is the ratio of fat to flour and that for this type of crust the ratio should be two to three. They will then be able to make any desired amount of it. A cook who understands (possesses the technê of pastry making) will know which ratios of flour to fat make the different kinds of pastry (flaky, shortcrust, etc.) and why only these ratios make satisfactory pastry.

It is hard not to see the influence of Pythagoreanism in this concept of what is involved in understanding what one is doing. Pythagoras was in Plato's time already known as a legendary mathematician, natural philosopher and founder of a quasi-religious fellowship, members of which Plato appears to have encountered while visiting Sicily. Pythagoras was credited, by legend, with the discovery that the reason two strings plucked together (or two pipes blown together) sounded harmonious, rather than discordant, had to do with there being an integral ratio between their lengths:

Interval	*Ratio*
octave	2 : 1
fifth	3 : 2
fourth	4 : 3

Now a note in itself is neither harmonious nor discordant, it is only the mutual relationship between notes which produces harmony or discord. Discord is the product of disagreement and disorder; it was thought to mark a departure from reason, from the ideal order. This suggested the doctrine that all forms of good (or intrinsically desirable) conditions could be expressed in terms of the ratios of whole numbers. Wherever one could find integral ratios between magnitudes, there was the harmony which made that bit of the universe intelligible. To look for a rational order as a system of ratios is thus to be directed away from individual things to the whole which they compose and to the structure of relationships within it.

A given structure of relationships can be instantiated in many different ways. Musical harmonies, for example, can be the result of ratios between vibrating strings or vibrating columns of air. In this way ratios of numbers, harmony, rationality and accounts of how things ideally should be, all came to have close connections in Plato's thought. (Just as the words for a numerical ratio and for rationality are etymologically linked in English, via Latin; the Greek word *"logos"* applies both to numerical ratios and to a person's ability to reason.)

The concept of ratio was also connected with that of measurement. For the ancient Greeks, who had no precisely fixed standards of measurement, it was obvious (more obvious, perhaps, than it is to us) that measurement itself involved this kind of relationship. A string has a length, but this length has no number except in relation to some other thing with length, a unit, which is used to measure it. To measure is to determine the ratio of one thing to another.

Moreover, if one knows the ratio of A to B is the same as that of B to C, and, for example, that A is one inch long and B two inches long, then one can conclude that C is four inches long (A : B = 1 : 2 = B : C = 2 : 4). If one knows that the area of a circle stands in a fixed ratio, π, to the square of its radius (area = πr^2), then to determine the area of a circle one only needs to measure its radius. The modern scientific conception of a law of nature as something which is expressed by means of an equation, such as Einstein's discovery that $e = mc^2$, embodies the same idea. Here the ratio of energy (e) to mass (m) is constant and equal to the value of the square of the velocity of light (c). With the development of mathematics, however, more complex forms of relations than the Greeks could ever imagine can now be used in the expression of laws.

Through a sequence of such inference steps one actual measurement can indirectly yield many others. In other words, ratios extend knowledge through a system of inter-relations to things which are not directly knowable. This was, and is, very important in astronomy, for example, because we are not in a position to make direct measurements of the heavenly bodies or their motions. The ability to extend knowledge in this way indicates the power, and hence the attractiveness, of this conception of what we can know and how we can reason about it. It is not surprising that the realization that human beings have this kind of ability encouraged mystical tendencies in Neoplatonic and Neopythagorean philosophy early in the Christian era. For inferences of this kind appear to confer the capacity to acquire a form of knowledge which transcends the limitations of human experience.

If human rationality is understood entirely in terms of Aristotelian demonstrations which do no more than chase understanding up the tree of Porphyry, then virtues of rationality will be the abilities to distinguish, to avoid incompatibilities and to recognize when one concept includes another. The association between rationality and harmony brings with it a notion of rational order and of coherence, which is not founded on the opposition of having or lacking a given quality, on the logical opposition of contrary qualities, or on observing what distinguishes one thing from another. Ratio and harmony are intrinsically relational concepts so that rationality in this other sense requires not merely distinguishing the distinct but also observing the connections among the related and noting how they form a structured whole.

It needs to be emphasized that having sprouted from the same stem, for a long part of their history there was no perceived tension between these two strands of the conception of understanding and of rationality. Porphyry was himself a Neoplatonist, who made little of what later scholars regarded as deep differences between Plato and Aristotle. He wrote an influential introduction to Aristotle's logic, which presented it as an important tool to be used in conjunction with Plato's philosophy.

It also needs to be stressed that the concept of understanding and rationality, which encourages organizing kinds of things in Porphyrian trees, can survive being divorced from Aristotelian demonstration. In the sixteenth century the influential logician, Peter Ramus, rejected Aristotle's account of demonstration along with its supporting metaphysics of species, genus and essence. But Ramus recommended the use of classificatory trees, or tables, as a form of organization which is natural to the human mind and which thus imposed a conventional linguistic order which could readily be memorized (see Ong, 1958).

Bacon too used such tables to convey his ideas about the organization of the various fields of learning, even though he is scornful of Aristotelian logic. He was also familiar with the projects of a number of people, whom he regarded as charlatans for the way they sought understanding based on the grasp of similitudes and harmonies, and he was consequently deeply suspicious of efforts to develop that alternative.

3 Signs and the Chemical Philosophy

Although mathematical relationships formed an important part of the initial conception of the kind of reasoning which seeks relationships and harmonies, it was extended to cover all forms of systematic analogical reasoning. The pattern of reasoning to find the fourth proportional – A is to B as C is to what? – is also the pattern for analogical reasoning. For example, gold is to silver as the sun is to what? – the moon. Moreover, the pattern A is to B as B is to C, used in indirect measurement, was frequently assimilated to the pattern of the syllogism, A–B, B–C therefore A–C, where via B, the middle term, a relation is established between A and C. The problem of finding a middle term (a branch on the tree of Porphyry) in order to establish a connection between two terms and so demonstrate a proposition was also often thought of as finding a common measure. So what would to us seem to be quite distinct kinds of reasoning and quite distinct kinds of rational order, were up to the seventeenth century frequently not distinguished.

A good illustration of this can be found in the elaborate logical system constructed by the thirteenth century Catalan philosopher, Raymon Lull (see Yates, 1982). Lull believed that the universe is ordered as a hierarchical sequence of levels, or orders, of being. God occupies the highest position, inanimate matter the lowest. Each level of being is itself ordered, its constituents classified and the structure of this order is the same at each level. This means that if we acquire knowledge of this structure at the levels where we can have direct experience (in the vegetable and mineral kingdoms for example) and can establish correspondences between key items across the levels (similitudes which allow a being of one order to be the sign of, or to signify, a being of another, higher order), this will suffice to enable us, by analogical reasoning, to gain knowledge of the higher levels to which we have no direct access. Step by step we can thus ascend the ladder of being (journey through the spheres) until we reach God (until we reach the outmost sphere and the Prime Mover). Lull made very extravagant claims for the power of his system. He specifically claimed that it could be used as a means of converting the Muslims of North Africa to Christianity, since it would bring them to a knowledge of the Christian God.

Lull's work was quite widely known in the seventeenth century and for a time had a certain vogue in Paris, where both Descartes and Leibniz encountered it. Leibniz was sufficiently sympathetic to have tried to adapt some of Lull's ideas, although his enthusiasm was far from unqualified. Bacon also knew of Lull's work and commented,

> There hath been also laboured and put into practice a method which is not a lawful method, but a method of imposture; which is to deliver knowledge in such a manner, as men may speedily come to make a show

of learning who have it not. Such was the travail of Raymundus Lullus in making that art which bears his name. (ALNA, p.167)

The hostility which Bacon expresses is typical of how Lull appeared from the standpoint of those seventeenth century trends which we now identify as "modern philosophy." One of the trends most responsible for this hostility involved the attempt to separate (what for the sake of brevity we can call) "logical" from "analogical" styles of reasoning and to purge scientific understanding of the latter.

The two structures of understanding and the two corresponding senses of rational order, which had emerged more or less together as Plato worked to develop a method of arriving at definitions, had continued to co-exist up to the seventeenth century without anyone feeling there to be a tension or opposition between them. Those whose outlook led them to emphasize one of the two aspects more than the other, did not do so with the aim of burying the other. The two forms of reasoning and the two corresponding patterns of rational order, logical and analogical, now appear to us as quite distinct. That they could be run together suggests that our assumptions about the way language works to embody knowledge, and the way words acquire meaning, differ in important respects from those held prior to the seventeenth century.

One of the ways in which two, parallel rational orders could be seen to be carried in the same language was through the contrast between literal and symbolic meaning. As good an Aristotelian as St Thomas Aquinas (Lull's contemporary) noted that things as well as words can signify, and he accepted the multiple ways of signifying, multiple models of understanding and multiple truths which were entailed by operating within a system of signs.

> Any truth can be manifested in two ways: by things or by words. Words signify things and one thing can signify another. The Creator of things, however, can not only signify anything by words, but can also make one thing signify another. That is why the Scriptures contain a two fold truth. One lies in the things meant by the words used – that is the literal sense. The other is in the way things become figures of other things, and in this consists the spiritual sense. (*Questiones quodlibetales*, quoted in Gombrich, 1972, pp. 13–14).

The system of signs rested on overlapping networks of relations of similitude of various kinds. One thing can signify, be the sign of, another if it occupies an analogous place in a system of relations and there is some similitude between them. Thus gold can signify the sun in virtue of its brightness in comparison to other metals and the sun's brightness relative to other heavenly bodies and because of their similar color. Gold may also signify the king or ruler and hence also the masculine. As Aquinas goes on to remark, there can be no authoritative dictionary of the significance of things, as distinct from words:

> It is not due to deficient authority that no compelling argument can be derived from the spiritual sense; this lies rather in the nature of similitude in which the spiritual sense is founded. For one thing may have similitude to many; for which reason it is impossible to proceed from anything mentioned in the Scriptures to an unambiguous meaning. For instance the lion may mean the Lord because of one similitude and the Devil because of another. (Ibid.)

It is not difficult to understand why Aquinas should have felt perfectly at home in such a system of signs. Literacy was relatively uncommon in thirteenth century Europe; reproduction of the culture, including the conveying of moral norms and religious doctrine, rested in part on the use of carvings, paintings and allegories. Images, which are sensible artificial signs, became fused with their significations, and were not distinguished from natural signs. The scriptures, read as vehicles of doctrine, were similarly assumed to have used the technique of allegory and of signs based on similitudes to communicate a spiritual message. St Augustine's general rule had been that whatever in scripture is not directly edifying must be figurative (Farrar, 1979, p. 237). In Aquinas this became the idea that the message cannot be gleaned by literal reading but can only be discerned by a learned deciphering of the esoteric, spiritual meaning.

The influences which tended to enforce the strict discursive practices, which Bacon advocates for science, are connected to the Reformation and to its struggles over religious authority. Luther rejected the notion of multiple meanings and the doctrine that the scriptures have a double meaning (literal and spiritual); he advocated what he saw as a return to one simple, literal sense (Farrar, 1979, p. 327). Protestants insisted that God's Word was accessible to all and argued that the illiterate should be taught to read rather than be fed on potentially misleading images. Reading the scriptures in their own language would enable people, using their literal understanding of it, to receive God's Word.

One could argue that a parallel debate occurred with respect to natural philosophy. One motive, canvassed in religious contexts, for the study of natural philosophy was that there were two routes to knowledge of God, through study of his Word (the Bible) and his Works (the natural, created world). The created world is a book which we should also learn to read. But should this reading of the world as a system of signs be, as certain "chemical philosophers" urged, allegorical, based on similarities between sign and things signified? Or should the reading be literal, where the relationship between sign and what it signifies is like that between a name and what it signifies, based in other words on a wholly contingent relationship?

This opposition is, like the religious opposition, associated with views on who can be an authority, who can have knowledge. The "chemical philosophy" (see Debus, 1977) derived from a Renaissance mixture of Neoplatonism, astrology and alchemy and its associated conception of knowledge was esoteric, an instrument of power which should not be widely disseminated. Authoritative readings of the analogies and similarities were not accessible to all, only to adepts. The "mechanical philosophers" – Boyle and Locke in particular, as well as Bacon – subscribed to much more democratic conceptions of knowledge.

Strong currents of iconoclasm ran through much of Protestantism. The use of images in worship was stigmatized as idolatry (hence the rhetorical force of Bacon's word "Idols" in a country which was officially, if not stably, Protestant). Images were at best an aid to memory, props to hold in place what the intellect needed for its work. For example Bacon, when writing of the use of emblems (concrete signs) in the art of memory says:

> Emblems bring down intellectual to sensible things; for what is sensible always strikes the memory stronger, and sooner impresses itself that the intellectual... And therefore it is easier to retain the image of a sportsman hunting the hare, of an apothecary ranging his boxes, a boy repeating verses, or a player acting his part, than the corresponding notions of invention, disposition, elocution, memory and action. (*De Augmentis* V V)

Images might be used to aid memory, but they were dangerous, and should not be relied upon. Images, signs and allegories were not to be confused with the route to true knowledge.

Bacon was far from being imbued with a Puritan distaste for icons; his writing is amply larded with image, myth and allegory. When he insisted that emblems were not proper instruments for understanding the natural world, it was not primarily Scholastics (or even medieval visionaries such as Lull) against whom he was defining his position, but against the natural magic of hermetic, or chemical, philosophers such as Ficino, Agrippa and Paracelsus. They took seriously (literally) the idea that an emblem could bring the intellectual down to sensible things. Their practice of natural magic rested in part on the belief that it was possible to call down astral influences of the semi-divine spiritual beings, which they identified with the planets. This was to be done by inscribing the astrological signs for the planets on a suitable material (one for which the planet had a natural affinity – gold for the sun, silver for the moon, etc.). Catholic, as well a Protestant, natural philosophers had reason to distance themselves from the dangerous heresies of this kind of natural magic. The move to treat the knowledge sought by natural philosophy as knowledge which could find expression in, and only in, literal uses of language was thus bound up with religious trends in several ways.

When Bacon illustrates how ambiguous language is liable to mislead us, the example he gives is of how the term "humid" (or moist) was used in alchemical theory. There it was an integral part of the theory of the four elements, Earth, Air, Fire and Water, each of which is characterized in terms of the opposed qualities hot-cold and dry-moist. He says:

> For it both signifies that which easily spreads itself round any other body; and that which is in itself indeterminate and cannot solidise; and that which readily yields in every direction; and that which easily divides and scatters itself; and that which easily unites and collects itself... accordingly when you come to apply the words, if you take it in one sense, flame is humid; if in another air is not humid; if in another, fine dust is humid; if in another, glass is humid. (*Novum Organum* I LX)

This is a fairly standard complaint made by those who were proponents of some form of mechanism against the various proponents of the chemical philosophy. There is a very similar criticism made by Boyle in his dialogue *The Skeptical Chymist*, in which he argues against the chemical philosophy.

Bacon's more detailed criticism of alchemy illustrates why his program for the reform of natural philosophy became linked to a program for linguistic reform and for establishing agreed, systematic nomenclatures. Alchemy was practiced as an esoteric art, one handed down from ancient authorities who, it was assumed, had knowledge of the

Language and Representation 141

great secret but who had concealed this knowledge in their writings lest it fall into the wrong hands. Alchemical texts were then read as sacred texts; their literal meaning was assumed to be but a key to their true "philosophical" meaning, which could be grasped only by intricate knowledge of the system of signs employed.

This, however, meant that the alchemist was not conducting experiments in order to learn from them by observation. He was trying to follow a recipe written in a foreign language, and his experiments served as a check on his translation. If he did not get the promised result, then he must have made a mistake somewhere.

> ...the Alchemist nurses eternal hope, and when the thing fails lays the blame on some error of his own; fearing either that he has not sufficiently understood the word of his art or of his authors... or else that in his manipulations he has made some slip of a scruple in weight or a moment of time (whereupon he repeats his trials to infinity)... (I LXXXV)

Modern historians trying to assess the status of alchemy have found it virtually impossible to repeat experiments described in alchemical texts because there is no way to be sure exactly what substances they were using. The nomenclature was unsystematic and variable so that even without an attempt at concealment there would be problems of replication (see Crossland, 1978, chapters 1 and 2).

The alchemist's assumption that his task is one of correct interpretation is natural in the context of assumptions which he made about any network of signs. Within such a framework the question of whether a sign has significance cannot be raised; by the fact that it occurs in the system, it must have relations to other signs and these relations confer significance on it. The only cognitive question which can be raised about a sign is that of its correct interpretation, in a particular context. (Does the sign for the planet mercury here signify the metal, mercury, or perhaps the metallic principle, mercury, which is common to all metals?) Within such a system of signs, interpretation leads from sign to sign, so that even when a word is interpreted as the sign for some physical entity, the next move is frequently to ask what that physical entity signifies. One of the effects of insisting, as Bacon among others did, that the book of nature be read literally was to displace this assumption and the conception of sign which supported it.

4 From Signs to Representations via the Way of Ideas

Michel Foucault contrasts two orientations to language in the early chapters of *The Order of Things*. His account treats one conception as completely dominating the sixteenth century and then giving way entirely to the other in the seventeenth. This both over-simplifies the patterns of intellectual domination in these two centuries and fails to situate the contrast in a wider historical context. Nevertheless his characterization of the contrast is valuable. The orientation which Foucault regards as dominating the sixteenth century is said to treat language as a "system of signs." In a system of signs, the relationship between sign and thing signified is based on analogies and resemblances; and in such a system language merges with the world in that things in the world can function as signs just as readily as linguistic entities do. Languages and the world form a single interwoven semeiotic fabric. It is clear from the preceding sections that this orientation can be found prior to the sixteenth century.

The orientation, which replaces the "system of signs," treats language (in Foucault's terminology) as a "system of representations." The relationship between a representation and what it represents is not based on similarity or analogy; the basis may be conventional or natural (in that one of two things causally related may represent the other). The qualities and associations of a representative do not contribute to determining what it represents; it has to be treated as transparent, read "literally." Its meaning is to be found entirely in what it represents so that there has to be a prominent division between representations and what they represent; a thing represented is not assumed to be itself a representation of something. (Obviously this use of "signs" and "representations" gives distinct technical meanings to two words which commonly function as near synonyms.)

In the present context the use of "representation" connects to the use of that word in the previous chapter (3.6). This is because, although Foucault does not do so, the development of the second orientation toward language needs to be considered in the light of the trend to rest cognitive authority on the ideas of individual conscious subjects and also in relation to the view of the world and events as contingently connected to one another to a radical extent (chapter 3.7). Ideas are treated by seventeenth century thinkers as constituents of a form of inner discourse, a language which everyone must translate into a publicly accessible form in order to communicate (cp. Hobbes,

Leviathan 1.4, "the general use of speech, is to transfer our mental discourse, into verbal..."). That this "inner discourse" is treated as taking precedence over public discourse, contributes in important ways to the conception of representation both in the seventeenth and in subsequent centuries.

To the extent, moreover, that objects and events in the physical world came to be thought of as only contingently related to one another, such things lost the capacity to function as representations (i.e., natural signs) of one another. Rational connections were reduced to respects in which the things to which one representation applied were included in, overlapped with, or were distinct from those to which another applied. A bare tree of Porphyry, stripped of any leaves of similitude, could serve to represent the order of things. One thing (object or event) could only be a representation of another through the mediation of an idea. Ideas thereby became the primary medium of representation; the natural world lost its independent capacity to represent. Even after ideas came to be abandoned as the primary medium of representation and it was accepted that such a medium must be public if communication is to be possible, language remained withdrawn from the world.

The transition in people's orientation from "system of signs" to "system of representations" is not, as Foucault suggests, discontinuous. Bacon bears witness to the possibility of being at home in a system of signs and nevertheless urging that certain parts of public discourse (those in which science will be recorded and communicated) be purged of features identified above as proper to a system of signs. By treating as a source of error the ambiguity (based on a network of similarities and analogies) present in the word "humid," Bacon flatly rejects the claims of those rival conceptions of natural philosophy which involved an esoteric, non-literal reading of the book of nature. And while religious trends and the political context may have provided precedents and motives for insisting on literal uses of language in natural philosophy, Bacon's demand is also intrinsically related to his reconception of the kind of knowledge which is the goal of natural philosophy. Practically useful knowledge, Bacon saw, must be written in a language which is unambiguous so that people will be able to apply successful procedures or repeat experiments performed by others.

Precedents for ways of communicating such knowledge already existed in books such as Georgius Agricola's *De Re Metallica*. Print technology had made it possible to produce texts with standardized wood block diagrams labelled in such a way as to make it quite clear what procedure or part of a machine an author was talking about. The same sorts of conventions came to be employed in the recording and writing up of experiments – Hales' *Vegetable Statiks* is an excellent example from early in the eighteenth century.

In this Bacon was surely correct. But the strictures inherent in labelling all ambiguity a source of error means that he, and those who followed his lead, rejected the use of analogies and metaphors in the expression of scientific knowledge. It is less clear that we should agree with this. At the level of the language of science the issue is whether words have univocal, literal meanings or whether they signify via a network which makes possible the use of metaphors, analogies and symbols. At the level of knowledge the issue is whether scientific knowledge can be expressed without resort to metaphors, analogies or symbols or whether (to put it in the jargon of twentieth century discussions) metaphors have cognitive content. At the level of metaphysics the issue is whether the world about which we talk and of which we seek knowledge is a multiplicity of independent particular objects, or whether it contains structured wholes, the multiple interrelated parts of which are such that the identity of each is dependent on its relations to all the other parts.

One of the reasons we might have misgivings about a wholesale rejection of the style of reasoning and associated framework that goes with analogies is that an integral part of Bacon's excision of this from natural philosophy is his rejection of the idea that mathematics can be used to construct theories which yield knowledge of nature. This is a move for which he has been heavily criticized – he failed to see one of the important aspects of what was to be modern science, that it would be mathematical science. Yet, as we have seen, tradition assimilated analogies to mathematical ratios and amongst Bacon's immediate predecessors there were figures such as John Dee who sought to make mathematics an integral part of their hermetic, natural magic. Even when the magical hermetic element is excised, as it is from Newton's *Principia* (if not from all of his natural philosophy), there remains a tension between the use of mathematics at the theoretical level and the conception that the language of science should be literal and wholly unambiguous. Leibniz and Kant both struggled with this tension, and it is an issue to which we shall return toward the end of the chapter.

Bacon's method of induction was designed to correct for the errors likely to be introduced through the use of language by insisting on the detailed and precise public recording of observations and experiments, where the language used is directly anchored in the phenomena described. His inductive procedures are in part designed to detect and correct ambiguities. By recording the things to which a term such as "humid" is applied, we may well conclude that this collection is too heterogeneous to form the locus of any investigation and that a more discriminative terminology should be introduced. Bacon, the public figure, thus envisioned the establishment of new institutional networks and new public authority structures as a means of establishing and maintaining a language which would be adequately tied to experience and sufficiently precise for use in the communication of natural philosophy, or as we would say, "scientific knowledge." When the Royal Society of London was established 34 years after his death it was entirely appropriate that Bacon should be enshrined as the Society's *"artium instaurator."*

Bacon's concern that language should aid rather than obstruct the pursuit of knowledge was a theme to which philosophers frequently returned during the century which followed his death. Thus, for example, we find Locke commenting:

> By their [sc. words'] *civil use*, I mean such a communication of thoughts and ideas by words as may serve for the upholding common conversation and commerce, about the ordinary affairs and conveniences of civil life... By the *philosophical use* of words, I mean such a use of them as may serve to convey the precise notions of things, and to express in general propositions certain and undoubted truths, which the mind may rest upon and be satisfied within its search after true knowledge. These two uses are very distinct; and a great deal less exactness will serve in the one than in the other... (*Essay* III IX 3)

It is during the seventeenth century that the project of developing a language adequate for science emerges. Amongst those who urged the cause of a new broadly mechanistic natural philosophy (from the authors of the Port Royal Logic through Locke, Leibniz and Comenius to Condillac in the eighteenth century) there was a general consciousness that their project required, as a condition of its success, wide-ranging reform of the classificatory terminology used to express knowledge of the natural world. Existing terminology could not be used to express the new knowledge; it had either grown up in a haphazard way, or incorporated a world view based on the four elements (Earth, Air, Fire and Water), astrology and a reading of the world's signs through relations of similitude. New precise terminology was required, terminology which revealed rather than obscured, which distinguished rather than confused. Nature would have to be observed closely for objective differences in which to anchor nomenclature; the differences when found were to be located in carefully constructed taxonomic trees. Out of the movement to reform language arose the taxonomies of Linnaeus and Cuvier.

In important respects, however, the strategies adopted by Bacon's successors to overthrow the Idols of the Market Place were not Baconian. Where Bacon clearly expected to rely on instruments of public authority in his campaign against idolatry, his successors looked to the authority of individual independent minds seeking personal epistemic salvation. The parallel between the moves made in respect of religious and scientific knowledge did not go unremarked. Thus Locke took a firmly Protestant stance: "The Romanists say it is best for men, and so suitable for the goodness of God, that there should be an infallible judge of controversies on earth; and therefore there is one. And I, by the same reason, say it is better for men that every man himself should be infallible" (*Essay* IV 12). Descartes put the epistemic point in terms drawn from the moral psychology of St Augustine:

> "It is a supreme perfection in man to act voluntarily or freely, and thus to be in a special sense the author of his own actions, and to deserve praise for them. We do not praise automata for precisely carrying out all the movements for which they were designed, since they carry them out by necessity; we rather praise the maker for fashioning such precise machines, because he fashioned them not by necessity, but freely. Similarly, it is more to our credit that we embrace the truth when we do, because we do this freely, than it would be if we could not but embrace it." (Haldane and Ross, 1955, I 233-4)

As these passages illustrate, the possibility of acquiring scientific knowledge was not sharply separated from issues of religious freedom and moral responsibility.

Locke also insisted that useful knowledge had to be appropriated by individuals; it could not be second hand.

> Perhaps we should make greater progress in the discovery of rational and contemplative knowledge, if we sought it in the fountain, in the consideration of things themselves, and made use rather of our own thoughts than other men's to find it. For I think we may as rationally hope to see with other men's eyes as to know by other men's understandings. So much as we ourselves consider and comprehend truth and reason, so much we possess of real and true knowledge. The floating of other men's opinions in our brains makes us not one jot the

more knowing, though they happen to be true. What in them is science is in us but opiniatry... such borrowed wealth, like fairy money, though it were gold in the hand from which he received it, will be but leaves and dust when it comes to us. (*Essay* I IV 24)

This echoes in many ways Plato's distinction between *epistêmê* and *doxa*, and it is the grasp of "ideas" which, verbally at least, makes the difference both for Plato and for Locke. But for Locke and many of his contemporaries the possession of ideas was not the possession of standards which functioned as explanatory principles, but of experience in which to anchor the words which convey the understanding.

In the seventeenth century ideas seemed to offer a resource for resisting both the tyranny of language and the external authority of those who claimed superior linguistic mastery. They were deployed to deflect and negate the claims of specific forms of philosophical discourse by insisting that words can have meaning for people only when they stand for ideas which they have. Words without associated ideas are as lacking in significance as the phrases uttered by a parrot (Locke, *Essay* III II 7). The mere ability to utter "Pretty Polly" or "Hello sailor" is not a mark of knowledge of any kind. The ability to discourse "learnedly," using terms such as "*suppositio,*" "*essentia,*" or "*substantia*" is similarly no automatic mark of knowledge. Ideas thus became crucial weapons in the skeptical disestablishment of knowledge claims; where there are no ideas, there can be no knowledge, only empty word play. Ideas were weapons whose use simultaneously circumscribed the domain of the humanly knowable.

The term and the use to which it was put to was by no means universally applauded. Section III II of Yolton (1956) cites a number of Locke's contemporaries who resisted the term because they feared that it led to pernicious skepticism or simply because it was not well understood. For example, John Sergeant (quoted on pp. 90-1 of Yolton, 1956):

> In a word, since *Ideas* are both *Unintelligible*, and altogether *Useless*, & (I fear) *ill Use* is made of them, contrary to the Intention of their Authors; it seems but fitting that the *Way of Ideas* should be *lay'd aside*; nay, that the very *Word* which has got such a *Vogue*, should be no longer heard of, unless a good reason may be given why we should use *such Words as no Man understands*. (Preface to *Transnatural Philosophy*, 1700)

The term "idea" indeed did not have a fixed descriptive meaning (signification) on which all (of what Sergeant called) "Ideists" agreed.

This did not prevent the term from playing a legitimating rôle in the language in which debates about knowledge were conducted. To dispute, as Berkeley did (*Principles*, Introduction 6–22) for example, the claim that there are any such things as abstract general ideas (of which the idea of matter was Berkeley's principal target (ibid., I 17, 81, 99)) is to dismiss as illegitimate claims to have knowledge founded on such ideas (in the case of matter, this would be knowledge of basic laws of mechanics).

But the appeal to ideas was not wholly skeptical, for the very term "idea" (as opposed to "idol") traditionally carried the loading "true image;" ideas give some sort of knowledge (truth) about something. To establish the scope and limits of (individual) human knowledge is, within the framework of the way of ideas, to investigate the extent of the domain of ideas, their possible source and their cognitive credentials. But how did ideas, located in the minds of individuals, come to be able to play this legitimating role? One way to answer this question is by tracing some of the moves by which ideas mediate the transition from the conception of language as part of a wider sign system to a representational conception of language and knowledge. Ideas effect this mediation by making possible a sharp distinction between linguistic and non-linguistic signs.

5 Natural Representations

Roots of the conception of a system of representations can be found in early fourteenth century nominalism. William of Ockham's nominalism influenced Locke's philosophy in a number of important respects and his doctrine of "signs" shows he thought them to be in important respects like a system of representations. Moreover, it shares the most significant and problematic feature of the representational thinking found in "the way of ideas" in that it locates the primary (and natural) system of representation "in the mind (soul)." Ockham, however, uses several terms ("concepts or intentions of the soul," "impressions of the soul") where Locke uses "ideas."

> I say that spoken words are signs subordinated to concepts or intentions of the soul not because in the strict sense of "signify" they always signify the concepts of the soul primarily and properly. The point is rather that spoken words are used to signify the very things that are signified by concepts of the mind, so that a concept primarily and naturally signifies something and a spoken word signifies that same thing secondarily... In

Language and Representation 149

general, whenever writers say that all spoken words signify or serve as signs of impressions, they only mean that spoken words secondarily signify the things [which] impressions of the soul primarily signify. (*Summa Logicae* 1.1)

Locke similarly uses the terminology of primary and secondary signification. "Words in their primary or immediate signification, stand for nothing but the ideas in the mind of him that uses them" (*Essay* III II 2). But they have a secondary signification which is to the things outside the mind that the ideas signify.

Although Ockham, like Locke, still uses the word "sign," by virtue of giving a privileged position to those signs which are concepts or intentions of the soul, he has moved toward treating these signs as (what Foucault would call) representations. In a system of signs anything can function as a sign, so that interpretative thought may move indefinitely along a chain of interpretants, never leaving the system, but also never failing to find some signification. By contrast, in a system of representations, interpretation involves moving from a representation to a determinate referent which is regarded as lying outside the system of representations, just as we move from a picture to what it is a picture of, where the latter is not usually another picture.

In a system of representations the important questions are about how a representation points (or refers) outside the system and about whether there really exists any such external referent. Just as pictures can depict mythical, fictional or even impossible things, so it is with other forms of representation: the existence of the representation does not guarantee the existence of what is purportedly represented, because the latter is presumed to lie outside the system of representations. (Indeed nominalism is the denial that there are objective realities corresponding to general terms.) Ockham's concepts or impressions of the soul constitute a separate subsystem of the realm of signs, whose function is to signify things lying outside their own subsystem (outside the soul). It is in this way that he laid the groundwork for Locke, Descartes and other seventeenth century philosophers to introduce a more explicitly representational conception of knowledge and language – one grounded in ideas, where ideas are treated as the constituents of an internal language.

But how did concepts or impressions of the soul come to be able to carry the sort of cognitive authority which is implicit in the shift to calling them ideas? Why suppose that there is any connection at all between these impressions and the truth of things? Why are words empty unless their use is informed by the ideas "that men have in their minds"? The answer is suggested by Ockham. "The concept or impression of the soul signifies naturally; whereas the spoken or written term signifies only conventionally... We can decide to alter the signification of a spoken or written term, but no decision or agreement on the part of anyone can have the effect of altering the signification of a conceptual term" (*Summa Logicae* 1.1). Ideas are *natural* signs. They are the mind's natural responses to external stimuli.

If we compare a linguistic sign to a natural sign we can see the force of Ockham's point. In the case of a natural sign we can allow our thoughts to move directly from the sign to what it signifies, from thunder to an impending storm, from a sneeze to something irritating the nasal passage. But in the case of a linguistic sign we cannot automatically move from the sign to the thing signified; we have to take into account what we know about the person who produced the sign. If we hear the sound "wren" (ren) we have to know whether it was spoken in English or Chinese; if we read the word "rot" we have to know whether it is written in German or in English. Even when we are confident that we know to what portions of the world a person would apply a certain word, we have to take into account the beliefs which that person holds about those portions of the world. Aristotle would have applied the word "*hudor*" to pretty much those portions of the world to which we would apply the word "water," but would have looked on those portions as basic material stuff (a simple body), where we look on water as a compound stuff. It is natural for us now to say that Aristotle's idea of water differed from ours, and that the same combination of Roman letters conjures up the idea of a color in a German speaker and the idea of a degenerate condition in an English speaker. There is thus clearly a need to find some way of expressing this personal grounding of the use of words. For Ockham conceptions or impressions of the soul perform this function, and for seventeenth century philosophers ideas performed the same role.

The additional assumption, which Ockham shares with many seventeenth century philosophers, is that human beings all have a common nature; that is, basically similar physical and intellectual capacities, so that people from different cultures will form the same idea when confronted with the same physical object. In other words, although they might not share the same language and so would use different words to signify that one object, they can do so and can mean the same thing by their words because they have the same idea. Ideas thus have a greater stability than words. The basic ideas which we get from experience are a direct and natural response to stimuli we receive from the physical world. They can thus serve as a reliable basis for knowledge of that world. This could not be said of all ideas, since some result from putting together simpler ideas into complexes which we have never experienced and to which there may be no corresponding existing thing (such as a mountain made of gold or a winged horse). Thus simple ideas, those received directly from sensory experience, came to occupy a privileged epistemic position for empiricist philosophers. Locke stresses their reliability in much the same terms as Ockham. He says that simple ideas,

> ...must necessarily be the product of things operating on the mind in a natural way and producing therein therein those perceptions which by the wisdom and will of our Maker they are ordained and adopted to. From whence it follows that *simple* ideas *are not fictions* or our fancies, but the natural and regular productions of things without us. (*Essay* IV IV 4)

Because they are linked in this way to a universal, God-given human nature, ideas, especially simple ideas, cannot in themselves be false, be sources of error.

This is a form of naturalism, one which is buttressed by theology. In a similar way Descartes' epistemology also relies on the goodness of God. The Christian God, it was assumed, is a benevolent creator who would not have created people with faculties which systematically mislead and deceive them. He gave human beings intellectual and perceptual faculties so that they would be capable of acquiring knowledge. The difference between a rationalist philosopher, such as Descartes, and an empiricist philosopher, such as Locke, is that Descartes presumes that as rational beings we have another, intellectual source of simple ideas (ideas which are not derived from experience). These too are to be relied on because they are part of our created nature and indeed they provide the categories in terms of which we should seek an understanding of the natural world. Ideas drawn from experience cannot provide an adequate vehicle for an intellectual, mathematical understanding of the world. Empiricists and rationalists share the view that it is only because of their own willful misuse of their God-given faculties, or because of their slothful failure to develop them, that people fall into error.

In short, what is natural is God-given and thus a source of knowledge. Within this framework the task of epistemology is to reveal the natural workings of the human mind, i.e., (1) to describe how the human mind works when it is functioning in the way that, by its nature, it *should* function; (2) to suggest and justify methods for training the mind into, or restoring it to, this proper (natural) way of working; and (3) on the basis of (1) and (2) to discern the scope and limits of human understanding. Once this has been done the links to language are conceived as being very simple. Words stand for ideas and a word can be meaningful only when there is an idea for which it stands. A word has a precise meaning only if it stands for a clear and distinct, or determinate idea; i.e., one which is such that we can perceive its internal structure and are clear about how it is made up of simple ideas, if it is not itself simple. The possession of scientific knowledge depends on acquiring ideas which are determinate in this way.

Thus, hand in hand with the conception of language as acquiring its meaning by relation to a system of mental representations went a technique for organizing what we know by painstakingly mapping the differences between things. The net result is an insistence on the kind of precision that Bacon had required for the language of science, but the theoretical grounding of this is very much more individualistic than Bacon envisioned. This individualism in the conception of knowledge and of its grounding in ideas was to prove problematic, for science is not an individual enterprise. Scientific knowledge is not the knowledge of a single individual, but is essentially shared, public knowledge.

6 Losing the Way (of Ideas)

Epistemological naturalism, based on ideas as natural signs and on the general reliability of our God-given faculties (when correctly used), was exposed to pressures which by the end of the nineteenth century sufficed wholly to undermine it. These pressures arose, in large measure, from the success of the natural philosophy, which "the way of ideas" had sought to promote, and of efforts to disentangle the study of nature from theological issues and from the authority of Aristotle. The rise of the new natural philosophy was accompanied by (and contributed to) a decline in the way religious concerns dominated all aspects of intellectual discourse. Ultimately this eliminated recourse to theology as a source of legitimation for knowledge claims and altered the concept of nature to such an extent that this kind of naturalism became incapable of justifying either scientific practices or their social organization.

Epistemological inquiries conducted under the assumptions dictated by the notion of representation, together with the recognition of the achievements of Newton, worked to displace the Aristotelian concept of nature (the conception under which each kind of thing has a nature) from Nature (the unitary system which is the created physical universe). Locke illustrates this phenomenon well. For all his insistence on needing to have our own ideas, he recognized that in natural philosophy the aim is to bring our ideas into line with the "truth of things."

> ...our names of substances being not put barely for our *ideas*, but being made use of ultimately to represent things... their signification must agree with the truth of things as well as with men's *ideas*. And therefore in substances, we are not always to rest in the ordinary complex *idea* commonly received as the signification of that word. (*Essay* III XI 24)

However, in the case of ideas of substances, natural kinds such as gold, there were difficulties.

Locke's conception of what would be required to bring our idea of gold into agreement with the truth of things is situated in a general framework which is still broadly Aristotelian (see chapter 2.5.). On this account, to know the "truth" ("real nature" or "real essence") of something such as gold would be to be able to give an account of what it is to be a thing of that kind, an account on the basis of which one would be able to explain its possession of a whole range of other properties. Among the properties to be explained would be those sensible properties by which gold was originally identified (yellow, fusible, ductile, soluble only in *aqua regia*...) and which constitute our complex idea of it. It is this complex idea which governs our use of the name "gold" in the absence of a grasp of the real essence of gold; Locke referred to this idea as the "nominal essence" of gold.

Locke believed that we can in some cases bring our ideas into conformity with the truth of things, because at least in the case of geometry we have achieved this kind of knowledge. We can say what a triangle is in such a way that we are able to explain why triangles must have the properties which they are observed to have (*Essay* III III 18), for example, interior angles which add up to two right angles. However, on Locke's account, geometrical knowledge of this kind is possible just because there is no distinction between real and nominal essence. Triangles just are what we define them to be. There is no independently existing natural kind to which our geometrical terms have to answer. But in the case of material substances, such as gold, where real and nominal essence do not coincide, achievement of this kind of knowledge appears to Locke to be highly problematic. The problem is to frame an account of what a substance such as gold is (to determine its real essence in a way) which will allow us to explain rigorously why it has the observable properties which it has and by which we identify it (the properties whose ideas together make up the nominal essence of gold) (Ibid., IV IV 9).

Here there are two difficulties. The first is that ideas are supposed, by Locke, to be mental effects of the mechanical action of material objects on our sense organs, and because, in general, the same mechanical effect can be produced in several ways, there is no reason to suppose that every time we see the yellow of gold, the same material organization of particles is responsible for producing it. But secondly, even without this problem, experience can afford us no concepts which would equip us to give any explanation of how a mechanical action can be the cause of an idea, so we could never demonstrate the connection between an idea of gold-yellow and a material organization of particles (even if we had "microscopical eyes" and could see the latter). As a consequence there is no account we could ever give which would allow us to understand why, when certain external objects exert causal influences on our minds, we form the ideas of certain colors, tastes, or sounds (Ibid., IV III 13).

Locke was keenly aware of this last difficulty, for it seems to stand in the way of our ever providing a satisfactory account of how it is that external objects produce in us the effects which they do. The difficulty may be traced to the respects in which Locke accepts from Descartes an account of human (mental) nature, which places it outside Nature, the material world governed by the laws of mechanics. Locke's conclusion amounts to a retreat from the Aristotelian aspiration to understand by grasping the essences of things: even if we cannot discover why the properties found in gold all have to coexist, we can rely on experience to teach us what reason cannot disclose (Ibid., IV XII 9) and thereby attain such knowledge of things as we actually need (Ibid., IV XI 8).

These considerations reinforce Locke's (nominalist) claim that general terms are all fictions of the mind (Ibid., III III 11). There is no account to be given of what unifies the diverse features that make up our complex general idea of something like gold, because that unity is entirely our invention, a creature made for our own use. But this doctrine tends to undermine the concept that kinds of things have natures independently of the way we associate ideas, and the erosion of this concept was continued by the force of Hume's treatment of the notion of necessary connection. Our experience gives us no basis for saying that certain combinations of impressions must occur together and other combinations are impossible. This argument arose from Hume's working out the consequences of treating statements of law within a framework of descriptive representations, where they can function only to represent the totality of what does happen, not what must happen or cannot happen. This in effect removes the possibility of any quality or event functioning as a natural sign of any other. "Natures" express our belief that certain properties naturally go together, but it follows from Hume's doctrines that we can attach no meaning to "the nature of [e.g.] gold" beyond the idea we currently have of a bundle of properties; and nothing in such a bundle can serve as a basis for explaining or predicting how it *must* be constituted.

If, moreover, "nature" can be no more than the idea we have of a thing (constituting a Lockean "nominal essence"), an idea fabricated by us for our own use, and if appeal to natures cannot in any case be used to explain the behavior of things, what must be said of human nature? How is it now possible to engage in foundational epistemology which initially rested its account of the scope and limits of human knowledge on presumptions about a shared human nature? If humans are a part of Nature, then it would seem that such a study could only be empirical, and should be looking for "laws of thought" – laws governing the working of the human mind. Thus Hume, self-consciously modelling his procedure on Newton's, proposed that laws of association between ideas could serve as the first principles from which to derive an account of the scope and limits of human understanding.

"Laws of association of ideas" however must be like any other "laws of nature," descriptions of some totality of what happens, but not able to represent how possibilities are limited, not able to set anything like "scope and limits." So how could such laws serve as first principles for an account of this kind? Since Hume denied the possibility of substantive *a priori* knowledge, such principles could only themselves be derived from experience and could never provide the kind of *a priori* guarantees required by the project of foundational epistemology to determine once and for all the scope and limits of human understanding. An empirical study could not possibly bear the weight that foundational epistemology would require of it.

A different kind of naturalism has recently attracted interest, one based on the thought that if human beings are the product of biological evolution, then their cognitive capacities and large portions of their beliefs may be underwritten by appeal to natural selection. If our cognitive capacities and crucial portions of our belief system were not reliable, the argument goes, nature would have dealt severely with the human species and it would not have survived. However, those who have explored this form of naturalism, from Dewey (1910, chapter 1) to Quine (1969, chapter 3) and Popper (1973, chapter 7), have in different ways repudiated the foundationalist project.

This strategy, moreover, does not justify the claim that either our beliefs or our theories are correct in any absolute sense; it does not justify the claim that they accurately represent the way things are in themselves. It could at best justify the claim that our faculties are adequate to provide us with ways of representing the world to ourselves which serve as broadly reliable instruments for coping with threats posed by our physical environment. There might well be more than one way of achieving this. Different people(s) facing different evironmental hazards might very well represent their world in different ways; instrumental adequacy relative to conditions for survival is all that can be underwritten by this type of account.

For foundationalists and others committed to the possibility of absolute representations, naturalism might well be an ill-advised strategy; perhaps humans are not a part of nature. Hume, after all, was vexed to find himself unable to locate the human subject within experience (which for him functioned as nature). His arguments carried him much further than did Locke's: we would seem to have no more right to the idea of the real essence of our selves than we do to the real essence of gold, but it is not even clear what could be the nominal essences of ourselves. Hume insisted that he had no idea of his self; he had only a contingently related series of impressions and ideas, and in that nothing which could be identified as his self. There is no idea, and hence no possibility of knowledge, of any being of which this series constitutes the experiences. If humans, at least in regard to their cognitive capacities, are not to be counted part of Nature, then a separate account must be given of how we have knowledge of our own cognitive capacities and of our relation to Nature. This was the route that was followed by Kant and later by Husserl.

By the end of the nineteenth century the concept of human nature had atrophied to the point where it was difficult to claim that any, even empirical, ideas had the status of natural signs. As a condition of performing their foundational epistemological rôle, ideas had been supposed to be immediately present to the consciousness of the person having the idea. The price to be paid for this immediacy was that an idea was then firmly locked in the mind of the person having it; no other person could have that same idea and so no other person could have any direct knowledge of that idea. Another person's ideas are not possible objects of my experience. This creates problems for the account of language which supposes that words have meaning by standing for ideas. So long as a common human nature could be assumed, it could with some justice be assumed that in the presence of the same physical stimulus two people would form the same, or closely similar, ideas. Likewise, a common nature meant common rational faculties and hence the same rational order of ideas and the same basic rational concepts. Common experience of a physical world would thus serve to ensure that people made sufficiently similar word-idea association to be able to communicate.

But as the common grounding in human nature weakened, the theory that language functions by having words stand for ideas became increasingly implausible. It could no longer serve as a basis for explaining how we manage to use it as a vehicle for communication, especially for the communication of objective, scientific knowledge about the natural world. With the professionalization of science its essentially public, institutional character was also becoming more apparent. The process of scientific discovery was less and less frequently an individual affair and the ratification of claimed discoveries was increasingly done through systematically organized forms of peer review. To attain the status of scientific knowledge a discovery had to have withstood public scrutiny. This status could not be conferred on the basis of any single individual's intellectual effort or understanding.

Thus by the end of the nineteenth century we find the attention of epistemology turning away from discovery and away from the basis of knowledge in the individual, toward justification and the public processes of argument, criticism and experimental testing which determines whether a claim is allowed or not allowed to stand as a certified piece of scientific knowledge. Language, as the vehicle within which this process is conducted and the knowledge recorded, has to be able to function publicly and an account of linguistic meaning thus has to be an account which explains how this public function is performed.

So, for example, we find Frege and certain of the logical positivists inveighing against the appeal to ideas as "psychologism;" the thought that some ideas might be natural signs had so little credibility that it was hardly mentioned. Frege's concern was with language as a vehicle for the expression of objective public knowledge, something which is inter-subjectively shared. He argued (1964, p. 17) that if the meaning of a sentence depended on ideas then it would be impossible for one person to know that another has the same thought in mind when debating the truth or falsity of "the Moon orbits the Earth." One person's thought might be quite different from the other's even though they are using the same words, since they might have associated different ideas with these words. Since neither can "see" what ideas the other has, they have no way to be sure that they mean the same things by their words. Thus if words stand for ideas, and their meanings are given, for each person, by the ideas for which they stand, communication of the precise form required in science and mathematics would be impossible. If objective knowledge is to be possible, if there can be public, shared knowledge, another account must be given of the meaning of linguistic expressions.

7 Ideal Languages and the Linguistic Turn

Early in this century epistemology moved away from ideas toward language; that is, interest turned away from attempting to secure knowledge of the natural world in individuals toward the logical and linguistic structure of public justification. This shift has been called "the linguistic turn." With this turn logic and language take theoretical precedence over thought and ideas. It is language and the expressive power of systems of linguistic representation that set the bounds on what we can think (and consequently know), and it is the aim of the philosophy of language to discern these bounds through an account of how language can function as a representational system.

With this renewed focus on language there was a revival of the project of constructing an ideal language for science – not one backed by determinate ideas – but one in which all names refer to genuinely existing objects and in which all general terms have a completely precise meaning, a meaning that would determine for any object whether the term does or does not apply to it. Thus Frege (1964, p. 90) claimed to have set out a system of logical notation which was adequate for expressing arithmetic, and in which it was impossible to construct a grammatically correct name which lacked a referent or a term which was ambiguous. The core conception of Frege's approach to language and logic, the core which was taken over by Wittgenstein in his *Tractatus*, by Russell and by the logical positivists, is as follows: If language is a vehicle for representing the world, then the linguistic unit to which one should look first, in giving an account of meaning, is the sentence, not the word. A factual descriptive sentence is either true or false depending on how the world is. Its truth or falsity is a matter of the relation between a linguistic item (a sentence) and the world. This relation holds or fails to hold independently of whether any person thinks or knows that it does. The truth-conditions of a sentence are the conditions which must pertain in the world if the sentence is to be true. Knowing the meaning of a sentence, knowing what it says about the world, can thus be equated with knowing its truth-conditions. To know the meaning of a word or expression is to know how it contributes to determining the truth conditions of sentences in which it occurs. Logical relations between sentences hold in virtue of relations between their truth-conditions.

Frege's work, transformed in crucial ways by Russell and Wittgenstein, was taken by Carnap and other members of the Vienna Circle to have provided the basic framework for an account of the meaning of linguistic expressions which could serve as a basis (empirical foundation) for an account of objective, public knowledge and its possible justifications. They saw that it would be relatively easy to adapt the key empiricist tenet, that all knowledge is rooted in experience, to this framework. Instead of having simple ideas derived from sense perception forming the basis of all knowledge, we have atomic sentences, i.e., the simplest possible sentences, expressing uninterpreted observations – the recording of measurements (thermometer reading 52 degrees centigrade at time, t, at place, s) or mere reports of what is given in sense experience, i.e., sense data reports (red column now next to mark "52"). Even if people perceive red differently, they can agree about when a column reaches a particular mark. The relation between column and mark is all that is significant for the truth conditions of the sentence. The sensed qualities which were taken to constitute ideas derived from sensory experience, do not form part of the objective, scientific meaning of empirically descriptive sentences (see Carnap, *Logical Structure*, section 16). Objective communication concerns the relations between publicly observable items.

Instead of looking to natural functions of the human intellect to discern what rational processes were available for building knowledge from this base, the logical positivists looked to what they believed to be the inherent logic of language conceived as a system of representations. Each atomic sentence is a basic unit which is either true or false (either representing the world correctly or not). Just as simple ideas had been assumed by Locke and Hume to be distinct and independent, it was assumed that the truth values of atomic sentences are mutually independent, so that knowing that one such sentence takes the value "True" or the value "False" tells you nothing about the truth value of any other such sentence; there are no logical relations between them, which are inherent in what they mean. These units can be combined to form more complex sentences using logical connectives, conjunction, disjunction, negation and conditional, which have roughly the meanings of "and," "or," "not," "if... then." These connectives are interpreted as truth functions, that is, as being such that if the truth value of the complex sentence is uniquely determined by the truth values of the component sentence.

The operators (known as "quantifiers") "all" and "some" were treated as infinite conjunctions and disjunctions respectively and thus reduced to truth functions. So "All men are mortal" would be treated as "Frege is mortal and Russell is mortal and...," where the conjunction of sentences would somewhere mention every human being. This formal logic, known as "extensional first order logic," was conceived as providing a kind of grammatical packaging for empirical content, all of which entered via the atomic sentences of the ideal scientific language. The grammatical packaging transmits content without altering it in any way, so that in principle it should be possible to trace the precise empirical content of a complex sentence by unravelling its logical grammar, or displaying its logical form. (This is nicely summed up in a slogan, which was coined by Quine, "Logic chases truth up the tree of grammar," Quine, 1970, p. 35.)

In this way epistemological problems are essentially turned into logical problems. These are of two kinds: (1) how to specify the logical form (and hence reveal the empirical content) of the various kinds of non-observation sentences used in science; (2) how to characterize and justify scientific reasoning which needs to draw theoretical conclusions from empirical data. This second is a problem because deductive logic will not license the move from any finite number of instances of the form "a is a swan and is white, b is a swan and is white..." to "All swans are white" (the conjunction of all those instances). For some the appropriate response to this problem was to develop a logic of induction. For others, such as Popper, the appropriate response was to articulate "the logic of scientific discovery" as a process of deductive falsification rather than inductive verification. The former aspired to provide a rational justification for accepting some scientific generalizations; Popper gave up this aspiration and urged us to think of science as consisting of vulnerable generalizations which have nevertheless survived attempts to falsify them (Popper, 1973, chapter 1). In either case the linguistic turn moves epistemology away from the psychology of the subject. It becomes the study of the relation between language and the world – "epistemology without a knowing subject," as Popper put it (Popper, 1973, chapter 3).

Some of the considerations which were later to be pressed against this project, were being canvassed even before it acquired much support. Frege's contemporary Duhem had already argued that scientific theories do not confront experiment one sentence or one law at a time (Duhem, 1962, VI.2). No such direct confrontation is possible. It is not individual sentences but theories as wholes which are used to derive testable predictions. If predictions are not verified, there is nothing in formal logic that will lay the blame on any one theoretical principle. One principle out of the total theoretical package has to be altered, but an empirical result contrary to what the theory predicts will not say which has to be altered. Thus, to take a common example, when the astronomer Roemer failed to obtain an observation predicted on the basis of Newton's celestial mechanics, this called into question a large theoretical complex which included the assumption that light takes no time to reach us from its source, as well as the fundamental laws proposed by Newton. Duhem's argument thus suggests that sentences are not the relevant unit of linguistic meaning for considering how scientific theories relate to empirical data; it should be whole theories.

Quine (1969, chapter 2) put Duhem's point together with mathematically proved results about theories written within extensional first order logic and argued that the attempt to ensure precise literal meaning within this kind of logically structured language undermines itself. The crucial question for any system of representations is, to what do its terms refer? But a formal logically structured representational system cannot, on its own, fix the reference of its terms. The system does not include information on how it is to be interpreted, and Tarski had proved that it could not do so without losing that characteristic deemed essential to any language suitable for the expression of scientific knowledge, viz. consistency. The upshot was that the problem of communication would not be solved by taking this linguistic turn.

One of the ways Quine presented his arguments (1960, chapter 2) was to examine (theoretically) the situation of someone who had to translate the speech of a community which had never before been translated into another language, the situation of "radical translation." From the difficulties this person was supposed to encounter (the difficulties are known as "the indeterminacy of translation" and "the inscrutability of reference"), Quine argued that we can never be sure that other speakers interpret sentences in the same way that we do. Quine did not, however, draw the skeptical conclusion that we cannot know the meanings of other people's sentences. Instead, he urged that since no evidence could settle the question it is a question which cannot sensibly be raised. Sentences do not have meanings, the notion of meaning should be discarded. There are just sentences which people have dispositions to assert or deny in specific situations, and communication is based on the systematic ability to anticipate those dispositions.

Quine's argument here was mounted from the standpoint of one who is external to a linguistic community, who observes the linguistic behavior of those in it and tries to construct an interpretation of their language on the basis of observations. Similar conclusions about the inadequacy of an ideal language conceived as a system of representations could be drawn from the work of Wittgenstein after he became convinced that the *Tractatus* (in which language is treated strictly within the framework of extensional, first order logic) did not offer an adequate account. One of the respects in which it fails to represent the way language actually works is in its assumption that there are atomic sentences which are logically independent of one another. Wittgenstein noted that even such simple observation statements as "This spot is red" do not qualify as atomic because they are not logically independent of other atomic sentences. To say that something is red is also to say that it is not blue, green or any other color than red. It is also to say that it is colored. To understand the use of the descriptive predicate "red" we must also already understand the use of other color words and also have some grasp of the concept of color, as opposed to shape.

This means that when we use even the simplest descriptive language we are already imposing conceptual structures, ordering and classifying, and to that extent interpreting what we see. The point is substantially Kant's argument (about the way in which experience is a result of the imposition of categories and concepts) transposed from the framework of mental representations to that of linguistic representations. This seriously undermines the hope of the logical empiricists to identify a secure, theory-neutral foundation for scientific knowledge within a purely descriptive language for recording scientific observations. There is no such neutral observation language; any description already involves an element of interpretation, or as the point was made in the philosophy of science, "all observations are theory-laden."

The consequences for that philosophy of science were spelled out in detail, albeit in different ways, by Kuhn and Feyerabend. Both argued that if one accepts a scientific theory and takes it and its language seriously as a representation of reality, then as a consequence of that serious participation one will interpret observations in the light of that theory. The very language used to report observation would already incorporate elements of theoretical interpretation simply in virtue of their being regarded as observations of the reality which the theory itself aims to describe. So, for example, to treat a measurement as a measurement of the mass of an object is already to use a theoretical concept in the description of what is experimentally observed, since mass is a concept which cannot be grasped outside the context of a theory of mechanics; it is not a directly measurable magnitude. Likewise our time measurements depend on theoretical connections of one kind or another.

Feyerabend, in his early work, makes the case in terms of the logical model of scientific language. He argues that on this model, since even atomic observation statements will involve theoretical terms and will not be independent of the rest of the theoretical framework, it will be impossible for two rival theories to come into logical conflict with one another. For example, one of the principles of classical mechanics is the principle of conservation of mass. This principle contributes to the meaning of the term "mass" which is a theoretical term whose content cannot be explained outside the context of its theoretical embedding. A theory, such as that of special relativity, which appears to deny this principle will in fact not contain any statement which is the logical negation of the original principle, for the term "mass" will have been given a new meaning by reference to its new theoretical context.

The consequence for science of treating its language as conforming to the framework of first order extensional logic is this: If we represent the world within the constraints of this framework and each sentence is supposed to have a precisely determined representational meaning, fixed by the theoretical framework, then the whole system will be so tightly constrained as to be incapable of change. Any modification to the theory would amount to the adoption of a new language (within that framework). Since rival theories cannot be expressed in the same language the choice between theories can receive no logical representation. For those who accept logic as the basis of scientific rationality, this (the "incommensurability of rival theories") would mean that theory choice can never be a matter of rational argument.

8 An Inadequate Ideal?

Feyerabend's argument can be dismissed as amounting to nothing more than the resurrection of an old sophism, one which argued that if two people disagree about something, e.g. whether Aristotle spoke with a lisp, (whether mass is conserved) they cannot be talking about the same thing because one is talking about a man with a lisp (a quantity that is conserved) and the other talking about a man who does not speak with a lisp (a quantity that is not conserved). But Feyerabend's argument can also be taken as symptomatic of what happens when one applies rigorously the principle that what an expression means consists entirely in the contribution which it makes to the truth or falsity of the sentences of which it is a constituent. This principle is, recall, the basis of this century's attempts to treat language as a system of representations. The lesson of the sophism is that if we treat the meaning of what two people are saying as consisting entirely of corresponding pictures they might draw, they will not draw the same pictures and communication between them will come to seem mysterious. The lesson of Feyerabend's argument may be that if the function of a scientific language is taken to consist entirely in representing (where this function is elucidated in terms of truth conditions) then communication, dispute and reasoned changes in belief will come to seem mysterious.

Wittgenstein's *Tractatus* account was based on what he called a "picture theory of meaning;" and the lesson which he drew, from what he came to perceive as its inadequacies, was that language has multiple functions. The implications of the direction taken in Wittgenstein's *Investigations* were that the representative function cannot by itself sustain communication, does not lie at the basis of the other functions necessary to sustain communication, and that the project of constructing an ideal language based on that function alone would be a wild goose chase.

Kuhn's approach to science was similar in that he called attention to the plurality of discursive practices found in science and in particular to the way certain solutions to problems functioned as paradigms or exemplars of how to proceed scientifically. It must be remembered, however, that the conception of language as a system of representations was part and parcel of a conception of what was required for objective knowledge of the natural world. Any dilution of the representational conception of language thus appears to threaten the concept of objective knowledge to which it was linked. This has been the source of most of the objections to Kuhn's work; he is viewed as undermining the image of scientific knowledge as objective and of science as a rational enterprise. It may be, however, that the conception of language as a system of representations has become an Idol of the Theater, scripted originally to warn us of the Idols which dwell in the Market Place, but now an obstacle to understanding our scientific achievements.

We have seen how modern discussions of language and knowledge are heirs to a tradition of thinking of language primarily as a system of representations. The characteristics of such a system are that there is a class of things represented which are not themselves representations, that a well constructed system distinguishes what is different and has referring expressions only for things which actually exist outside the system of representations. In this account the properties of the representational sign and the images and associations which it stimulates are strictly irrelevant to its function. The representational sign must be treated as transparently presenting what it represents, must read "literally." Figurative language is confined to strictly decorative and rhetorical functions.

There is a clear respect in which an experimental natural science which aims at practically applicable knowledge must make use of language which functions in this way. It needs precise systems of classification in order to ensure unambiguous description of experimental and technological procedures. Nevertheless, the tradition based on the system of signs, which the mechanist philosophers sought to exclude, encouraged ways of thinking about the world which are still part of our science but which the representational conception finds it difficult to recognize. What, in particular, tend to be obscured are efforts which theorists of natural science make to relate phenomena into harmonious wholes. Science does not attempt merely to distinguish and classify but to find patterns which reappear in widely differing circumstances. If one went by the notion that scientific knowledge is no more than a system of linguistic representations one might conclude that these impulses are not part of science. But these impulses and forms of thinking have in fact remained an important part of scientific practice since the time of Bacon, and one could argue that, as mathematics is used more and more widely, they form an ever greater part of science.

Systems of signs were taken to be founded in relations of similitude, which could of course be resemblances that were wholly adventitious and superficial (as in much of the practice which accompanied the doctrine of signatures), but they could also be based upon important measurable invariances. Ratios can exist only between things which have some (measurable) attribute in common. What the notion of harmony encouraged was the search for another structure, another intelligible order, to be discerned beneath the classificatory order of genera and species. It encouraged natural philosophers (or scientists) to look for definitions of terms, to identify things and distinguish one from another in order to discern the underlying structure which they form – the harmoniously unified order of universal principles which underlie the diversity of appearances. Natural philosophers, on this (Platonic) model, should distinguish parts within the whole in order to find out how these are related and so to discern through change and diversity an unchanging unitary structure of relationships, which can be realized in various ways and ultimately be expressed as relations between numbers.

This is the ancient idea that the goal of natural philosophy is to discern the *harmonia mundi* (the harmony of the world). It is found expressed frequently in the sixteenth and seventeenth century figures who were influenced by Renaissance Neoplatonism but who were also important to the development of modern science, including figures such as Kepler and Newton. John Dee, who in 1570 wrote the preface to the first English translation of Euclid's *Elements of Geometry*, for example says, "The entire universe is like a lyre tuned by some excellent artificer, whose strings are the separate species of the universal whole..." (p. 127). Newton, in his *Opticks*, also makes reference to a universal monochord (pp. 126–8, 295, 305). We find a strikingly similar idea expressed by a modern theoretical physicist, talking about string theory:

> "In most of the string theories there is basically one kind of string. You see one kind of string can excite many different kinds of motion. If you think about a violin, a violin string when you play on it can vibrate at many different frequencies, called harmonics... In the case of the violin string the different harmonics correspond to different sounds. In the case of a superstring, the different harmonics correspond to different elementary particles. The electron, the graviton, the photon, the neutrino and all the others, are different harmonics of a fundamental string just as the different overtones of a violin string are different harmonics of one string." (Edward Witten, 1988, pp. 92–3)

The persistence in our scientific culture of the image of strings tuned to a subtle harmony, which it takes the mind of a mathematician to discern, is itself interesting, but by no means the most important manifestation of the aspects of modern science which fail to fit comfortably into the conception of scientific knowledge as embodied in the sentences of a language whose terms are to be read literally. As mentioned above (chapter 3.7), the decline of the notion that we should seek knowledge of individual (specific) natures was accompanied by the rise of a notion, which Bacon championed, that we should seek knowledge of nature's laws of action. Bacon did not encourage natural philosophers to try to express such laws in mathematical terms; he stressed only one of what Whitehead in this century identified as the two main ingredients of the new natural philosophy, a "passionate interest" in measurable details. What was added to this by others, such as Descartes and Newton, was an "equal devotion" to theories articulated mathematically. "It is this union of passionate interest in the detailed facts, with equal devotion to abstract generalisation which forms the novelty of our present society" (Whitehead, 1967, p. 3). Laws expressed in the form of mathematical equations took over from natures the rôle of expressing the first principles by reference to which all events must be explained.

The successes of mathematical physics, its theories of mechanics, of electromagnetic and thermodynamic phenomena, all of which have spawned whole new technologies, call for an explanation. As Wigner (1969) asked, what is the souce of "the unreasonable effectiveness of mathematics in the physical sciences?" This problem presents an acute challenge to those empiricist philosophers who insist that scientific knowledge can only be a representation of actual objects or events, and that the content of any generalization is exhaustively given by facts about the individual particulars to which it applies.

One way of answering this challenge appeared along with the work on language which led to the reformulation of the conception of representation in terms of an improved logic. Frege developed his formal logic with a view to showing that arithmetic reduces to logic. This suggested, first to Russell and later to the logical positivists, a more ambitious claim, viz. the whole of mathematics reduces to logic. In other words, mathematics is simply an elaborate part of that necessary grammatical structure of our thought (or language), which transmits empirical content unaltered. The use of mathematics adds nothing to our knowledge, it adds only to the facility in handling what we know, by providing transparent packaging of empirical content into convenient bundles. That we appear to achieve knowledge of some harmonious whole when we characterize an invariance in mathematical terms, is an artifact of the way we organize what we really know.

This strategy for circumventing the embarrassment of the successful use of mathematics in science, known as logicism, was never successfully carried out in a manner that met adequate standards of logical and mathematical rigor. The strategy still, however, tempts some people in spite of Gödel's incompleteness theorem and various results in formal logic which are interpreted by others as showing definitively that the reduction cannot be carried out. In the light of the historical associations of the use of mathematics in scientific theorizing, however, it is more plausible to take the difficulties encountered by the reduction of mathematics to logic as an indication of the inadequacies of that particular formal logical framework as a framework for modelling scientific knowledge, theorizing and reasoning.

What, after all, does mathematics enable us to do when thinking about the natural world? It enables us to express complex relationships between measurable magnitudes. It enables us to model complex structures in a remarkable variety of ways. It enables us to make calculations and predictions on the basis of these models. But a representation or model of a structure of relationships is not a description of any specific portion of the world. It has application wherever we can find a sufficiently similar structure exhibited amongst items in the natural world. Because it deals essentially in relationships and structures many applications of mathematics have more in common with modelling, and hence with the use of analogies and analogical reasoning, than with giving literal descriptions and the drawing of deductive conclusions from them. At the very least the extensive use of mathematics in modern science suggests that we should not too readily assimilate the characterization of structure to literal description and should re-open some questions about what would constitute a justified claim to have objective knowledge of structures of the world (of patterns in nature).

There are many uses of mathematics in science as well as many uses of descriptive language. Once we make the move, which Kuhn encouraged us to make, away from thinking only about scientific knowledge as embodied in theories to thinking of scientific knowledge as an integral part of a whole complex of practices, we will be forced to recognize the justice of Bacon's view that the language we use, even for scientific communication, will always be imperfect and open to misunderstanding and error. The lesson of the intervening centuries of epistemology is that efforts at wholesale control of the Market Place are futile and the hope of transcending its pressures forlorn. We should not overlook Bacon's warning that the Market Place attracts trade in junk that serves only to clog the intellectual economy. Since we cannot avoid the Market Place, vigilance, discrimination and honesty are the only ways to keep it from becoming a prison.

5
Idols of the Cave: *Human Science and Human History*

Idols of the Cave take their rise in the peculiar constitution, mental or bodily, of each individual; and also in education, habit and accident.

Novum Organum I LIII

1 Human Nature and Human Knowledge

Whereas Idols of the Tribe are a product of what is universal in the human condition, Idols of the Cave are a product of peculiar circumstances, which frequently play an important but unacknowledged rôle in shaping the way we think and what we are prepared to believe. Obstacles to the improvement of knowledge are generated by the way the light of nature is refracted and discolored as it passes through the private "cave or den" of the "lesser world" (*Novum Organum* I XLII) created by individual predilections, regardless of whether they arise from some innate personal disposition or from acquired habits, from general education or even from special experience gained in the pursuit of science.

Bacon saw the last of these as the source of the errors of the alchemists and of his contemporary Gilbert, who had made a thorough study of the loadstone and was prone to find the principles of magnetism in everything. Aristotle, Bacon believed, had in a similar way exaggerated the importance of logic (I LIV). There are also several opposing thought styles which cut across intellectual party lines and disciplinary boundaries. People will insist that knowledge consists in whatever it is that satisfies their minds, whether it be broad resemblances between things or the subtle respects in which things differ (I LV). Some will insist that understanding requires analyzing things into their smallest constituents and explaining all in terms of the properties of the constituents, others will insist on seeking to explain things in terms of the comprehensive structures which they form (I LVII). Some have regard only for what has a lengthy history; others have faith only in novelty (I LVI).

The division between the Idols of the Tribe and the Idols of the Cave rests on the distinction between what is universal in, and what is peculiar to, the circumstances of human beings. Any attempt to say in advance which is which depends on something like Aristotle's distinction between what can be assigned to nature (in this case human nature) and what is accidental. But even in Aristotelian terms, the Idols of the Cave would be a doubtful topic for inclusion in any theoretical discussion of knowledge. Theories are designed to be general in application and for this reason Aristotle denied there could be *epistêmê* of accidents (*Metaphysics* 1026b3), for accidents are precisely what we cannot say anything systematic and general about. We can perhaps offer rule-of-thumb advice such as Bacon's caution to "every student of nature" to be particularly suspicious of "whatever his mind seizes and dwells upon with particular satisfaction," and when dealing with such matters exercise much more care "to keep the understanding even and clear" (I LVIII). But we cannot offer any systematic treatment of such obstacles. An epistemology which looks for universal principles governing the justification of claims to know, or which seeks to discern the general scope and limits of human understanding, will not concern itself with Idols of the Cave.

But how then can any epistemology distinguish between what is contingent and what is universal as regards human capacities to acquire knowledge and the limitations to which they are subject? It seems that in order to proceed, any epistemology will either have to presume an account of human nature as its starting point, or will have to admit to some dependency on the sciences, such as psychology, sociology, anthropology and history, which study human beings. But shouldn't a theory of knowledge also incorporate an account of the nature and possible status of our knowledge of human nature, or of human beings? Here there is clearly a danger of circularity. This could be benign, if the accounts are all self-consistent, but if they work to undermine one another the position will be unstable. The only escape from this circularity would be to find some way of making the discussion of knowledge independent of any claims or presuppositions about the nature of human beings.

It was one of the strengths of Descartes' epistemology that he recognized the need for an account of knowledge to take on a reflexive character. He turned his proposed method (of analysis/synthesis, chapter 3.5) for acquiring all knowledge onto the problem of acquiring knowledge of himself and his own cognitive capacities (Haldane and Ross, 1955, I 24f.), arguing that it enabled him without difficulty to know his own nature. His consequent identification of himself with his mind, treating the body as not part of his essence, meant that as far as his knowledge was concerned such aspects of his material embodiment, as race, sex and social class were irrelevant. His confidence that he could know his mind better than his body or anything in the material world, meant that when he applied the method of doubt, he need have no fear about the success of his efforts to suspend his beliefs and to refrain from reaffirming any until they were properly grounded. A mind, a personal den or cave, could be purged once and for all by doubt and would then no longer discolor or distort its contents.

This Cartesian response to Idols in general (that is, to the need to recognize that our beliefs may not merely be inadequate but may stand in the way of the improvement of our knowledge and understanding) places the Idols of the Cave in a peculiar limbo. For the Cave becomes the center of the foundation of our claims to be able to know. Once he had the assurance of the existence of a benevolent God, Descartes could evade all the Idols in Bacon's cataloge; but even before he secured this assurance, he was in a position to rid himself of the contingent determinations which generate the Idols of the Cave. Unless, that is, like Gilbert, who saw magnetism in everything, and Aristotle, who imposed demonstration on everything, Descartes was the victim of an Idol of his own Cave. In other words, his belief that he could purge his Cave was, perhaps, no more than a fantasy based on mistaking his genuine achievements in mathematics for the key to all knowledge. Can one so easily break free of the perspective shaped by the contingencies of education, profession, or social standing? Are these influences so obvious that all it takes is a comprehensive vow to suspend one's beliefs in order to avoid those influences?

Being able to assure oneself that one has no prejudices is, after all, a good way to insulate one's prejudices. Unless Descartes' views of human nature and knowledge can themselves legitimately claim freedom from any contingent determinations, proponents of alternative conceptions would be justified in suspecting that these views and the epistemology which rests on them embody the kind of bias that arises when the perspective of one individual or group of individuals is over-generalized and claimed to be universal. This is the stance from which feminists, marxists and others have criticized epistemology in the Cartesian tradition.

Challenges of this sort to the validity of Cartesian epistemology face a strategic problem. Just as Bacon recognized that because he was challenging traditional conceptions of knowledge and of human dignity, to enter into detailed disputations with the Schoolmen would require participation in the framework he was challenging, critics of Cartesian epistemology have realized that they cannot argue with their opponents in terms those opponents would find convincing. By the same token those defending a broadly Cartesian, (and as they see it) strictly philosophical conception of epistemology, must treat as impertinent the suggestion that their standpoint is a limited perspective masquerading as universal. To acknowledge the dependence of their theories of knowledge on disputable conceptions of human nature or of knowledge would be to undermine the foundations of their own position. Unless, that is, they could achieve the kind of reflexive closure sought by Descartes and Kant and give, by their own criteria, solid *a priori* arguments for the exclusive correctness of these conceptions.

We have seen (chapters 3.5 and 4.6 above) that the possibility of this kind of closure depends upon being able to separate the object of knowledge of the empirical sciences (the natural world) from the system (the knowing subject, language, or culture) in which the knowledge is embodied, and to claim a more favorable epistemic access to the latter. The way of ideas (chapters 2.6 and 4.5 above) was premised on taking the ideas of the knowing subject to be the system in which knowledge is embodied, assuming a universal human intellect whose nature was transparent to its own reflective introspection. What tended to discredit this (narrowly) Cartesian attempt to secure closure in the Cave was the (anti-psychologist) fear that, however thorough the applications of Descartes' method of doubt, each person's Cave might remain a grotto filled with Bacon's Idols (chapter 4.6). Reaction to the undercutting of this seventeenth and eighteenth century route to epistemology was, not surprisingly, different depending on whether the route from Descartes had been empiricist or rationalist. In fact both of these positions proved to be unstable, once their conception of knowledge was applied to knowledge of human beings. Consider first the empiricist alternative.

2 *Epistemology as an Empirical Science of Human Nature*

We have already seen (chapter 3.7 above) some of the tensions in Hume's position which result from his abolishment of the traditional rôle for the concepts of nature, cause and agency. Although Hume rejected the way Aristotle treated the concept of human nature as a set of capacities and potentialities, he did not set out specifically to displace the concept of human nature. In fact he felt sufficiently confident about its applicability to write *A Treatise of Human Nature*, which set out to provide a foundation for the rest of the sciences.

> If therefore the sciences of Mathematics, Natural Philosophy and Natural Religion, have such a dependence on the knowledge of man, what may be expected in the other sciences, whose connexion with human nature is more close and intimate? The sole end of logic is to explain the principles and operations of our reasoning faculty, and the nature of our ideas: morals and criticism regard our tastes and sentiments: and politics consider men as united in society, and dependent on each other... In pretending therefore to explain the principles of human nature, we in effect propose a compleat system of the sciences, built on a foundation almost entirely new, and the only one upon which they can stand with any security. (*Treatise*, Introduction)

What notion of nature could provide this new foundation? Simply the thought that in all people, at all times, a single set of principles govern the association of ideas, just as natural scientists take the universe to be governed by an unchanging set of natural laws. Hume did not hesitate to compare his project to the practice of the leading natural philosopher of his age, Newton.

> Astronomers had long contented themselves with proving, from the phaenomena, the true motions, order, and magnitude of the heavenly bodies: Till a philosopher, at last, arose, who seems, from the happiest reasoning, to have also determined the laws and forces by which the revolutions of the planets are governed and directed. And the like has been performed with regard to other parts of nature. And there is no reason to despair of equal success in our enquiries concerning the mental powers and economy, if prosecuted with equal capacity and caution. It is probable, that one operation and principle of the mind depends upon another, which again may be resolved into one more general and universal. (*Enquiries*, I I).

The method to be followed is that of experience and observation. Newton begins his *Principia* by setting down definitions of key terms followed by a list of axioms or laws of motion employing them. He says that these principles "have been received by mathematicians, and are confirmed by abundance of experiment" (*Principia*, I p. 21). Hume similarly begins by giving definitions and by setting down principles of the association of ideas. He goes on to give examples, claiming that people can confirm his principles by reference to their own experience. Here, like Descartes, he assumes that the mind is equipped to look into itself to gain at least the experience and observation necessary to conduct a self-study as an empirical science. In the *Enquiries* (I I) the task is described as creating a "mental geography, or delineation of the distinct parts and powers of the mind." The distinctions that need to be made will all be apparent to the (self) reflective consciousness.

Although this initially appears to put us in a position of privileged epistemic access with regard to acquiring knowledge of our own minds, Hume's own arguments work to undermine any right to claim this. Although he has twice been quoted immediately above as speaking of inquiring into the mind's "powers," it is a consequence of Hume's arguments that we cannot apply the concept of power to nature or to ourselves. We have no impression either from the operation of our own minds or from our observation of nature which can supply an idea of power (*Treatise* I III xiv). Likewise, Hume finds that there is no rational ground for the belief that nature is governed by unchanging laws.

But where does Hume find the standard, by reference to which he can judge that there is no rational legitimation for this belief? Hume's conception of reason is of a faculty of perceiving relations between ideas. He presumes that since ideas are in the mind and complex ideas are the product of associations made as the mind functions according to laws, the complexity of an idea will be something which can be known with certainty, since reflection gives us complete and accurate knowledge of our own ideas and hence a complete basis for perceiving any relations there may be between them. Here we have a vestige of Descartes' procedure; the epistemological asymmetry which affords Hume a rational standard is a product of the Cartesian transparency of the mind to its own reflective rational gaze.

Nevertheless, although Hume needs this absolute point of reference to be able to make his skeptical claims, the remainder of his account of the operation of the mind, and of causal reasoning in particular, works to undercut the assumption that standards of reasoning will be uniform across cultures and historical periods. Hume claims that because we habitually make inferences from effect to cause, and cause to effect, we tend to think that there is some necessary connection between them, a law which underwrites the validity of our inferences. We think that where there is smoke there must be fire, so it is correct to draw the conclusion that there is fire. But Hume claims that the habit of making the inference is prior, and it is this habit projected onto the world, which we suppose to be a connection between things, which matches that between our thoughts. Now if this is so, it follows that different peoples, in different settings developing different habits of thought in response to their experiences, will come to regard different patterns of inference as valid and different kinds of connections between events as possible, necessary or impossible.

Thus, for example, Galen and his followers formed a set of beliefs about disease and its causes according to which disease is the product of an imbalance amongst the four humours, blood, phlegm, black bile and yellow bile, and their experience would be interpreted within this framework. A Galenic physician would see fever as a symptom of too much blood and prescribe bleeding. Modern Western physicians would regard such a treatment as quite irrational and obviously harmful. Their beliefs about disease might lead them to suspect a bacteriological infection and they would prescribe antibiotics. These doctors approach patients with different mind-sets, which include different views about the human being, the relation between mind and body, as well as different views about what is evident in experience and how evidence should bear on their theories and their practices.

From Hume's standpoint the most that could be said is that both are equally wrong to be confident of the framework within which they reason; neither has any rational justification, even though both may think they do. This opens the way to an empirical study of belief formation and patterns of justification. In other words we could embark on a social-psychology of knowledge, where the goal would be to determine what occasioned people to come to think, in the way that they do, by reference to psychological, social, economic or political factors, i.e., factors which do not justify but which explain in terms of an assumed common psychology of motivating factors and non-rational mental principles (such as Hume's principles of association).

This is indeed the kind of account for which Hume himself offers a basis. His "mechanics of the mind" is an account of the psychology of belief; i.e., a framework for explaining why people come to have the beliefs they have, which does not offer any justification for those beliefs or portray the beliefs as justified. Hume's principles of the association of ideas are analogs of Newton's law of gravitational attraction. Hume claims that we believe those things which are presented to the mind with the most force and vivacity. Association transmits force and vivacity (much as impact transmits momentum) so that if a forceful and vivacious idea of smoke is present and this is associated with fire, the force and vivacity of the idea of smoke will be transmitted to that of fire and the result will be belief that there is a fire. This account describes the preservation of belief through a chain of inferences not as something justified by the truth preserving character of the rules of inference applied, but as a natural product of psychological laws.

It is also used to describe the "weighing of evidence" in cases where our experience, such as that of the association of a particular kind of weather with a particular time of year, has not been "uniform." People in Northern Europe will believe more strongly that there will be frost some time in January than those from more southern parts of Europe. This is because they have more experience of this being the case, so the force and vivacity of these experiences outweighs that of experiences of cases where there has been no frost (*Enquiries* I vi). Hume's psychology of belief thus gives a common set of evidentiary principles which will be found to be employed by everyone, but which does not justify the beliefs formed on that basis.

There is, however, a real problem with Hume's position. It is one which he himself to some extent acknowledged but did not resolve. It is possible to regard Hume's arguments as an amusing intellectual exercise, but what of their effects? Hume, like many philosophers of the period, is anti-dogmatic. He wants to undermine claims to absolute knowledge and so urge the cause of tolerance, especially religious tolerance. His arguments in other words should have the effect that (on the basis of self understanding) people change the way they think and should not, for example, believe unconditionally in the principle of the Uniformity of Nature, and should not treat associations of ideas as rational connections.

Suppose people did alter their behavior in this way. They would be people to whom Hume's psychology of belief would apply in an importantly different way. Assuming self-understanding has the desired effect, people would not associate ideas in the same casual manner as those who were not persuaded by Hume's arguments. There is even the possibility that by accepting this account of human nature people might start arranging the world and behaving in such as way as to make it correct. Skeptical arguments, which convince them of the ineffectiveness of any reasoning, might persuade them to pay no regard to reasoning, thus making it empirically true that reasoning has no effect, where it might well have had some before. In which case Hume's psychology of belief would have come to give a correct description because it was believed and only after it had been propounded and accepted. It would not be universally correct because it would not have been correct at the time of its proposal.

Suppose, on the other hand, as Hume did, that his views are descriptively correct at the time of writing. On the basis of his own psychology of belief Hume was able to see why as matters then stood people on the whole were not persuaded by lengthy reasoning such as that contained in his own arguments. Hume expressed both pessimism over the effectiveness of his efforts and perplexity over the rôle which norms ("what ought to have influence on us") have in his project.

> Shall we, then, establish it for a general maxim, that no refin'd or elaborate reasoning is ever to be receiv'd? Consider well the consequences of such a principle. By this means you cut off entirely all science and philosophy...and you expressly contradict yourself; since this maxim must be built on the preceding reasoning, which will be allowed to be sufficiently refin'd and metaphysical...For my part I know not what ought to be done in the present case. I can only observe what is commonly done; which is that this difficulty is seldom if ever thought of; and even where it has once been present to the mind, it is quickly forgot, and leaves but a small impression behind it. Very refin'd reflections have little or no influence on us; and yet we do not, and cannot establish it for a rule, that they ought not to have any influence; which implies a manifest contradiction. (*Treatise* I IV vii)

In other words if what he said was right, he was not going to achieve anything by writing a book giving lengthy philosophical justifications for his views.

The paradox is that if Hume is right about belief formation, his arguments will have no effect, but if he is wrong they could possibly achieve the desired effect. If the point of undertaking a science of human nature was (as Hume suggested) to achieve a self-understanding, which would put all the sciences on a new and secure footing, then this science is (perhaps in spite of itself) part of a project of self-improvement. When we understand ourselves better we will be able to do things in new and better ways and will not repeat old mistakes, old habits of thought, including an over-reliance on reason and an unhealthy contempt for our natural inclinations. To be effective self-understanding has to have an impact on the beings who are the object of study. Hume cannot both treat human science as continuous with the natural sciences, viewed as capable only of giving empirically accurate descriptions, and as part of the project of making new ways of thinking and acting possible.

The project of the natural sciences, as reflected in the epistemology of representation, was founded on the presumption that improvements in our state of knowledge have no effect on the object that we are seeking to understand. The thing known is the way it is independently of our attempts to learn about it. This presumption is built into the principle of the Uniformity of Nature. Hume's epistemology transfers the presumption to human science. He himself argued that there is no sense in looking for a human nature in anything other than empirically established "laws" of behavior. If coming to know those laws has the potential to modify the behavior they are supposed to describe, then the study of human behavior cannot be modelled on the natural sciences. Hume's position is thus problematic because he tries to base an epistemology on what can only, according to that very epistemology, be regarded as empirically established laws of human thought. But part of the project of that epistemology was to effect changes in the way people "reason" or form their beliefs. And if it is possible for behavior to be changed in that way, it is not possible to believe that human thought is entirely governed by empirically discoverable laws.

These problems reveal that a necessary condition for a universal, normative epistemology to be modelled on natural science, one which is conceived as aiming to yield descriptively correct laws, is that the system in which knowledge is embodied be something which can be treated by analogy with a natural object, i.e., as something which is not modified either by our attempts to come to understand it, or by the impact of the norms proposed. In other words, the system and its interconnections would have to be independent of human attempts to acquire knowledge and of their behavior. This rules out natural language and culture for both are highly dependent on human belief and behavior. It seems that to transcend the Cave and its Idols it will be necessary to reach for Plato's Forms (the project is after all in some respects analogous to Plato's; see above, chapters 1.4 and 3.1). Thus in recent literature we find Popper's "third world" (Popper, 1973, chapter 3) and Armstrong's epistemology (Armstrong, 1983) based on real universals. For the empiricists, however, this creates another problem. How can we ever get knowledge of such a non-empirical realm? Here we have come full circle. The knowledge project seems to require the kind of old-fashioned metaphysics against which empiricism originally defined itself.

3 Epistemology as an Experimental Science of Human Nature

Empiricism is defined by its opposition to the claim that there can be any substantive knowledge that is not derived from experience; in Hume's terms, all knowledge takes the form either of relations of ideas (analytic, necessary, *a priori*) or of matters of fact (synthetic, contingent, *a posteriori*). This not only rules out metaphysics but it rules out the possibility of there being anything which might claim the status of synthetic *a priori* knowledge: something non-trivial not known by reference to experience but which applies necessarily within the realm of experience. This hostility to synthetic *a priori* knowledge is in turn due to pursuing rigorously something which appears to be involved in possessing objective knowledge.

Subjectivity is commonly the result of the subject's unwarranted contribution to whatever system (ideas, beliefs, theories) embodies knowledge. We consequently know (objectively) to the extent that we render ourselves passive and allow the system which embodies knowledge to be shaped by whatever will make it reflect accurately what it is we hope to know (cf. Descartes' quest for the point at which the will has to submit). Anything we might want, anticipate, or imagine must be excluded. It is this attitude which ultimately pressures empiricists to adopt toward their own practice the stance of someone observing and describing but not venturing to interfere. And it calls into question any privilege which subjects might claim for the access they have to the system which embodies knowledge.

In Decartes' epistemology, however, objective knowledge is not so relentlessly shaped by the idea that objective knowledge is the product of passive determination. For his method is also premised on the idea that objective knowledge can only be achieved through active critical reflection. The passive way in which we allow our beliefs to accumulate through everyday experience gives rise to conflicting beliefs, not to knowledge. Only active doubt, pushed to its limits, can reveal what must, objectively, in spite of our activity, be the case. Here Descartes has based his epistemology not on mere self observation in the detached sense of observing the normal course of his trains of thought – the observation to which Hume appeals for confirmation of his principles of the association of ideas. Instead, Descartes is inviting subjects to conduct an experiment, pushing their minds out of the normal course. The experiment is conducted to see whether there is a point at which doubt must stop. The point about experiments is that we can claim the special knowledge, which agents have of their own intentions, to relate what was done to the result obtained. To this extent Descartes can be read as basing his epistemology on the experimental method which he, like Bacon, advocated as the way to use experience to learn more about the natural world.

This element of agency in Descartes' conception of himself may well have contributed to his general confidence in the transparency of his mind, but he nowhere considers carefully the rôle of the mind's activity as an element in what is known, or whether he satisfactorily strikes a balance between the active and passive functions of the mind in knowing. His emphasis on method is an emphasis on knowledge as the product of activity, but its justification through the method of doubt provides a criterion in terms of passivity – genuine knowledge consists of the clear and distinct perceptions which force themselves on us, which we are incapable of doubting, no matter how hard we try. The separation between idea as neutral presentation of content and the attitude which we take toward it by an exercise of will, encourages a conception of intellect as passive and separate from the active will. Judgment is an exercise of the will. This does not fit easily with Descartes' discussion of what is required of reason in the implementation of method, where, for example, he says that one must go over chains of inference repeatedly in the mind to secure understanding of them.

There is a similar oscillation in Descartes' geometry, which is the source of his conception of a general method for acquiring knowledge (chapter 3.5 above). Descartes linked geometry and algebra by considering a geometrical curve to be defined by the equation of the motion of a point that would trace out that curve. That is, definition describes a construction. Yet Descartes then takes the static contemplation of the equation as the paradigmatic state of knowledge – having a clear and distinct idea – something which is quite timeless and which can appear to stand outside time. This made it possible for both empiricists, who came to emphasize the passivity of the intellect, and the later rationalists, who emphasized intellectual activity, to take their cues from Descartes.

Where Hume read the success of Newtonian natural science as the success of empirical methods of induction from observation, Kant read it as the success of the merger of rational, mathematical methods with experimental methods. His critique of pure reason based its claims to scientific status, to yielding knowledge of reason and its system of representations, on its use of experimental method. Thus

Kant says: "What we are adopting as our new method of thought, namely that we can know a priori of things only what we ourselves put into them" (*Critique of Pure Reason* B xviii). The footnote to this passage then begins, "This method, modelled on that of the student of nature, consists in looking for the elements of pure reason in what admits of confirmation or refutation by experiment." In the next footnote Kant draws an analogy between the "analysis of the metaphysician" and experiments in chemistry. Chemists start with naturally occurring substances which they regard as compounds of simpler substances and seek, by experiments, to analyze them into their components and to discern laws of chemical composition and interaction. A thorough understanding of the chemical composition of say, sugar, would be confirmed if it were possible to take the chemical components and from them manufacture synthetic or artificial sugar. Kant started from items of empirical knowledge (experience), which he presumed to be composite, sought to analyze them and by so doing to advance to a theory of knowledge in the same way that chemists advance to chemical theories.

The difference is that whereas naturally occurring chemical compounds have not been put together by us, so that we are ignorant of the principles of composition as well as of the nature of the ingredients, in the case of empirical knowledge it has been put together by the operation of our minds. Kant presumes, like Descartes, that the mind has privileged access to the principles of its own operation. Experience is a product of judgments which we make, and we have special access to the concepts and principles which structure our experience, because we may be assumed to know what form of judgment we are making when we make it. *A priori* knowledge is possible because we impose these forms on all that exerts influence on our sensibility. *A priori* knowledge is justified because if we do not impose these forms, concepts and principles, experience is not possible.

Kant's account of how mathematical knowledge is possible forms a crucial bridge between his view of natural science as successful because experimental and his hopes for a philosophy which starts with a theory of knowledge. The basis of Kant's explanation of how mathematics can provide us with demonstrations of statements, which are not true solely in virtue of the concepts involved (are not analytic), is found in his account of the imagination. The forms of judgment are not the only respects in which mental activity makes a contribution to knowledge. There are in addition forms (of space and time) which are imposed on experience by our sensibility, that is by our capacity to have objects presented to us. These forms constrain not only what we can perceive but also what we can imagine.

But our imagination can function in such a way as to generate (construct) objects which have no properties other than those determined by these forms, i.e., it can construct, or create, without empirical material being given to it. When constructing "out of nothing" in this way the products only have properties which arise from their mode of construction. Since there are no component materials there can be no properties which derive from that source. Since we actively perform the construction in imagination we know the principle of construction (a general procedure) and have insight into how this procedure relates to the construct produced.

The syllogism, which demonstrates "All Greeks are mortal" from the premises "All men are mortal" and "All Greeks are men," only shows us what is contained in our concept of being a Greek. Mathematics, Kant believed, could go beyond reasoning "from concepts;" it could reason "from the construction of concepts." For example, what makes geometry a science that can demonstrate that all triangles have interior angles equal to two right angles (in the traditional sense of showing why all triangles must have this property) is that it is possible to exhibit the universal principles embodied in a concept, such as a triangle, by using the imagination to "construct that concept."

By "constructing a concept" Kant had in mind the procedure by which mathematicians in the course of a proof will generate an example, in order to show what is embodied in the principles which govern the construction of any example of the concept under consideration. Thus, a line will be drawn through the apex of a triangle parallel to its base. That this may be done is not contained in the definition of a triangle but follows from the principles which permit the construction of a triangle; and these principles are taken by Kant to reflect a spatial structure which our sensible intuitions must have. The key, Kant believed, to understanding how there could be significant *a priori* knowledge in mathematics, was to be found in the mind's own activity.

Kant's emphasis on the respects in which the mind must be active in knowing thus not only provided an answer to Hume's attack on the possibility of non-trivial (synthetic) knowledge which was both necessary and universal (*a priori*), it breathed new life into the Cartesian project of an epistemology based on special insight which humans have into their own nature. However, Kant's epistemology, it must be noted, rests on some substantial assumptions about the universal and unchanging forms within which humans are able to think and articulate their knowledge. He assumes that we are all equipped with the same forms of intuition, space and time, and that our faculties of imagination, judgment and reason all function according to the same principles and employ the same forms. It is the assumption of fixed and universal forms of thought which allows Kant to offer a justification for the claim that reason can conduct a complete and exhaustive self-examination on the basis of which the scope and limits of human understanding can be set once and for all. Only thus can a critical examination of the forms, which our understanding must take, set these limits in such a way that *a priori* knowledge of substantive first principles of physics is possible.

But what happens to this enterprise if the assumptions about these universal and unchanging forms no longer appear secure? Consider, for example, the forms of sensibility. Since it was assumed in Kant's day that there was only one science of geometry, Kant was confident that our sensible intuitions have but one *a priori* spatial structure. Subsequent developments of alternative (non-Euclidean) geometries called into question the principle used in the example given above. One may assume there are no lines through the apex parallel to the base of the triangle, or one may assume there are many different lines through the apex parallel to the base. Each assumption generates a different geometry with a different answer to the question, "What is the sum of the internal angles of a triangle?"

There is a tradition some two millennia long based on the assumption, which governed not only geometrical demonstrations but also the practice of measurement, that the first principle (there is exactly one line parallel to the base of any triangle) is correct. The assumption was so strong that to conceive any other alternative was a singular mathematical achievement. Is this because of the way we naturally organize our sensory experience, and is it therefore an (inescapable) Idol of the Tribe, as Kant suggested? If it were, it would be not merely difficult but impossible to conceive these alternatives and give them application in the empirical world. Yet non-Euclidean geometry plays a crucial role in Einstein's theories of relativity. Acceptance of Einstein's theories in physics means that the conviction that Euclidean geometry was founded on self-evidently true first principles must now be regarded as a long standing Idol enshrined in the caves of those who pursued the science of geometry or based their physics on it.

If all Kant can establish is that there have to be forms, concepts and principles which structure experience, but cannot determine which, if any, are universal and unchanging, then his project will not be able to reach a standpoint free of the contingencies which generate Idols of the Cave. His transcendental philosophy cannot, any more than Descartes' method of doubt, claim to pave the way to a universal perspective. But it did not necessarily require the development of non-Euclidean geometry and non-Newtonian physics to make this apparent. Kant was aware enough of the possibility of change to have raised serious questions about the universality of the standpoint his epistemology tried to take up.

The conception of reason as a basis of action and a force for change led Kant to a view of reason as not merely a set of fixed capacities, which form part of the nature of each individual, but as something whose projects and development transcend individuals. By the eighteenth century it had become clear that the project on which the natural sciences had embarked required the cooperative work of many people and would require many generations of such work. The conception of a full understanding of the natural world as something which could be embodied in an individual (something still possible with Descartes and Leibniz) was already recognized to be unrealistic. This puts a strain on the Cartesian approach to epistemology which emphasizes and can provide a foundation only for individual knowledge. The lack of analogy between religious knowledge needing to be grounded in inner conviction and knowledge of the natural world as proposed by the Baconian project became clearer as the natural sciences developed.

Kant's route to externalizing the projects of theoretical reason was opened for him by the stress he placed on the importance of practical reason, which includes governing the activities of theoretical reason (chapter 3.8 above). It was widened by his arguments for a morality based on reason and the demands of living in a community whose other members are also recognized as rational beings. Once we recognize that a human lifetime is too short for the full development of human rational potential, we have to hope that the development achieved by one generation will be handed down to the next. Without believing in this cumulative progress, we would never be motivated to work on or contribute to projects which we know we are as individuals incapable of completing. The projects of natural science make sense only for individuals in the context of an enduring community of rational beings. Thus Kant says, "In man (as the only rational creature on earth) these natural capacities which are directed to the use of his reason are to be fully developed only in the race, not in the individual" (*On History*, p. 13).

But how can Kant or any individual philosopher, writing from within history, be assured that their rational powers are developed to the full extent necessary to be able to discern the scope and limits of human understanding? How can any philosopher pretend to stand outside history? The difficulty is that Kant seems to have made reason both historical and outside time, both relative to individuals and their historical contexts, and universal. Time for Kant was, after all, like space, only a form of intuition; it formed the frame of the empirical world of appearances not of the unknowable world of things in themselves. It is this division, replacing Descartes' dualism of mind and body, which Kant argued to be essential if reason was not to come into conflict with itself. For without this dualism the mind would represent to itself an exhaustive empirical reality within which its own activity could not be located (chapter 3.8 above). Yet Kant's dualism cannot be unproblematic if reason itself must be regarded as having a history.

The division between empirical reality and things in themselves was eradicated in different ways by both Hegel and Marx, but in each case with the effect of making human beings, their knowledge structures and their culture, into fully historical beings. Where Hegel removes the division in favor of reason so that the rational becomes the real, Marx removes it in favor of the material dimension of human life, so that ideas and ways of thinking and reasoning arise out of the concrete relations which human beings must sustain with one another in order to provide their own material necessities. In both cases, the thought structures of individuals and societies are essentially historically embedded. They owe their character to their historical location. The same ways of thinking are not open to everyone at every historical period or in every cultural situation.

Both Hegel and Marx continued to think of this history as having a goal, as a progress toward a society in which human fulfillment is possible, even though they had very different conceptions of that goal and of the forces which propel humanity toward it. Both face the problem that the statement of their philosophic positions seems to require them to occupy a standpoint outside history, whereas the positions themselves claim no such standpoint to be possible for individuals. To be rendered self consistent their claims seem to cry out for their efforts to be limited to reflecting on the ideals embodied in the culture of nineteenth century Europe, in which both are situated. But this would not be internally consistent either, for the content of those ideals included the very universalist claims which Hegel and Marx made. The attempt, to find a philosophically coherent expression of the project of progress through reason and through the development of scientific knowledge, gets caught in a conflict between its need for ahistorical foundations (a clean break with the past, the possibility of ignoring the conditioning of past history) and its own historicity, its view of itself as a project with can only be achieved through time.

4 Humans as Historical Beings

In a sense this problem was inevitable. It had already been approached early in the eighteenth century by Vico, who took a more direct route because he started from a thorough rejection of Descartes' philosophy. Vico set out by pursuing, more vigorously than Kant, the epistemological implications of the idea that it is through their constructive activities that human beings are able to acquire scientific knowledge. Ultimately this led Vico to a distinctive version of the claim that we can know ourselves better than we know anything in the natural world, but the object of this knowledge was not a self which stands outside history unconditioned by the contingencies of human existence.

Vico's first philosophic publication involved taking Descartes to task for having failed to appreciate the nature of his own achievements in geometry. Descartes proposed clarity and distinctness as the criterion of the truth of his ideas. He derived this criterion from his confidence in what he took to be his knowledge of mathematics, as well as the confidence he felt in his proof of his own existence. This criterion encouraged the conception of the intellect as passive, forced to acknowledge truth by the clarity and distinctness of what was presented to it. But even Descartes acknowledged the possibility that what he took to be clear and distinct was neither correct nor undistorted. To secure his criterion, he needed to establish the existence of a benevolent God.

Geometrical knowledge, Vico insisted, is true not because of its clarity and distinctness, but because geometrical figures are things we construct. It was the similarity of this claim to Kant's doctrine that mathematics gives us (synthetic *a priori*) knowledge "through the construction of concepts," which aroused interest in Vico's thought among followers of Kant over a century later. We can know the objects of mathematics because their only properties are those which our activities put into them. When our constructions make those properties manifest there is no possibility of misperception. Thus Vico says,

Mathematics are commonly thought to be contemplative sciences and not thought to give proofs from causes; when in fact they alone among all the sciences are the truly operative ones [*operatrici*] and give proofs from causes since, of all the human sciences, they, uniquely, make their way in the likeness of divine science. (*De antiquissimus Italorum sapienta, Opera filosofiche* (p. 77) quoted in Lachterman, 1989, p. 8)

In other words we stand to mathematics as God stands to his creation, our mind has a perfect grasp of its objects because it has made them.

But we do not stand to nature in this cognitively favorable relationship. As Vico saw it Descartes had attempted to understand nature by expressing its principles in geometrical concepts and explaining its phenomena by means of geometrical demonstrations. But while geometry might provide the study of nature with a method of discovering probabilities, it could not provide it with demonstrations. "We demonstrate geometrical things because we make them; if we could demonstrate physical things we would make them" (*Selected Writings*, p. 41). Vico appears here to be claiming in opposition to Descartes that we cannot have knowledge of the natural world because it is not our creation, but because Vico is not taking "knowledge" (*scienza*) in quite the same sense as Descartes, his confrontation with Descartes is less than perfectly direct. Vico clearly has Descartes in mind when he chides, "Men who do not know the truth (*il vero*) of things endeavour to cling to the certain (*il certo*) in order that, since they are unable to satisfy their intellect with knowledge (*scienza*), their will may at least rest upon consciousness (*coscienza*)" (*Selected Writings*, p. 162). Descartes, of course, hoped to find the truth of things in certainty, but he realized he had to establish the existence of a benevolent God to do so. Vico, as we will see shortly, rejected the possibility of doing this, but his principal complaint is that Descartes treated certainty as a sufficient criterion of *scienza*, when traditionally one could not claim *scienza* (Italian "*scienza*" = Latin "*scientia*" = Greek *epistêmê*) unless one knew why the object of knowledge had to be that way. In other words, Vico, like Kant (chapter 3.7 above), was committed to the traditional distinction between knowing that and knowing why, and to treating only the latter as worthy of being called "science" (a body of adequately justified claims to know).

But in his efforts to sustain this distinction Vico went well beyond Kant in the way he pressed the principle that having constructed something places one in a privileged epistemic position with regard to that thing. In this respect Vico differs as much from the tradition, whose distinction he accepts, as he does from Descartes. Vico maintained the thesis (first put forward in the context of engaging Descartes) that "the criterion and rule of the true is to have made it" (*Selected Writings*, p. 55). "In Latin *verum* [the true] and *factum* [what is made] are interchangeable or, in the language of the Schools, convertible terms" (*Selected Writings*, p. 51). This apparently paradoxical thesis arises from identifying truth with the object of *scienza* – in other words there is no truth where there is no grasp of the reason why – and adopting a highly conservative attitude toward what could put a human being in a position fully to know "the why" of anything. Here having made it and being responsible for its properties is, Vico believes, the only guarantee of being able to know "the why" and thus attain *scienza*, which is what we have when we have grasped the truth.

This was not a wholly novel development of the tradition. Vico was building on that part of the tradition which held that to understand anything is to discern that wherein its perfection lies. This includes the natural world and one must not pretend to "know" (in the favored sense equivalent to "understand") anything until one has grasped how it reflects intelligent purpose directed at the good. The revisionary identification of the "true" with the "made" was accompanied in Vico's philosophy by an orthodox (Platonic) identification of the true with the good. "Just as for God the criterion of the true is, in the act of creating, to have communicated goodness to his thoughts – 'and God saw that it was good' – so among men the criterion is to have made the truths which we perceive" (*Selected Writings* p. 56). As long as Descartes was read (by no means charitably) as committed to "science" in the traditional sense, the *verum* is *factum* thesis could be pressed not only against the possibility of natural science (physics) but against two other central pillars of Cartesian philosophy. For someone to attempt to demonstrate the existence of God would be not only to undertake the impossible but to proceed with impiety, "For this would be tantamount to making himself the God of God, and denying the God whom he seeks" (*Selected Writings*, p. 65). And the assumption that we know our own minds better than we do the natural world is likewise a serious mistake, "For while the mind perceives itself it does not make itself, and because it does not make itself it does not know the genus or mode by which it perceives itself" (*Selected Writings*, p. 55). Of course Descartes was not claiming to "know" either his own mind or the existence of God in the traditional sense; he was involved in a movement which ended by changing the goal of inquiry from *scienza* to *coscienza*.

Vico's philosophy was not merely a rejection of the philosophy of Descartes; its positive side included an endorsement of experimental natural science and the suggestion that geometrical method was better employed in the design of experiments than in the articulation of general theories (*Selected Writings*, p. 75). Implicit in Vico's approach was an important limitation on human aspirations; our efforts to understand the natural world will lead at best to an understanding of principles which govern what we can do in the natural world, but not to any theory that might claim to represent the natural world as it is in itself (or as God made it), independently of human involvement in it. We can know the world only through our active involvement with it.

This leads to a conception of scientific knowledge and its ground which is the inverse of that proposed by the empiricists, who require total disengagement, or non-interference, before there is any right to claim knowledge. This is because the conceptions of knowledge are different. Where Vico sought knowledge as the form of understanding possessed by a creator, the empiricists sought knowledge of how things are in themselves from the point of view of the universe, not from the point of view of man. These two conceptions can be run together when the point of view of the universe is that of a creator-God. This happens with Descartes, whose disengaged meditations nevertheless made knowledge dependent on his own activity. Vico did not, any more than Bacon, hold that to escape the Idols of the Tribe we must attempt to transcend our humanity altogether.

Vico had worked out and published this much of his philosophy within the first decade of the eighteenth century. After a pause of fifteen years he published the first edition of the *Scienza Nuova*, which contained an important amplification of his position, in that it assigned a privileged status to a certain newly conceived science of "the nature of nations." Two subsequent editions of the *Scienza Nuova*, each a virtual rewriting of the previous edition, refined and broadened what began primarily as an attempt to understand the necessary and universal features of legal institutions. From the outset the sources from which Vico sought the principles of this new body of understanding – viz. common ideas (e.g. providence, eternal and universal justice); institutions of religion, marriage and burial; myths, metaphors, emblems, poetry, language, etc. – collectively pointed to the study of what we now conceive as human culture.

Vico claimed the status of science for this study on the grounds that it is possible for humans to grasp the necessary and universal principles which constitute the causes of human cultural institutions because humans are the authors of those institutions. Here he does not mean that humans are the authors of their own institutions in the sense of having consciously decided to construct them and having then done so according to principles. Rather he means that these institutions are the product of human activity. Participating in human culture does not automatically provide a grasp of its necessary and universal principles. A participant's unreflective rôle in a cultural institution yields only particular experience, and this can form the basis only for that second grade of knowledge, consciousness (*coscienza*), whose object is certainty.

Although Vico acknowledged Hobbes as an important theorist of human society, his thought at this point moves well away from Hobbes. Hobbes treated the acts by which humans make the commonwealth as though they were, or could be, deliberately established conventions. Vico appreciated the circularity in treating human society as established on the basis of interactions (such as reaching an agreement to observe a convention) which presuppose an already constituted human society. Human society for Vico was established by divine providence, which was the term under which he conceived the way that, in interacting with one another, humans modify each other's behavior so as to constitute unreflectively, i.e., without deliberation or intention, a permanent structure of regulated behavior.

Vico's conception of how one attains *scienza* of human society is not easy to grasp because it combines elements which in more familiar accounts of knowledge are supposed to stand in opposition to one another. It does not involve merely placing experience of (participation in) a particular institution under or along side a grasp of abstract laws. Rather the experience has to be linked to an imaginative reconstruction of the earlier forms of institution, out of which the present (participated in) institution developed. It also has to be linked to imaginative constructions and reconstructions of other possible forms of institutions, which might have developed from similar starting points. While there are a number of possible alternative forms, it is clear that Vico believes the number is not unlimited. There are constraints on what is a possible primitive social institution and constraints on what can develop out of a given institution. The hope in Vico's program of being able to generate a science, with universal and necessary explanations, rests on its being able to discover those constraints. But the abstract grasp of these constraints expressed as laws will not constitute Vico's science. The constraints have to be grasped in such a way as to govern the imaginative construction of particular phenomena.

This is not wholly unlike the way in which thought experiments are used in natural science, or the way in which mathematical or physical models are used in attempts to understand particular types of phenomena, such as the behavior of pendulums, interference of waves or complex molecules. These are all cases where understanding is sought through imaginative construction. Commonly these steps are not given any epistemological significance, but are treated as "heuristic," aids to discovery, which are irrelevant to the justification of any knowledge claims which result. Vico, on the contrary, is claiming that the ability to construct, because it reveals "the why" (the cause; see chapter 3.3 above) is the locus of justifications and is therefore of central epistemological significance.

Thus for Vico the hope of founding a demonstrative science of human institutions rests on being able imaginatively to project our minds into genuinely possible social forms, in which we do not participate and which may indeed not actually exist or exist any longer. Such imaginative projecting informed by knowledge of constraints on possible forms will effect the required demonstrations as the (re)constructions of the social forms, since according to the dictum, "*verum = factum,*" "to prove [the true] by means of causes is to effect [it]" (*Selected Writings*, p. 64). Just as geometry cannot demonstrate without the imaginative construction of geometrical objects, Vico's science cannot demonstrate without the imaginative construction of forms of human institutions.

The need for the use of the imagination is so prominent in Vico's work that it is easy to identify his project with later (nineteenth and twentieth century) views of historical method which recommend imaginative projection into the minds – what Bacon would call the private caves or dens – of one's historical subjects. However, Vico's project comes to rest on what we call "imaginative projection" not because he placed any special epistemic value on the individual experience of historical figures, but because of the way he conceived of demonstrations in science and hence in his new science. Demonstrations are based not on projecting into the minds of other individuals, for this could give at most another participant view, another particular experience. What is required is the disciplined, imaginative construction of another society as a possible object of experience.

This requires not a subjective or empathetic projection but in fact a disciplined putting aside of presumptions based on the experience of one's own current situation. We have to put aside the assumption that all people think like we think. From Vico's standpoint it could be argued that Hobbes failed to found a science of human society precisely because he uncritically projected his own mentality – that is umptions, values, expectations, and perceptions of what onto people in a state of society which afforded no access imptions, values, expectations, and perceptions of what

By doing so he cut himself off from appreciating the different kinds of constraints under which different peoples operate. Vico regarded the key to his conception of a new science to be the realization that primitive humans spoke and thought "poetically;" (see *The New Science*, Book II). That is, he suggests that certain (tendentiously labeled "primitive") cultural forms generate very different ways of thinking, or, as might now be said, give rise to different "mentalities."

Because of the temporal dimension introduced by differentiating between primitive and more developed social forms, Vico called his new science "history." Vico proposed, however, to do more to the concept of history than shift it from a collection of facts to a demonstrative science (recall from chapter 3.7 that for Wolff and Kant "historical knowledge" was a term for attested judgments unaccompanied by explanations of why they should be so). The imaginative constructions and reconstructions required for Vico's science of history should do what the constructions of mathematical science manifestly do not, i.e., tell a developmental story. Each nation (i.e., system of institutions) has, to be sure, its own pattern of development. But Vico would not dignify with the term "science" simple narratives which tell of such developments. The narratives have to convey the "whys" and "wherefores" which reveal what are the preconditions, and what are the possible consequences, of a given system of institutions. The temporal dimension of Vico's history implies more than the mere dating of facts.

5 Humans as Self-Creators

Vico's significance does not lie in the influence his thought exerted on subsequent generations, for he was largely ignored until well into the nineteenth century. There are, however, at least three enduring strands in his thought. The first is a particularly uncompromising version of the claim that we have no alternative but to understand the world around us in terms of what we are able to make or construct. This means that scientific knowledge is viewed as the kind of understanding of a thing which is associated with knowing how to construct it. This is very different from the conception of knowledge as accurate representation, so that the issue of justification and the criterion of truth play out quite differently in the context of Vico's philosophy. Full justification of a claim to know in this context rests on the disciplined use of the imagination to carry out constructive activity.

The second is the claim that different cultural institutions sustain – and require if they are in turn to be sustained – fundamentally different ways of thinking, fundamentally different "thought styles" or "mentalities." An institution is a structure of customs; customs are shared habits of procedure. One may like Hobbes assume that there is a single core set of shared habits of procedure, variations of which generate different institutions. Or one may realize that habits of procedure not only rest on but create and reinforce expectations and perceptions of what is possible. Expectations and perceptions of what is possible cannot change without changing people's habits and habits cannot change without modifying expectations and perceptions of what is possible. Expectations and perceptions of what is possible are what constitute assumptions, what is taken for granted, and they shape what people will value, what they will reach for if given the opportunity and try to secure in the face of threat. These are what constitute ways of thinking and they are inextricably tied via shared habits to the institutions which constitute a culture.

The third is the claim that human institutions must be understood as phenomena which develop, each stage constrained by previous stages. We may well be able to formulate laws or principles governing these developments, but they will not be such as to make prediction possible. They will be laws of the operation of constraints rather than laws of determination. The first strand in Vico's thought implies that we will be able to grasp these principles only to the extent that they allow us imaginatively to describe (i.e., construct) institutional forms which explain how and why actual forms have the characteristics which they do. The second strand has the consequence that difficulties we face may be the result of our own inability to free our thought from the assumptions and values which are required for participation in our own institutional forms. In other words we may stumble because we have not identified and put aside the Idols of our Caves.

Obviously this enterprise presumes that we can identify and suspend assumptions and values which are conditions of participating in our own institutions. As long as we do not imagine that this has to be done on a wholesale basis, it is not an unreasonable presumption. People moving between cultures and even between different sub-cultures have to adjust their expectations and perceptions of what is possible. It is common enough to undergo the process with a certain amount of reflective awareness and consequently to be able to use information about a culture to imagine what would be involved in the transition to participating in that culture. It is possible to undertake this imaginative exercise in a disciplined way so that one can continue to participate in one's own culture while grasping what it would be to have to live and think in a different framework of shared habits. Clearly this is something which is never done completely, but the benefits of even limited success are an increased self-awareness and access to a much wider range of values and perceptions of what is possible.

The implications of these strands of Vico's philosophy can be either intoxicating, threatening or merely disquieting. Philosophers, whether empiricist or rationalist, who worked within the framework shaped by Descartes assumed that, whether or not it is a part of physical nature, humans have a fixed nature, which includes the cognitive, intellectual functions by which they come to know the world around them. They assumed, moreover, that we have special access to that nature and to those cognitive, intellectual functions. These two assumptions together are necessary presuppositions of the strategy of turning the methods of natural science onto the human mind in an attempt to provide a self-consistent justification of the claim that the methods of science do lead to objective knowledge, whilst at the same time setting the scope and limits of such knowledge. The self-knowledge necessary to be able to claim to have put the Idols aside must not itself be distorted and hence must itself be a product of the method which claims to banish Idols. But this demand of reflexivity proves, as we have seen, to be destabilizing.

If a knowledge system has to include knowledge of itself, sufficient to establish its own reliability, it must be either inconsistent or incomplete (this may, if you like, be thought of as Gödel's first incompleteness theorem rather freely generalized). It follows that one must either abandon the demand that the system conform to familiar standards of rationality (i.e., consistency) or accept that there is scope for development and opt for some kind of historicized view of the system.

For empiricists, this means a particularly stark choice. It appears that the only way to be fully consistent with their empiricism is to give up the foundational, justificatory project of normative epistemology. The only kinds of studies of knowledge which can be conducted are locally applicable empirical studies of belief formation, of the processes which in particular communities lead to the establishment of what is there accorded the authority of knowledge. Such studies would, even when drawing normative conclusions, have to acknowledge that ultimately their conclusions are strictly descriptive of norms which apply in a particular context and carry no authority outside that context. This is the position adopted by advocates (Barnes and Bloor, 1982) of the strong program in the sociology of knowledge. In all self-consistency participants in this program have to acknowledge that the cognitive standards, which they themselves employ, could be the object of such a study. They can advocate that others adopt their position and study the social institutions which generate and legitimate claims to knowledge in a purely descriptive manner, but they cannot claim theirs to be the only legitimate position. It is the only one consistent with their cognitive standards, but these, they must acknowledge, are not universal.

Rationalists can yield on the claim of completeness and accept that there can be no complete foundational epistemology. The forms of judgment and of experience are historically and culturally conditioned. Nevertheless since there are such forms, and knowledge is a product of their imposition, it remains possible to give a locally applicable theoretical account of knowledge using critical methods analogous to Kant's. What cannot be claimed, however, is that the empirical world, as the world of possible experience for human beings generally, is identical to that of the world of experience as represented in, or given through, one particular set of forms. This means that synthetic *a priori* principles have their necessary applicability secured only relative to particular frameworks. Internal recognition of this incompleteness would require acknowledgment that there is no basis for expecting the synthetic *a priori* principles of one framework to be recognized by people operating in another (in other words, cultural relativism).

Neither of these positions affords any underpinning to the idea that apart from mere accumulation there can be development, let alone progress, in or through the acquisition of knowledge. Both empiricist and rationalist positions were developed on the basis of what was presumed to be a static human intellectual nature. When converted into local studies of knowledge, they still remain static, yielding no prospect for understanding or underwriting either cognitive development or social development. Any "progress" would have to be judged relative to the values of a particular framework. The correct response may be that this is because there is no such understanding or underwriting to be had. The whole notion of progress (in some absolute sense) is another of those Idols which should be banished. But if that is the case, at least we might ask for some understanding of this Idol's powerful allure, for it still does play a very prominent role in Western ideology.

The constellation of conflicting ideas about human beings, their knowledge and their capacity for self-improvement through knowledge, is not of specifically modern, or specifically European, origin. Nevertheless, the particular configurations which are driven by the notion of progress are specific to Western culture as it has developed since the seventeenth century. In the Italian Renaissance we can see the re-emergence of a view of human beings which is neither classical Greek nor medieval Christian in spirit. The spirit is found expressed in a rather varied collection of texts known as the *Corpus Hermeticum*, which were determined (by Isaac Casuabon early in the seventeenth century) to have been written in the first century AD by Alexandrian Greek Neoplatonists. But from the time of their recovery up to that point they were regarded as the work of an ancient Egyptian, known as Hermes Trismegistus, and were thought to date from the time of Moses. This over-estimate of their antiquity gave them an undue influence in a society which revered ancient wisdom because it regarded the history of mankind as one of decline from an original state of grace and knowledge (symbolized in the expulsion from the garden of Eden). Thus the older a text the more reliable, it was thought, was the wisdom contained in it.

The *Corpus Hermeticum* was translated into Latin by Ficino (1464) and was an important inspiration for the Renaissance conception of natural magic, a revitalized combination of alchemy and astrology (it was essential to this conception that it be applied within what in chapter 4.4 was called "a system of signs"). The vision embodied in these works was given a distinctive interpretation by Renaissance enthusiasts. Pico della Mirandola's essay *On the Dignity of Man* (1487), for example, was a widely read work in which this new vision was forcefully articulated. In this essay Pico proclaimed a new relation between man and the material universe, and between man and God. Man, he said (and as Bacon was to say over a century later), should not disdain nature, but should seek dominion over it and so reveal the godlike powers latent within him. Man is not part of nature, subject to fate and necessity, but master of his own destiny. He is made in the image of God, capable of exercising god-like powers over nature. Pico begins his oration with a reference to a passage from the Hermetic text, *The Asclepius*:

> Man is a marvel then, Asclepius; honour and reverence to such a being! Man takes on him the attributes of a god, as though he were himself a god; he is familiar with the daemon kind, for he comes to know that he is sprung from the same source as they; and strong in the assurance of

that in him which is divine, he scorns the merely human part of his own nature. (Hermes, I p. 295)

The Asclepius claims that man is god-like because he has himself the power to create gods; "man is the fashioner of the gods who dwell in temples and are content to have men for their neighbours" (II.23b p. 339). A little further on it becomes clear that this is a reference to automated statues made for temples. We have a record of the kind of technology that could have been used for these in the works of Hero of Alexandria. His devices rely mostly on hydraulic or steam power. The ability to make self-moving devices (automata) is significant for this Alexandrian conception of the relations between man, God and nature just as it was to be for those who drew on it when it was rediscovered in the fifteenth and sixteenth centuries. (In chapter 3.4 above we noted the fascination which automated figures had for Descartes and his contemporaries.)

Pico describing the creation of man says:

He [God] took up man, a work of indeterminate form; and placing him at the midpoint of the world, He spoke to him as follows:
We have given to thee, Adam, no fixed seat, no form of thy very own, have no gift peculiarly thine, that thou mayest feel as thine own, have as thine own, possess as thine own the seat, the form, the gifts which thou thyself shalt desire. A limited nature in other creatures is confined within the laws written down by Us. In conformity with thy free judgement, in whose hands I have placed thee, thou art confined by no bounds; and thou wilt fix limits of nature for thyself. I have placed thee at the centre of the world, that from there thou mayest more conveniently look around and see whatsoever is in the world. Neither heavenly nor earthly, neither mortal nor immortal have we made thee. Thou, like a judge appointed for being honourable, art the moulder and maker of thyself: thou mayest sculpt thyself into whatever shape thou dost prefer. Thou canst grow downward into the lower natures which are brutes. Thou canst again grow upward from the soul's reason into the higher natures which are divine. (pp. 4–5)

In *Heptaplus* Pico says: "Now for the first time we perceive in him [man] the image of God, through which he has power and command over the animals. Man was so constituted by nature that his reason might dominate his senses and that by its law all the madness and craving of anger and lust might be curbed" (p. 125). What this suggests is that man, by his own efforts, can create his own nature in the sense of determining his own dominant characteristics. Moreover, we see here the theme of domination over both the natural world and over the sensual, bodily component in man himself.

This is not formulated in the context of mechanist natural science, but in that of natural magic, where it was hoped to renew and develop the sciences of alchemy and astrology to harness the power of planet-gods. But we find this conception of man as responsible for his own destiny reiterated by those who had moved to advocating mechanistic natural science. Thus Bacon remakes the wielders of esoteric powers into benefactors of mankind:

> What I purpose is to unite you with things themselves in a chaste, holy and legal wedlock; and from this association you will secure an increase beyond all hopes and prayers of ordinary marriages, to wit, a blessed race of Heroes or Supermen who will overcome the immeasurable helplessness and poverty of the human race... ("The Masculine Birth of Time," p. 72)

Kant, in a passage which even more strongly echoes Pico's, stresses both the moral right and the moral obligation to strive in this way:

> Nature has willed that man should, by himself, produce everything that goes beyond the mechanical ordering of his animal existence, and that he should partake of no other happiness or perfection than that which he himself, independently of instinct, has created by his own reason... it seems not to have concerned Nature that he should live well, but only that he should work himself upward so as to make himself, through his own actions, worthy of life and well-being. (*On History* pp. 13-14)

Renaissance figures like Pico, who drew heavily on the *Corpus Hermeticum*, revering it for its antiquity, whilst at the same time proclaiming a vision of man which suggests a future-directed project of self-improvement and mastery over nature, are pivotal figures, neither medieval nor modern. Bacon puts antiquity more firmly behind him. It is not to the writings of the ancients that we should look for the knowledge necessary to this project of self-improvement, but to active experimental investigation of the world. We cannot expect to improve upon what has already been achieved in the mechanical arts without systematic investigation. If a self-conscious break with the past coupled with the sense of having embarked on a project to fulfill human destiny, a project in which progress must be made from one generation to the next, is central to what has been called "modernity," Bacon is a modern philosopher.

Again, let a man only consider what a difference there is between the life of men in the most civilized province of Europe and in the wildest and most barbarous districts of New India; he will feel it to be great enough to justify the saying that "man is a god to man", not only in regard to aid and benefit, but also by a comparison of condition. And this difference comes not from soil, not from climate, not from race, but from the arts. (*Novum Organum* I CXXIX)

Kant's philosophy illustrates the view of the human race as actively progressing toward its own fulfillment by creating the conditions for the possibility of that fulfillment and also illustrates the way in which this was based on the view of a universal and unchanging human nature, which is primarily and essentially rational. Reason is the progressive force. "Reason in a creature is a faculty of widening the rules and purposes of the use of all its powers far beyond natural instinct; it acknowledges no limits to its projects" (*On History*, p. 13). A rational being is therefore not defined by natural instincts (these become contingencies of existence) and in this sense has no fixed nature. It is reason, with its projection of ideals to be attained that motivates the quest for knowledge and for an ever more detailed and comprehensive understanding of phenomena. At the same time, as we have already seen, Kant's epistemology presumes that reason is unchanging and thus that there is a very substantial component of his intellectual character that man does not in any way shape or mould.

This is the implicit limitation which runs through all the above quotations. It is a limitation which seems necessary to the whole vision that it is through the exercise of reason and the acquisition of knowledge (which yields power to dominate both their material world and their own natural instincts) that human beings can take responsibility for their own nature and transform themselves. Yet it leaves reason no power to transform itself. It in effect sets a very definite line between what is universal in human beings, reason or intellect, and what is contingent, everything to do with embodiment and embroilment in the material world.

If domination of self were understood as renunciation and taken as the means to self transcendence this would reiterate familiar religious themes and would not necessarily be subject to the kinds of internal conflict that have been explored in this chapter. For the religious context provides an external, non-human source of human knowledge of the route to human fulfillment (or salvation). Pico portrayed Adam as having the vital knowledge revealed to him by God. Asclepius had the knowledge passed to him by Hermes Trismegistus.

If however, as in Bacon, domination involves active intervention to alter the material conditions in which people live, this means fulfillment is not being regarded as separate from material existence. Implicitly this is to acknowledge that material embodiment is also a fixed and essential part of what it is to be human. In this case the knowledge which makes it possible to alter the conditions of human life also alters human beings. But the idea that human beings are responsible for their own nature and can transform themselves, through the acquisition of knowledge which yields the power to dominate their own natural instincts and natural environment, is inherently problematic. It suggests a single path to the fulfillment of human potential – knowledge that leads to domination of a natural world whose nature is fixed independently of these attempts at knowledge and domination. Yet at the same time it also suggests that humans can take responsibility for their own nature, and hence set their own goals and standards of achievement (they can choose to live with the animals or with the gods).

This is reflected in the way in which discussion of morals and codes of behavior are divorced from discussions of knowledge. This separation, however, masks rather than relieves tension between the universalist assumption that increased knowledge, which yields technological power, constitutes progress toward human fulfillment, and the relativization of goals and values (including religious orientation) which comes from regarding these as matters of human choice and hence not subject to universalization. There is religious tolerance, but set against a backdrop of a displacing, universalist vision of what constitutes progress toward human fulfillment. Science becomes the route to salvation (see Midgley, 1992). Science claims a non-human standard for its authority, the non-human, material world. But a world conceived as the legitimate object of domination cannot also be the source of knowledge of human nature, including knowledge of what would constitute human fulfillment. Human flourishing is not a possible object of knowledge for a science which has banished teleology (chapter 3.4).

However, if there is no external non-human source to reveal to humans this knowledge of their own nature, then conceptions of human fulfillment can only be based on human self-understanding, understanding which may be limited and imperfect and which will be subject to change as human beings change in response to changing conditions. The boundary between what is universal and fixed and what is contingent or mutable in human nature will shift as human self-understanding changes. Projections of what constitutes human fulfillment presuppose a presently imperfect state, one which can be modified in ways which are within the power of human beings. But can it be presumed that these powers will remain constant through change?

Here we get the full impact of the conception of man as self-creating. Individuals are constrained by the society in which they live to act and think in certain ways; there is a framework of customs, laws, and language which set the bounds of what is possible for them to do or think. To this extent all individuals are "made" by others, or are a product of their culture. But as participants in society they can deliberately, by discovering new ways to do things which are picked up by others, change aspects of their culture. With these changes come changes in conceptions of what is and what is not humanly possible.

The idea that there have been fundamentally different "thought styles" or "mentalities" and that these are an integral part of a culture, must necessarily reflect back, first onto our conception of ourselves, and then onto our thoughts about knowledge and the project of epistemology. It is an example of the way in which theories about human beings and their institutions reflect back into views about the status of knowledge and hence of those theories themselves. If Vico (or Hegel or Marx) is right, then we ourselves think in ways which are a product of our cultural and historical embedding. If these frameworks set bounds on what it is possible to think or imagine, and if justification depends on being able to see possibilities and constructively realize them, at least in thought or imagination, then different cultures' views on justification, on the kinds of justification possible for knowledge claims, may be different. And there could be no way to set limits in advance on all possible forms of justification that might be available to human beings in some culture at some time or other.

This means that epistemology, even when it focuses attention on justification rather than discovery, can only be the epistemology appropriate to a particular culture at a particular point in its history, which has to acknowledge the limitations placed on it by historical and cultural location. In other words, tracing the consequences of the view of the intellect as active in its own self-perfection, or more neutrally, formation, we are led inevitably to a developmental conception of humans as historical beings which in the end undermines the project of an epistemology which hopes to ignore the contingencies of historical and/or cultural location.

6 Epistemology as Idol Knowledge

In this chapter, and throughout the book, we have sought to portray the Baconian reorientation of human knowledge as a contingently conditioned redefinition of a human project. Modern Western culture inherited from the ancient Greeks the idea that the acquisition of knowledge was both integral to living the fulfilled life of a human being and necessary to creating the conditions under which such a life would be possible. But as we have seen the Greek focus was on determining what constitutes the good, (fulfilled) life for a human being and on how to live it. Detailed technical knowledge of the natural world was not an integral part of this project. Bacon's writings reveal that he was conscious both of the extent to which he was drawing on tradition and the extent to which he was redirecting it in a way which marked a decisive break. The connection between knowledge and human fulfillment is retained, but the conception of fulfillment and the route to it is different. Since the reason for which knowledge is to be sought and valued is different, the kind of knowledge sought and valued is also different. It is not contemplative understanding, but the detailed "mechanic's" understanding of how things work and can be made to work that is required.

If the project of science is historically and culturally conditioned, then to remind ourselves of this is to guard against being taken in by an Idol. The conceit, which is internal to (and which indeed has driven) investment in scientific and technological development, is that it is the one route to human progress, a precondition of all others, and one which must be universally acknowledged for its successes. When this is assumed as absolute, when its human origins are forgotten, it becomes an Idol. To put an Idol aside does not necessarily mean rejecting everything that was seen under its distorting influence. This would be a consequence only if one adhered to a strictly representational conception of knowledge, one which we have also seen (chapter 4) is internal, not to science, but to the philosophical theories of knowledge developed to legitimize its project.

Bacon regarded the senses as a source of Idols only to the extent that they were trusted as giving a direct, undistorted view of the material world. To be delivered from their illusion is not to reject them as sources of information, since indeed they are the vehicle of our interaction with the world. It is to recognize that the information they yield must be treated with circumspection, that thought has to be given to the question of exactly where to rely on them, how they can be supplemented and so on. Similarly, much modern science has proved itself through conferring ability to intervene in the material world (it has provided reliable sources of electricity and appliances which use it, for example). To the extent that we value those powers of intervention, we must accord authority to the scientific and technological knowledge which makes them possible. On the other hand, to the extent that the goal, domination of nature, was humanly conceived it may be questioned. Adoption of a modified goal would require reassessment of existing knowledge in the light of its value for contributing to that goal.

The science and technology developed in a Baconian spirit are very much a part of present human reality. To insist that the development of science and technology is a human project is to say that as with any such project our view of it can be expected to change as we proceed to execute it and have to confront the realities, the obstacles, in the way of completing it. Work on these projects also changes us, as we are forced to think in new ways, as we come to live in new ways, made possible or required by the introduction of technology. Our freedoms and constraints change and with them our conceptions of ourselves as human beings. Recognition of this as a human project may serve to remind us that we have a certain responsibility for the science we produce – the scientist is not being dictated to by the world, merely recording its pronouncements. The positivist image of science, with its conceptions of factual objectivity, a standard set by a non-human world, presents science as containing no place either for human values or creative thought. It explicitly sets up an opposition between the scientific and the human as a projection of the opposition between subject and object.

One of the lessons of the history of science in the twentieth century is that what were once taken as scientific certainties, principles not within reach of empirical verification or falsification, may come to be questioned and rejected. When such a change occurs standards and methods of justification also inevitably change. Use of what could once be assumed without justification, Euclidean geometry for example, now needs justifying by reference to the context of use. Thoughts that it would be impossible to entertain within the old framework become thinkable, such as the local warping of space-time by strong gravitational fields. At the empirical level too, new technologies have made whole new kinds of experiments possible. Computers have changed and continue to change the way theories are tested, experiments are done and data collected. These developments are not things which could have been foreseen by nineteenth century physicists. They were not visible, not thinkable. This is the sense in which methods and techniques of justification within science, whether at the theoretical or experimental levels, are context dependent.

But it might be claimed that there are overarching methodological principles governing the practice of the natural sciences, which free them from cultural context dependence and which justify their claim to value neutrality and legitimate their claim to universal authority. This would be the claim that scientific methods have been formed around the sort of strategy suggested by Bacon, the strategy which institutionalizes mechanisms for exposing Idols and the distortions they produce (chapter 2.8 above). Theories are discussed and criticized, papers in scientific journals as well as research proposals are subject to peer review, experimental results are published and attempts made to repeat them. Non-repeatable results are treated with extreme suspicion, if not rejected outright. The scientific community is an international community and should therefore be drawing on people from sufficiently varied backgrounds to allow individual and cultural biases to be cancelled out in these processes. Claims which survive and become established knowledge, ought to be neutral and should, by commanding respect within the scientific community, deserve universal respect.

But the standards of peer review are those of the methods and justificatory framework of a particular discipline at a particular time. The only criticisms of a view or theory that can be recognized and thus heard are those that can be articulated within that framework. Similarly, the only claims that will be seriously considered are those that fit into the framework, unless the people suggesting them have already established themselves as pre-eminent in their field. The operation of these kinds of pressures in the development of molecular biology in this century is illustrated by the relative isolation of Barbara McClintock and the subsequent recognition of the value of her work (see Fox Keller, 1983).

The problem with institutions is that, like language, they are resistant to change and can never be merely institutions concerned with ensuring the evaluation of knowledge simply as regards its likely truth or falsity. As currently established, institutions of peer review are also vehicles for funding and for professional power and prestige. These problems are not just human failings which could be eliminated in principle; they are inevitable consequences of knowledge being a source of authority and hence power.

Moreover, the project of modern science carries contradictory tendencies within it. The ideal of openness to pluralistic criticism comes into conflict with the vision of steady progress to a unified truth and claims to scientific authority. In practice criticisms are limited, channelled and deflected. Lapses from the idealized standard of openness to criticism are normal. Dogma is inevitable, since some things must be held fixed in order for problems to be framed and inquiries undertaken. To have any goals at all, is to take some things for granted.

A more detailed understanding of the ways in which knowledge achieves authority status is a necessary part of the self-knowledge, knowledge of present constraints and possibilities, required for any reorientation in the conception of the goals of knowledge and hence of the nature of knowledge. The ideal of openness to pluralistic criticism, unrealizable in day-to-day scientific work, can nevertheless be invoked in service of the project of periodically renegotiating the vision of truth and the nature of its unity.

7 Skeptical Strategies

To persuade people to put aside their Idols, you must first shake their faith (the skeptical task) and then convince them that there is something which can take their place. It is necessary to share and build upon their commitment to pursue existing goals, channelling it in a new direction. The exposure of Idols (as Foucault has taught us) is part of the politics of knowledge. But one's purpose might be more, or less, radical than reform. The skeptical stage may be an end in itself, being deployed for conservative or for anarchistic ends. The skeptic persuades us of the status of our Ideas as Idols, as graven images created by human beings, denying them the status of true religion or true knowledge. If we want religions or knowledges, we will have to make do with human-made ones, no one of which can claim moral or cognitive superiority.

One response made in the sixteenth and seventeenth centuries by Roman Catholic theologians to Protestant challenges was to use skeptical arguments to discredit Protestant claims to religious knowledge (see chapter 2.3). They argued that human reason is incapable of being deployed to yield religious knowledge. Individual human beings cannot, by their own efforts, acquire this form of knowledge. Religious knowledge is granted to the chosen few in revelations. For the remainder the important religious attitude is that of faith, acceptance of authority grounded in trust. In this case skepticism served conservative forces in their resistance to change and in their attempt to retain authority.

During the same period humanist scholars were using similar arguments to discredit all traditional authorities on matters of moral and political organization. They argued that since knowledge of any uniquely best moral or political formation is impossible for human beings, they should just get on with using their experience to create what seemed to them to be workable systems of laws, customs and political practices. This served not only as a basis for pluralism, but also as an argument for a separation of Church from State and removal of the Church from secular political power, without disputing its claims to religious authority.

Both of these strategies (and many variations) can be seen in play today with Western technological science substituted for the Catholic Church. Science disputes the cognitive credentials of its critics, encouraging skepticism with respect to their methods and claims. Environmentalists, humanists and feminists seek to limit the scope of the authority of science, examining its methods and arguing that it really cannot claim decisive authority in matters social and environmental.

Philosophy itself has not been immune from this power play. The credentials of epistemology, that branch of philosophy which concerns itself with knowledge and its nature, with knowledge claims and their possible justification, or as Locke put it, with the scope and limits of human understanding, has itself been challenged. If the skeptics are right, if the edifice of science is the most elaborate and most powerful Idol yet, if the whole project of overthrowing Idols in search of true knowledge is bankrupt because finally realized to be not only impossible but also highly dangerous, then the theory of knowledge is the theory of nothing. It must itself have been part of the mystificatory rites of the cult of (scientific) knowledge.

Some of the critics of epistemology, of whom Richard Rorty would be a leading example, take the conception of epistemology as given and urge its total abandonment; philosophy should not concern itself with knowledge, but should restrict itself to the humanistic task of stimulating edifying conversation. We do not advocate this route. It seems to us that it amounts to an abdication of responsibility on behalf of philosophy in an age in which authority rests on high technology and as part of a culture in which the cult of the expert flourishes. Even those opposed to the values they think to be inherent in science and technology, who reckon them to be false Idols, cannot bring about their downfall merely by ceasing to believe whilst continuing the rituals of worship embodied in life in a technologically developed country. So long as knowledge is power and the exercise of the power is prominent in shaping the society and environment in which we live, and so long as we seek to have the sort of understanding of society which is a necessary condition of dissent and political challenge, then it seems to us that there is a rôle for critical reflection on the knowledge process, whatever name one wishes to give it.

Thus we wish to take the reformist route. This involves altering the conception of epistemology rejected by Rorty. It can be admitted that much of what has gone under the heading "epistemology" has played the rôle its critics assign to it without accepting that this is all that epistemology ever has been or could ever be. All the moves discussed above, moves in which Idols are detected and denounced, counter-proposals made and modified, only to be challenged later from other quarters, count for us as part of philosophical discourse on knowledge (epistemology). It is within the theory of knowledge that these arguments take place, arguments involving conceptions of what constitutes knowledge, why it should be pursued, how it can be acquired and by whom. We urge that the epistemology of early and mid-twentieth century analytic philosophy be discarded as a false Idol, and that epistemology be reconnected to the larger and broader tradition of philosophical engagement with the politics of knowledge.

Authorities

{Numbers in curly brackets indicate sections in which the entry is cited or mentioned.}

Agricola, Georgius *De Re Metalica* (1533), tr. H.C. Hoover and L.H. Hoover 1970. New York: Dover Publications. {1.5}

Aristotle, *The Complete Works of Aristotle*, Jonathan Barnes (ed.), 1984. Princeton: Princeton University Press. [References are by Bekker number.] {2.5, 3.1, 3.2, 3.3, 3.8, 5.1}

Armstrong, David M. 1983: *What is a Law of Nature?* Cambridge: Cambridge University Press. {5.2}

Augustine, *On Free Choice of the Will*, tr. A.S. Benjamin and L.H. Hackstaff 1964. Indianapolis: Bobbs-Merrill. {3.6}

Bachelard, Gaston 1984: *The New Scientific Spirit* [*Le Nouvel Espirit Scientifique* (1934)], tr. A. Goldhammer. Boston: Beacon Press. {2.8}

Bacon, Francis [References not otherwise marked are to the *Novum Organum*, by book and aphorism number] *The Advancement of Learning* [1605] *and the New Atlantis* [1627] [ALNA] 1906. London: Oxford University Press. {1.1, 1.5, 1.6, 1.7, 2.9, 4.3}

—— *De Augmentis*. In John M. Robertson (ed.) from the translation of Ellis and Spedding, 1905, *The Philosophical Works of Francis Bacon*, New York: Books for Libraries Press. {3.4, 4.3}

—— *The Masculine Birth of Time*. In *The Philosophy of Francis Bacon*, tr. Benajmin Farrington, 1964. Chicago: University of Chicago Press. {5.5}

—— *The New Organon* [*Novum Organum*] (1620), Fulton H. Anderson (ed.), 1960, from the translation of Ellis and Spedding, Indianapolis: Bobbs-Merrill. [Page references to the Great Instauration, GI, are to this edition.] {1.5, 1.6, 1.7, 2.1, 3.1, 3.3, 3.4, 4.1, 4.3, 5.1, 5.5}

Barnes, Barry and Bloor, David 1982: Relativism, Rationalism and the Sociology of Knowledge. In Steven Lukes and Martin Hollis (eds), *Rationality and Relativism*, Oxford: Basil Blackwell. {5.5}

Berkeley, George 1975: *Philosophical Works*, London: Everyman. {4.4}

Biringuccio, Vannoccio *The Pirotechnia* (1540), tr. C.S. Smith and M.T. Gnudi (eds), 1990. New York: Dover Publications. {1.5}

Boyle, Robert *The Skeptical Chymist* (1661), 1911. London, Everyman Library. {4.3}

Carnap, Rudolph 1959: The Elimination of Metaphysics through Logical Analysis of Language. In A.J. Ayer (ed.), *Logical Positivism*, New York: Free Press. {3.1}

Authorities

—— 1967: *The Logical Structure of the World.* Berkeley: University of California Press. {4.7}
Cicero, *De Natura Deorum* and *Academica*, tr. H. Rackham, 1933. London: Loeb Classical Library. {2.2, 2.3, 2.4}
Crossland, M.P. 1978: *Historical Studies in the Language of Chemistry.* New York: Dover.
Debus, Allen G. 1977: *The Chemical Philosophy* (2 vols). New York: Science History Publications. {4.3}
Dee, John *Propaedeumata Aphoristica*. In Wayne Shumaker, 1978 (ed. and tr.), *John Dee on Astronomy*, Berkeley: University of California Press. {1.5}
—— "Mathematical Preface" to *The Elements of Geometry of the most aunciect Philosopher Euclide of Megara*, tr. Sir Henry Billingsley, London 1570.
Descartes, Rene *Descartes' Conversation with Burman* (1648), tr. John Cottingham, 1976. Oxford: Oxford University Press. {2.6, 3.4}
—— *Descartes: Philosophical Letters* (1629–1649), tr. Anthony Kenny, 1981. Oxford: Basil Blackwell. {3.6}
—— *Discourse on Method, Optics, Geometry and Meteorology* (1637), tr. Paul J. Olscamp, 1965. Indianapolis: Bobbs-Merrill. {3.5}
—— *Le Monde, ou Traité de la lumierè* (1633), tr. Michael Sean Mahoney, 1979. New York: Abaris Books. {3.6}
—— *Oeuvres de Descartes*, Charles Adam and Paul Tannery (eds), 1912. Vol. 11, Paris: Cerf. {3.4}
—— *Philosophical Works of Descartes* tr. Elizabeth Haldane and G.R.T. Ross, 1955. New York: Dover. {2.5, 2.6, 2.7, 2.8, 3.4, 3.5, 3.6, 4.4, 5.1}
Dewey, John 1910: *The Influence of Darwin on Philosophy.* New York: Henry Holt. {4.6}
Diogenes Laertius, *Lives of Eminent Philosophers*, tr. R.D. Hicks, 1925. London: Loeb Classical Library. {2.4, 2.7}
Duhem, Pierre 1962: *The Aim and Structure of Physical Theory.* New York: Athenum. {4.7}
Eddington, Arthur 1929: *The Nature of the Physical World.* Cambridge: Cambridge University Press. {2.5}
Epicurus: Letters and a list of "Key Doctrines" are quoted in Diogenes Laertius, Book X (above). References are to this book. {2.3, 2.4}
Erasmus, Desiderius *On Free Will* (1524). In *Erasmus-Luther: Discourse on Free Will*, tr. Ernst F. Winter, 1961, New York: Fredrick Ungar. {2.3}
Farrar, Frederic W. 1979: *History of Interpretation* (1886). Grand Rapids, Michigan: Baker Book House. {4.3}
Feyerabend, Paul K. 1965: Problems of Empiricism. In R. Colodny (ed.), *Beyond the Edge of Certainty*, Englewood Cliffs, New Jersey: Prentice Hall. {4.7}
Feyrabend, Paul K. 1981: On the "Meaning" of Scientific Terms. In *Philosophical Papers*, Vol. 1, Cambridge: Cambridge University Press. {4.7}
Foucault, Michel 1973: *The Order of Things.* New York: Vintage Books. {4.4}

Frege, Gottlob *The Basic Laws of Arithmetic*, tr. M. Furth, 1964. Berkeley: University of California Press. {4.6, 4.7}

Galen, On Medical Experience. In *Three Treatises on the Nature of Science*, tr. R. Walzer and M. Frede, 1985. Indianapolis: Hacket. {2.2}

Galileo Galilei, *Discoveries and Opinion of Galileo*, tr. S. Drake, 1957, for "Excerpts from *The Assayer*" (1623). New York: Doubleday Anchor Books. {2.5}

Gombrich, E.H. 1972: *Symbolic Images*. London: Phaidon. {4.3}

Gould, Stephen Jay 1984: *The Mismeasure of Man*. Harmondsworth, Middlesex: Penguin Books. {Introduction}

Haldane, Elizabeth and Ross, G.R.T., 1955: *Philosophical Works of Descartes*. New York: Dover. {2.5, 2.6, 2.7, 2.8, 3.4, 3.5, 3.6, 4.4}

Hales, Stephen (1727) 1961: *Vegetable Staticks*. London: Macdonald. {4.4}

Harré, H. Rom *Varieties of Realism: a Rationale for the Natural Sciences*, 1986. Oxford: Blackwell. {2.8}

Harvey, William *The Circulation of the Blood* (1628, 1649), tr. K. J. Franklin, 1963. London: Everyman. {3.4}

Hermes Trismegistus, *Hermetica*, tr. W. Scott, 1985. Boston: Shambhala. {5.5}

Hobbes, Thomas *Leviathan* (1651), London: William Collins, 1962. {4.4}

Hume, David *A Treatise of Hume Nature* (1734), ed. L.A. Selby-Bigge, 1975. Oxford: Clarendon Press. [References are by book, part, and section.] {3.6, 3.7, 4.6, 5.2}

—— *Enquiries* (1748), ed. L.A. Selby-Bigge, 1963. Oxford: Clarendon Press. {3.1, 3.6, 5.2}

Husserl, Edmund 1962: *Ideas: General Introduction to Pure Phenomenology*, tr. W. Boyce Gibson. New York: Collier Books. {4.6}

Jones, Howard 1989 *The Epicurean Tradition*. London: Routledge. {2.3}

Kant, Immanuel *Critique of Judgement* (1790), tr. J.H. Bernard, 1951. New York: Hafner Press. {3.8}

—— *Critique of Pure Reason* (A = 1781, B = 1787), tr. N. Kemp Smith, 1965. New York: St Martin's Press. {3.7}

—— *Idea for a Universal History from a Cosmopolitan Point of View* [On History] (1784), tr. L. White Beck, R.E. Anchor and E.L. Fackenheim, 1963. Indianapolis: Bobbs-Merrill. {5.3, 5.5}

Keller, Evelyn Fox 1983: *A Feeling for the Organism: the Life and Work of Barbara McClintock*. New York: W.H. Freeman. {5.6}

Kuhn, Thomas 1970: *The Structure of Scientific Revolutions*. Chicago: University of Chicago Press. {4.8}

Lachterman, David Rapport 1989: *The Ethics of Geometry*. London: Routledge. {5.4}

Locke, John *An Essay Concerning Human Understanding* (1690), 2 vols. London: Everyman's Library, 1965. [References are by book, chapter, and paragraph.] {2.5, 4.4, 4.5, 4.6}

Long, A.A. and Sedley, D.N. 1987: *The Hellenistic Philosophers*, Vol. 1. Cambridge: Cambridge University Press. {2.3, 2.4, 2.7}

Lucretius, *The Nature of the Universe*. Harmondsworth, Middlesex: Penguin, 1951. {2.4}

Luther, Martin *The Enslaved Will* (1525) (excerpts). In *Erasmus-Luther: Discourse on Free Will*, tr. Ernst F. Winter, 1961, New York: Fredrick Ungar. {2.3}

Midgley, Mary 1992: *Science as Salvation: A Modern Myth and its Meaning*. London: Routledge. {5.5}

Nagel, Thomas 1986: *The View from Nowhere*. Oxford: Oxford University Press. {2.1}

Newton, Isaac *Opticks* (1730). New York, Dover Publications, 1952 {1.6, 4.4}

—— *Philosophiae Naturalis Principia Mathematica* (2 vols, 1686), tr. A. Motte, revised by F. Cajori, 1971. Berkeley: University of California Press. {3.7, 5.2}

Ockham, William of *Ockham's Theory of Terms (Summa Logicae, Part I)*, tr. Michael J. Loux, 1974. Notre Dame, Indiana: University of Notre Dame Press. {4.4, 4.5}

Ong, Walter 1958: *Ramus: Method and the Decay of Dialogue*. Cambridge, Massachusetts: Harvard University Press.

Palladio, Andrea *The Four Books of Architecture* (1570), tr. I. Ware, 1965. New York: Dover. {1.5}

Piaget, Jean 1929: *The Child's Conception of the World*. London: Routledge and Kegan Paul. {2.1}

Pico dela Mirandola, Giovanni *On the Dignity of Man, On Being and the One, Heptaplus*, tr. C.G. Wallis, P.J.W. Miller and D. Carmichael, 1965. Indianapolis: Bobbs-Merrill. {5.5}

Plato [references are by Stephanus page number] *Apology* and *Euthyphro* in *The Last Days of Socrates*, tr. by H. Tredennick, 1954. Harmondsworth, Middlesex: Penguin. {1.2}

—— *Cratylus*, tr. H.N. Fowler, 1926. London: Loeb Classical Library. {3.2}

—— *Euthydemus*, tr. R. K. Sprague, 1965. Indianapolis: Bobbs-Merrill. {3.3}

—— *Gorgias*, tr. W. Hamilton, 1960. Harmondsworth, Middlesex: Penguin. {1.2, 3.2}

—— *Laches*, tr. I. Lane. In Trevor J. Saunders (ed.) *Early Socratic Dialogues*, 1987. Harmondsworth, Middlesex: Penguin. {1.2}

—— *Parmenides*, tr. H.N. Fowler, 1926. London: Loeb Classical Library. {1.3}

—— *Philebus*, tr. J.C.B. Gosling, 1975. Oxford: Clarendon Press. {4.2}

—— *Protagoras and Meno*, tr. W.K.C. Guthrie, 1956. Harmondsworth, Middlesex: Penguin. {1.2, 1.3}

—— *Republic*, tr. D. Lee, 1974. Harmondsworth, Middlesex: Penguin. {1.1, 1.2, 1.3, 1.4, 3.3}

—— *Theaetetus*, tr. J. McDowell, 1973. Oxford: Clarendon Press. {2.1, 2.2, 2.6}

Popkin, Richard 1964: *The History of Scepticism from Erasmus to Descartes*. New York: Harper Torchbooks. {2.3}

Popper, Karl 1973: *Objective Knowledge*. Oxford: Clarendon Press {4.6, 4.7, 5.2}
Putnam, Hilary 1975: *Mathematics, Matter and Method*. Cambridge: Cambridge University Press. {4.1}
Quine, Willard van Orman 1969: *Ontological Relativity*. New York: Columbia University Press. {4.6, 4.7}
—— 1970 *Philosophy of Logic*. Englewood Cliffs, New Jersey: Prentice-Hall. {4.7}
—— 1960 *Word and Object*. Cambridge, Mass.: MIT Press. {4.7}
Ramelli, Agostino *The Various and Ingenious Machines of Agostino Ramelli* (1588), tr. M.T. Gnudi, 1976. New York: Dover. {1.5}
Rorty, Richard 1980: *Philosophy and the Mirror of Nature*. Oxford: Basil Blackwell. {Introduction, 5.7}
Sextus Empiricus, *Against the Logicians (Adversus Mathematicos* VII, VIII), tr. R.G. Bury, 1935. London: Loeb Classical Library. {2.2}
—— *Outlines of Pyrrhonism*, tr. R.G. Bury, 1933. London: Loeb Classical Library. {2.3}
Spinoza, Benedict *Ethics* in *The Collected Works of Spinoza*, Vol. I, tr. E. Curly, 1985. Princeton: Princeton University Press. {2.7}
Stewart, M.A. (ed.) 1979: *Selected Philosophical Papers of Robert Boyle*. Manchester: Manchester University Press. {2.5}
Vico, Giambattista *The New Science of Giambattista Vico*, tr. T.G. Bergin and M.H. Fisch, 1970. Ithaca: New York. {5.4}
—— *Selected Writings*, tr. L. Pompa, 1982. Cambridge: Cambridge University Press. {5.4}
Whitehead, Alfred North 1967: *Science and the Modern World*. New York: Free Press. {4.8}
Wigner, E.P. 1969: The Unreasonable Effectiveness of Mathematics in the Physical Sciences, In T.L. Saaty and F.J. Weyl (eds), *The Spirit and Uses of the Mathematical Sciences*, New York: McGraw-Hill. {4.8}
Winter, Ernst F. see Erasmus, Luther
Witten, Edward 1988: Interview with the editors in P.C.W. Davies and J. Brown (eds), *Superstrings, A Theory of Everything?* Cambridge: Cambridge University Press. {4.8}
Wittgenstein, Ludwig 1963: *Philosophical Investigations*, tr. G.E.M. Anscombe. Oxford: Basil Blackwell. {4.7, 4.8}
—— 1961 *Tractatus Logico-Philosophicus*, tr. D.F. Pears and B.F. McGuinness. London: Routledge. {4.7, 4.8}
Wolff, Christian *Preliminary Discourse on Philosophy in General* (1728), tr. R. J. Blackwell, 1963. Indianapolis: Bobbs-Merrill. {3.7}
Yates, Frances A. 1982: *Lull & Bruno*. London: Routledge and Kegan Paul. {4.3}
Yolton, John 1956: *John Locke and the Way of Ideas*. Oxford: Clarendon Press. {4.4}

Name Index and Biographical Glossary

Academy, school founded by Plato, dominated by skeptics during third and second centuries BC, 54–5, 75
Aenesidemus (1st century BC), Greek philosopher, 54–5
Agricola, Georgius (1494–1555), German scholar and mining engineer, 25, 143
Agrippa, Cornelius (1486–99), German physician and writer, 140
Aquinas, St Thomas (*c.* 1225–74), Italian Dominican theologian and philosopher, 40, 107, 137
Aristotle (384–322 BC), Greek philosopher and tutor to Alexander the Great, 5, 12, 29–31, 36, 46–8, 51, 56, 62, 67, 84–100, 177, 130–2, 135, 150, 152, 164, 169, 171, 173; Aristotelian, 70, 91, 99, 100, 101, 107, 113, 123, 129, 134, 137, 154
Armstrong, David M., contemporary Australian philosopher, 178
Augustine of Hippo, St, (354–430 AD), North African-born theologian, philosopher and Church Father, 107, 110, 138, 146

Bachelard, Gaston (1884–1962), French philosopher, 81–2
Bacon, Francis (1561–1626), English statesman and philosopher, 5, 8–11, 13, 24–45, 61, 64–7, 78, 80, 82, 84–92, 94, 97, 99–102, 107–9, 112, 114, 116, 123–6, 127–9, 135–41, 143–6, 152, 166–8, 169–72, 184, 189, 191, 196, 198, 200, 202
Barnes, Barry, contemporary British sociologist of knowledge, 195
Berkeley, George (1685–1753), Irish philosopher and Anglican bishop, 148
Biringuccio, Vannoccio (1480–1538?), Italian metallurgist, 25
Bloor, David, contemporary British sociologist of knowledge, 195
Boyle, Robert (1627–92), English natural philosopher, 139, 140

Casaubon, Isaac (1559–1614), French theologian and scholar, 196
Carnap, Rudolph (1891–1970), German-born philosopher, 86, 159
Cicero, Marcus Tullius (106–43 BC), Roman statesman, orator and philosopher, 51
Comenius, *or* John Amos Komensky (1592–1670), Czech theologian and educator, 145
Condillac, Etienne Bonnot (1715–80), French philosopher, 145
Copernicus, Nicolaus (1473–1543), Polish (or Prussian) astronomer 46, 91
Cuvier, George (1769–1832), French zoologist, 146

Dee, John (1527–1608), English philosopher and mathematician, 26–7, 144, 160
Democritus (c. 460–c. 370 BC), Greek philosopher, 32, 46–9, 53, 58–60, 64
Descartes, René (1591–1650), French mathematician and philosopher, 3–5, 40, 46, 61, 63–5, 69, 70–81, 87, 100–12, 117, 122–3, 136, 146, 151, 167, 170–2, 174, 179–82, 184, 186–9, 194, 197
Dewey, John (1859–1952), American philosopher, 156
Duhem, Pierre (1861–1916), French physicist and historian and philosopher of science, 65–6

Eddington, Arthur Stanley (1882–1944), English physicist, 65–6
Einstein, Albert (1879–1955), German-born physicist, 134, 183
Epicurus (341–270 BC), Greek philosopher, 32, 47, 57–63, 65, 67, 69, 71, 74–7
Erasmus, Desiderius (1466?–1536), Dutch humanist scholar, 53, 57–8

Feyerabend, Paul, contemporary Austrian-born philosopher, 162–4
Ficino, Marselio (1433–99), Italian philosopher and scholar, 140, 196
Foucault, Michel (1926–1984), French philosopher, 142–3, 149, 205
Frege, Gottlob (1848–1925), German mathematician and philosopher, 157–9, 161, 167

Galen (c. 130–c. 200 AD), Greek physician and writer, 50–1, 175
Galileo Galilei (1564–1642), Italian natural philosopher, 46, 66–7
Gassendi, Pierre (1592–1655), French natural philosopher, 58, 65
Gilbert, William (1540–1603), English physician and natural philosopher, 169, 171
Gödel, Kurt (1906–78), Czech-born mathematician, 167, 194

Hales, Stephen (1677–1761), English physiologist and chemist, 144
Harré, H. Rom, contemporary New Zealand-born philosopher, 82
Harvey, William (1578–1657), English physician and anatomist, 101
Hegel, George W. F. (1770–1831), German philosopher, 185, 201
Heraclitus, (died 480 BC), Greek philosopher, 49–51, 56
Hellenistic Philosophy, Greek philosophy 322–31 BC, 5, 37
Hermeticism, *Corpus Hermeticum*, 196–200
Hero of Alexandria (1st century AD), Greek natural philosopher, 197
Hobbes, Thomas (1588–1679), English philosopher, 142–3, 190–1, 193
Hume, David (1711–70), Scottish philosopher and historian, 58, 86, 112–19, 121, 125, 154–6, 173–80
Husserl, Edmund (1859–1938), German philosopher, 156

Kant, Immanuel (1724–1804), German philosopher, 5, 87, 111, 115–26, 144, 156, 162, 172, 180–7, 195, 198–9
Kepler, Johannes (1571–1630), German astronomer, 166

Name Index and Biographical Glossary 215

Kuhn, Thomas, contemporary American historian and philosopher of science, 162, 164, 168

La Mothe Le Vayer, François (1588–1672), French writer, tutor to Louis XIV, 57
Leibniz, Gottfried Wilhelm (1646–1716), German philosopher and mathematician, 129, 136, 144, 145
Linnaeus, or Carl von Linne (1707–78), Swedish botanist, 146
Locke, John (1632–1704), English philosopher, 40, 64–8, 139, 145–51, 153–5, 206
Lucretius, Titus (96–55 BC), Roman philosopher and poet, 47
Lull, Ramon (1235–1315), Catalan philosopher and logician, 136–7, 140
Luther, Martin (1483–1546), German theologian and religious reformer, 53–4, 57–8, 70

McClintock, Barbara, contemporary American geneticist, 204
Marx, Karl (1818–83), German-born political philosopher and social theorist, 185, 201
Mersenne, Marin (1588–1648), French cleric and natural philosopher, 58
Midgely, Mary, contemporary British philosopher, 200
Montaigne, Michel (1533–92), French essayist, 57

Nagel, Thomas, contemporary American philosopher, 45
Neoplatonism: developments of Plato's philosophy, especially during the first and third centuries AD and during the Italian Renaissance, 93, 134–5, 139, 166, 196
Neopythagoreanism: revivals of Pythagorean thought, often forms of Neoplatonism (especially in the 4th century AD) which stressed the Pythagorean elements in Plato's thought, 134
Newton, Isaac (1642–1727), English natural philosopher, 35, 65, 112, 116, 144, 155, 161, 166–7, 173, 175, 180

Ockham, William of (c. 1285–1349), English Franciscan friar and philosopher, 148–51

Palladio, Andrea (1508–80), Italian architect, 25
Pappus, Alexandrian mathematician (4th century AD), 103
Paracelsus, Theophrastus (1490–1541), German physician, 140
Piaget, Jean (1896–1980), Swiss psychologist, 44
Pico dela Mirandola, Giovanni (1463–94), Italian philosopher, 196–8
Plato (c. 428–c. 348 BC), Greek philosopher, 5, 8–24, 29, 46–7, 49–52, 54, 62, 69–70, 85–8, 92–5, 97–9, 102–3, 107, 110, 113, 127, 130, 131–3, 135, 137, 147, 166, 178, 188
Popper, Karl, contemporary Austrian-born philosopher, 82, 156, 160, 178
Porphyry (c. 232–306 BC ???), Greek philosopher, 131, 134

Port Royal Logic (1662): name commonly given to *L'Art de Penser* by Arnauld and Nicole, after the Cistercian abbey which was the center of a Jansenist community, 145

Protagoras (*c.* 485–*c.* 420 BC), Greek philosopher, 47–56, 59

Putnam, Hilary, contemporary American philosopher, 128

Ptolemy, Claudius (2nd century AD), Alexandrian astronomer, 91

Pyrrho (*c.* 365–270 BC), Greek philosopher, 54–5; Pyrrhonism, 54–6, 70, 74

Pythagoras (6th century BC), Greek philosopher and mathematician, 133

Quine, Willard, contemporary American philosopher, 156, 160–2

Ramelli, Agostino (*c.* 1531–*c.* 1610), Italian engineer, 25

Ramus, Peter (1515–72), French philosopher, 135

Roemer, Ole (1644–1710), Danish astronomer, 161

Rorty, Richard, contemporary American philosopher, 3, 206–7

Russell, Bertrand (1872–1970), English philosopher and mathematical logician, 158–9, 167

Sergeant, John (1622–1710), English Roman Catholic controversialist, 147

Sextus Empiricus (2nd century AD), Greek physician and philosopher, 53–5, 57

Spinoza, Benedictus (1632–1727), Dutch philosopher of Portugese Jewish descent, 75, 77

Socrates (*c.* 470–399 BC), Greek philosopher, 11–16, 49–50, 54

Stoicism (4th century BC to 3rd century AD): Greek philosophical school named after the *Stoa Poikilê* in Athens where its members first met, 74–7

Tarski, Alfred, contemporary Polish-born mathematical logician, 161

Vico, Giambattista (1668–1744), Italian philosopher, 5, 186–92, 201

Vienna Circle (1920s and 1930s): a group of logical positivists (including Carnap and interacting with Wittgenstein and Popper) centered on Vienna University, many of whom emigrated to Britain and the US with Hitler's rise to power, 159

Whitehead, Alfred North (1861–1947), British-born mathematician and philosopher, 167

Wigner, E. P., contemporary American scientist, 167

Witten, Edward, contemporary American physicist, 166

Wittgenstein, Ludwig (1889–1951), Austrian-born philosopher, 158–9, 162, 164

Wolff, Christian (1679–1754), German philosopher and mathematician, 116, 192

Subject Index

References in bold indicate pages where the term is explained or used in such a way as to make its meaning evident.

agency, 112, 114, 121–5, 173, 180
alchemy, 140–1
analogy, 135–41
analysis-synthesis, method of, **103**, 171
analytic philosophy, 1, 2, 75, 112, 207
analytic statement, **181**
anticipation of nature, 30, 38, 66, 91, 116
appearances 20, **56**, 75; in Kant, **118**, 120
a priori, 64, **85**, 102, 116–20, 124–5, 155, 172, 179, 181–2; synthetic *a priori*, **179**, 182, 195
artifacts, 97, 179
atomic sentence, **159**–160, 162–3
atomism, 32, **50**–1, 59–60, 64–6
authoritative, authority, 7–8, 10–13, 15, 19, 21, 26, 39–43, 45–9, 52–3, 56–7, 59, 63, 65, 70, 79, 90, 93, 107, 108, 120, 122, 138–9, 145–7, 149, 152, 194–5, 200, 203–5, 207

being, 23, 84–5, 108, 136
belief, 15, 44–5, 53, 55, 57, 60–2, 77, 82, 111, 113–15, 128, 150, 155–6, 164, 171, 175–9, 194
bias, 5, 33, 80, 82, 171, 204

categories, Kant's, **118**–19
causes, **30**, 31, 104; Aristotelian, **96**–7; Hume on, 113–14, 119, 121, 154, 173–5, 187, 189, 191; as Kantian category, 119–20; *see* teleology
cave, Plato's, 18, 22, 37–8, 102; Bacon's Idols of the Cave *see* Idols
chemical philosophy, **139**–40
Christianity, 29, 37, 38, 46–8, 53–5, 56–7, 69–70, 79, 93–5, 107, 136, 140, 151, 205
clear and distinct, 102–3, 106, 109, 111, 152, 180, 186
clocks, 63–4, 100–1
competence, mental, 72–3, 76–7
conduct, 8, 24, 55–6, 61, 76, 78, 114
conscious being, subject, 81, 97, 119, 142
consciousness, 74, 77–8, 110, 118, 156, 174, 187, 190; content of, 78, 80; public, 12; of self, 44, 119, 174

Subject Index

construction of concepts, 182, 186, 191
contemplation, 28, 80–1, **92–3**, 114, **124**, 146
contingency, contingent, 111, 115, 120, 139, 156, 170–1, 186, 199, 200
Copernican, **46**, 91
corpuscularian, **46–7**, 50, 62–3, 69
craft, 9, 12, 24–5, 36, 93–4
critical philosophy, **116–17**, 179
crucial experiment, 34
cultural relativity, 52, 150, 174, 193–4, 201
culture, study of, 189–94

definition, 14, 39, 85, 89–90, 127–32
demon, Descartes' evil, 72–3, 78, 111
demonstration, Aristotle on, **12**, 88–92, 129–30, 132; Bacon on, 40, 84, 88–90; Vico on, **187**, **191**–2
determinism, 111
dialectic, **22**–3, 92, 103, 107, 127
dogmatic philosophy, **116**
domination of nature, 28–9, 31, 77, 100, 109, 114, 123, 125, 196, 198, 200, 203
doubt, Cartesian, 71–2, 78, 80, 172, 179, 180, 184
doxa, **15–16**, 146
dreams, 71–7
dualism, **110**, 123, 185

ego, transcendental vs. empirical, **121**
eidôlon, **37**, 38, 68–9
empeiria, **13**, 62; *see* experience vs. understanding
empiricism, empiricist, **86**, 112, 115, 124, **151**, 159, 167, 172–3, **179**, 189, 194, 195; *see* logical positivism
Enlightenment, 77
epagôgê *see* induction
epistêmê, **11–12**, 13, 15–16, 18, 22, 62, 70, 85, 88, 96, 109, 130, 132, 146, 170
epistemology, **1–5**, 42, 53, 55, 65–6, 73, 80, 109, 114, 126, 151, 155, 158, 160, 168, 170, 172, 177–80, 182, 195, 201, 206; Cartesian, 68–79, 101, 112, 115, 170, 172, 184
essence, 30, 90–1, **130–1**, 153–5, 156, 171; *see* nominal essence
experience (*empeiria*) vs. understanding (*epistêmê*) **62**, **88**, 113, 116, 187, 192
experience(s), 5, 13–14, 46, 49, 51–2, 62–3, 68–75, 86, 113, 117–18, 124, 134, 136, 147, 151, 154–9, 173–6, 179, 190–1, 195, 206; Bacon on, 25, 27–8, 32, 34, 40, 108, 124, 145; transcending, 85–6, 90, 112, 114–16
experiment, 25, **30–31**, 32–4, 38, 64, 80–2, 84, 97, 99, 102, 113, 116–17, 141, 143, 157, 163, 165, 173, 179–81, 189–90, 198, 203, 204

expertise, 11–17, 19–20, 24–5, 88, 94, 206
explanation(s), 12, 16, 23, 30, 36, 61–2, 64, 66, 70, 88–92, 96, 113–14, 128, 130, 147, 169, 170, 173, 175, 181, 187–8, 192–3

fact–value distinction, 99
faith, 53–8
feminist criticisms, 27–8, 171
first philosophy, 85, 109
forms, Aristotle's, 37, 85, **93**; Bacon's, 30–1, 33, **36**, 99; forms of judgment, 181; Plato's, **16–18**, 19–24, **36**, 37, 46, **68–9**, 85, 93–4, 97, 123; Form of the Good, 23–4, 93–4, 107; vs. matter, 85;
foundationalism, **107**, 153–6, 194–5
foundations, Descartes', 72, **106–8**; empirical, **159**, 162
freedom, **121**, 77, 93, 111, 121–2

geometry *see* mathematics
goals of knowledge/inquiry, 24, 27, 31, 41, 77, 92, 100, 109, 115, 123, 125, 205
God, 10, 26, 37–8, 46, 48, 69, 71–4, 77, 80, 107, 110–12, 120, 138, 151, 186–9, 196, 197

habit, 2, 18, 20, 61, 169; bad, 18, 35; of discrimination, 75, 77; of thought, 113, 174–5, 177; shared, 127–8, 193, 199
harmony, 133–4, 165–7
human nature, 150–1, 154–7, 170–3, 177, 182, 195, 200
hypothesis, hypothesize, **22**, 34, 64

ideas, **68–9**, 142–3, 147–8; in Descartes, 73, 80, 103–**10**; in Hume, **112**–13, 173–6, 179; in Kant, 117, **121–2**; simple, 151–2; way of, 69, **147**–8, 152, 172; *see also* representation in Kant; forms, Plato's
Idols, 5–6, 35, **35–42**, 69, 102, 108–9, 126, 139, 171, 194–5, 202, 204–7; of the Cave, 38–9, 169–72, 183–4, 191, 193; of the Market Place, 39, 127–9, 146, 165, 168; of the Theater, 39–40, 84, 86–7, 92, 112, 114, 117, 122, 125, 164; of the Tribe, 43–5, 80, 82, 122, 170, 189
imagination, 117, 182–3, 190–1, 193
induction, Bacon's, **33**, 41, 86, 107, 144–5; Aristotle's *epagôgê*, **89**, 103, 106; problem of, 114, **160**
institutions, 7, 8, 18, 22, 24, 53, 73, 82–3, 145, 189–93, 195, 201, 205
interpretation, of nature, 30, 33–5; of ideas, 110
intuition, in Descartes, **106**; in Kant, **117**–18, 120–1, 182–3

judgment, in Descartes, 109–11, 180; in Kant, 118–19, 181–2
justify beliefs, claims to knowledge, 3, 20–2, 53, 79, 115, 156–9, 168, 170, 175–6, 180–1, 187, 191–4, 201, 203–4, 206; concepts, words, 120, 128, 171; practice, 102, 137, 160

know-how, 9, 11–13, 25, 93–4, 165
knowledge, concepts of, 1 4, 8, 12, 16, 27, 31, 62, 68 9, 74, 87, 100–2, 108–10, 113, 116, 118, 132, 134, 148–9, 171–2, 178–9, 187–92, 202, 205; of human beings, 26, 100, 124, 171–2, 200; religious/moral, 26, 48, 53–4, 57, 70, 121, 136, 139, 146; through the senses, 47, 50, 67, 64, 69, 118, 159; *see also* goals of knowledge, objects of knowledge, scientific knowledge, self-knowledge, social-psychology of knowledge, sociology of knowledge

language, 39, 52, 61, 127–9, 142, 144–5, 147–9, 152, 156–8, 162, 164, 167, 172, 178; *see also* science, language of
law, natural, 31–2, 99, 102, 109, 111–14, 121, 155, 167, 173–4, 178–9
linguistic turn, **158**, 160
literal, **137–43**, 161, 165–6, 168
logic, 173; Aristotelian, 29–**30**, 85, 89, 91, 132, 169, 182; extensional first order, **160**–3, 167–9; Kant on, 118–19; Lull on, 136; *see also* reasoning
logical connectives, **160**
logical positivism (logical empiricism), 86, 129, 157, **158–9**, 162, 167, 203; *see also* Vienna Circle in Name Index
logicism, **167–8**

madness, 73–7
magic, natural, **101**, 140, 196–8
mastery of nature see domination of nature
material well-being, 9, 10–11, 25, 45, 61, 123, 200
mathematics, 20–2, 26, 71–2, 102–7, 109, 111, 133–4, 144, 151, 153, 158, 167–8, 171, 173, 180, 182, 183, 186, 190
measure, 43, 46–7, 49, 52, 67–8
measurement, 134, 136, 163
mechanical philosophy, mechanistic outlook, 63, 70, 77, **100**–2, 106, 110, **139**–40, 165, 198
mentality, 191–2, 193, 201
mental realm, 68–9, 73–4, 110
metaphysics, 30, 32, 66, 70, **84–5**, 86, 98, 101, 112, 115, 123, 135, 179; in Bacon, 99, 101; dogmatic vs. critical (Kant), **115–17**, 120, 122
method, 4, 29, 33, 41–3, 102–8, 173, 180, 189, 194, 204; of analysis-synthesis, **103**; of division, 130–2
mirror (distorting), 38, 41, 43, 102, 125
modern philosophy, **3**, **42**, 137, 198
moral(s), 11, 12, 24–7, 37, 47, 57, 61, 76, 79, 82, 93, 95, 121, 123–4, 146, 198, 200, 205–6

naturalism, 37, **151**–2, 155
natural history, **31**, 114, 116
natural kinds, 31, 153

natural philosophy, **3**, 25, 27, 30, 39, 58, 78, 95, 97–9, 107, 112, 133, 139–40, 144, 165–6, 173, 190; *see also* science
nature (Aristotle), 90, **97**; attitude to, 28; light of, 106; Nature vs. natures, 99, **153**, 166–7
necessary connection, 154, 174; *see also* causes, Hume on
nominal essence, **153**–5
nominalism, 148, **149**, 154

objective, objectivity, **43**–5, 52, 73, 78–9, 82–3, 107, 126, 146, 157, 159, 164, 168, 179, 194, 203
objects of knowledge, 11, 26, 35, 37, 62, 79, 106, 107, 112, 115, 119, 123, 125–6, 128, 172, 186–7, 200
observation, 30–5, 38, 40, 62, 64, 81, 86, 89, 91, 93, 98, 101–2, 108–9, 113–14, 141, 144, 146, 150–63, 169, 174, 177, 179, 180
observed phenomena, 30, 63, 90, 103, 106, 154
obstacles, 5, 6, 35, 44–5, 86, 165, 169, 203
opinion, **16**, 38, 113, 116, 146
organon, **29**

passive, cognitive functions which are ideally, 92, 101, 114, 117–18, 121, 179–80, 186
perspective, limited, 5, 50, 56, 63, 73
phantasia, **59**, 69, 75
phenomena, 30, 56
phenomeno-technique, 81
philosophical framework, 1–5, 29, 117, 144, 148, 153, 194, 203
political affairs, issues, considerations, 3, 27, 77, 79, 94, 143, 175, 206
political authority, 10, 26, 49, 206–7
political practice, understanding, 21–2, 24, 93, 95, 206
politics of knowledge, 205–6
postmodernism, **2**, 52
power, human, 33, 35, 39, 61, 72, 122, 139, 173–4, 185, 196–201, 203, 206; natural, 10, 25, 30, 66–7, 112, 114, 121, 174; social, political, 7, 26–7, 204–6
practical abilities, knowledge, 93–5, 109; *see also* know-how
practical concerns, consequences, 3–5, 78–80, 92, 124–5
practical reason 122–6, 184
practically useful, applicable, 30, 35, 40, 62, 80, 114, 143, 165
practice, 12, 21, 24, 78
preconception (*prolêpsis*), **60**, 63
prejudice, 44, 80, 82, 171
presentation, **59**, 60, 63, 75–7, 110–11, 117, 180
principles, 24–5, 27, 30, 62, 88–90, 91, 92, 99, 102, 116, 120, 125, 173, 176, 182
progress, 11, 185–6, 195–6, 200, 202
psychologism, **157**

qualities, primary vs. secondary, 64-8
quantifiers, 160

ratio, 133-4, 165
rational argument, demonstration, 91, 131, 159, 163
rational capacities, faculties, 26, 77-8, 108, 157, 184-5
rational conversation, discourse, thought, 12, 20, 22, 79, 88
rational creature, 78, 107-8, 114, 123, 184, 199
rational foundation, grounding, guarantee, 12, 79, 113, 115, 125, 174
rational justification, 79, 113, 161, 174-5
rational knowledge, understanding, method, 14, 104, 111, 116, 146, 180
rational order, connections, structure, 130, 133-4, 136-7, 143, 157, 175
rationalism, rationalists, 85, **115**, 124, **151**, 172, 180, 194-5
rationality, conception of, 132-5, 163, 184, 194, 199
realism (Piaget), **44**; empirical (Kant), **125**,
reality, 17, 24, 76, 95, 87, 108-10, 112, 115, 123, 174
reason, faculty of, 18-20, 59, 72, 80, 106-7, 122-3, 125-7, 133, 146, 154, 173-4, 177, 180-1, 183-6, 197-9, 205; in Kant, 115-17, **121**
reasoning, 15, 30, 33, 40, 68, 72, 76, 84, 86, 91, 103-4, 129, 134-7, 144, 160, 168, 174-8, 182, 185
reasons, 12, 15, 20, 29, 55, 133, 164
reductionism, **65**, 106
relativism, 46-7, **48**, **52**, 59, 195; *see also* cultural relativity
representation, 42, 108, 110, 125, 142-3, **149**, 155-6, 158, 163, 167-8, 177; absolute, 156; in Kant (*Vorstellung*), 117-20, 122, 124
representations, system of, **142**, 143, 148-**9**, 158, 161, 164-5
rhetorical devices, 27-9, 165

saving the phenomena, **91**
science, conception of, 79, 106, 109, 112-14, 116, 160, 165, 172-86, 188-92; language of, 129, 138, 143-5, 152, 158-60, 163-4, 168; modern, 46, 52, **61**, 65-6, 81-2, 98, 100, 116, 123, 134, 144, 166, 189, 205; as a social enterprise, 10, 26, 39, 82-3, 152, 157, 166, 184, 195, 204
scientific attitude, inquiry, studies, 3, 67, 81, 117
scientific knowledge, 43-4, 46, 48, 52, 81-2, 100, 106-7, 109, 116, 121, 128-9, 137, 144-6, 152, 157, 161-2, 164-8, 186, 189, 192, 206
scientific principles, proof, 3-4, 125
Schools, Scholastic, **40**, 128, 140, 172
self-knowledge, understanding, 41, 76-9, 107-8, 110-11, 119, 156, 171-2, 174, 176-7, 179, 186, 188, 194, 200
senses, sense experience, sense perception, 38, 45-52, 55, 58-61, 63, 71, 74-6, 80-1, 89, 110, 112, 117, 140, 151, 182-3
signs, 139, 148; natural, 150, 155-6; system of, 137, 141, **142**, 143, 148, **149**, 165, 196

Subject Index

skeptic, skepticism, 38, **47–8**, 53–9, 69, 70–2, 74–6, 79, 108, 115, 147–8, 161, 174, 176, 205–7; mitigated, **58**, 62
social-psychology of knowledge, 175
sociology of knowledge, 195
sophists, **12**
speculation, 25, 85, 87, 90, **92**, 98, 114, 116, 122
standards, 20, 40–1, 52
Stoicism *see* Name Index
style, writing, 29; of thought, 38, 144, 193, 201
subject of experience (knowing subject), 107–8, 110, 120, 142, 156, 160, 172, 203
subjective, subjectivity, **43–4**, 73, 78, 119–20, 172, 179, 203
succession of appearances vs. experience of succession, 118–19
synthetic *a priori* knowledge, **179**

tables, Bacon's, 33–5
technê, **11–13**, 21, 88–92, 94, 132–3
technology, 197, 200, 202–3, 206
teleology, final causes, **87**, 95–102, 109, 111, 123–4, 200
theology, 25–7, 37, 53–8, 69–70, 85, 93–4, 98–9, 123–4, 151–2
things-in-themselves (Kant), 120, 156
tradition(s), 3, 39–40, 70, 108, 202, 206; philosophical 2, 4–6, 24, 40–1, 46, 53, 78–9, 116, 125, 128, 165, 171, 187–8
tree of Porphyry, **131**, 134, 143
truth conditions, **158–9**, 164
truth, criterion of, 32, 53–8, 60, 70–3, 74–5, 186, 188, 193
truth(s), 27, 32, 47–8, 53, 56, 62, 77, 86, 89, 92, 110–11, 125, 137, 146, 149, 153, 187–8, 205
truth function, **160**
truth values, **159**, 160

understanding, 14, **16**–18, 20, 23–4, 92, 114, 127, 146, 152, 183–4, 188–9, 192, 206; not a dry light, 38, 44; *see also* experience vs. understanding
universal perspective, 5, 19, 44, 46–8, 52, 63–4, 67–8, 77, 91, 98, 120, 171–2, 185, 189, 199; *see also* representation, absolute
utopia, 8, 10, 26, 82

vacuum, void, 32, 50, 61
value neutrality, 82, 99

wax, Descartes' piece of, 81
will, 72, 80, 109–11, 179, 180

yardstick (*kanôn*), 60, 71